SERO · SE D · SERIO

THE CECILS
of Hatfield House

DAVID CECIL

BOOK CLUB ASSOCIATES
London

This book was designed and produced
in Great Britain by George Rainbird Limited, London

Printed and bound by Jarrold & Sons Limited, Norwich
Colour plates and jacket originated and printed
by Westerham Press Limited, Kent

House editor: Yorke Crompton
Design: Pauline Harrison
Indexing: Ellen Crampton

First published in 1973
This edition published in 1973 by Book Club Associates
by arrangement with Constable & Company Limited

Reverse of frontispiece
The Cecil coat of arms on the Minstrels' Gallery
in the Marble Hall, Hatfield House

Frontispiece
Lady Cicily Alice Gore, 4th Marchioness of Salisbury,
with her son Lord David Cecil, painted by
James Shannon in 1908

This book
by a Cecil of Hatfield
is dedicated to the illustrious memory
of Queen Elizabeth I
in homage and
gratitude.

Contents

Colour Plates

A lively desire of knowing and of recording our ancestors so generally prevails, that it must depend on the influence of some common principle in the minds of men. We seem to have lived in the persons of our forefathers; it is the labour and reward of vanity to extend the term of this ideal longevity. Our imagination is always active to enlarge the narrow circle in which Nature confined us. Fifty or an hundred years may be allotted to an individual, but we step forward beyond death with such hopes as religion and philosophy will suggest; and we fill up the silent vacancy that precedes our birth, by associating ourselves to the authors of our existence.

Edward Gibbon

Preface

I must ask leave of my readers to offer them two words of explanation. The first concerns the content of this book. It is not so much a history of the Cecils of Hatfield as a series of family portraits. The most important Cecils have been statesmen absorbed in public and political affairs; and a full history of their lives would be largely a political history of the periods in which each flourished. Since I am not by profession a political historian, I am not qualified to write such a history. I have therefore treated my subjects not as statesmen but as men, including only such history as I found necessary to illustrate their personal characters.

My second word of explanation concerns the form of my book. Its first two parts treat of persons long dead, about whom I have, like other students of history, learned from books and manuscripts, and whom I have described in the objective, impersonal mode of historical biography. But, from the middle of the nineteenth century, I am concerned with people whom I have known at first hand, or at second hand from the memories of my immediate elders. I have therefore written of such characters in the openly personal mode of the writer of reminiscences. To do so seemed more natural and also more likely to be true to my subject. My parents and even my grandparents are part of my own experience; they have contributed, I realize, to my own identity. But when I peer back through the mists of the past in search of more distant ancestors, I find myself confronting the faces of those who, though they may bear the same name as mine, are in fact strangers, with whom I feel no sense of personal connection, and who, however much I study their stories, will always remain for me figures in a history book. My vision of my subject is incurably heterogeneous; surely, then, my picture of it should be equally so.

I must add some words of gratitude to the Sixth Marquess of Salisbury for permission to consult manuscripts and reproduce pictures from Hatfield, also for his unfailing and sympathetic help in my researches; for other help in my researches to Mrs Grant and Mr Harcourt Williams, Librarians at Hatfield; to Lord Blake, Professor Joel Hurstfield and Dr A. L. Rowse for invaluable advice and information; to the Dowager Lady Manners, the Lady Mary Howick and the Hon. Guy Strutt for information drawn from their own memories; and to Mr Laurence Whistler for permission to reproduce a drawing by Rex Whistler.

David Cecil

Prologue
THE HOUSE

BUILT IN 1611, Hatfield House now confronts at close quarters the modern world. The railway station faces its main gates; and these gates are only eight minutes' walk from the house. Meanwhile, in the last fifty years, the twentieth century has taken possession of the surrounding district. The old town of Hatfield has become embedded in an ever-expanding urban development; across this development thunders the traffic of a huge motorway; while overhead the air reverberates with the roar of planes landing and taking off from an aircraft factory barely half a mile away. Yet – as the visitor discovers, when he has taken his eight minutes' walk and is face to face with it – Hatfield House has not been subdued by its twentieth-century situation. It may represent the past, but not the dead past. Like the plays of Shakespeare, this massive architectural monument of Shakespeare's age somehow still manages to speak to us with a living voice.

Who should recognize this voice better than I? I spent my childhood there and, because I was the youngest of my family by seven years, my relation to the house was close and private. Not that I was a lonely child. The place was generally full of my elders and I spent a great deal of time with them. But I played on my own too and sometimes, if the rest of my family was away, I was at Hatfield alone but for the household. Then I had the place spiritually to myself. It became my single companion; it engaged the concentrated attention of my imagination. For hours on end I roamed the apparently endless ramifications of its passages and staircase and landings, its great rooms and small rooms and chapel and library and attics and kitchen, and rambled about the different levels of its leaden roof, whence I would gaze out over the gardens to where the turf and trees of the park faded into the Hertfordshire distance. Thus, in company or in solitude, gradually I was penetrated by the spirit of the place; thus I grew intimate with its changing moods and the varied aspects of its complex personality.

Hatfield House: the centre of the South Front, hardly altered since it was designed as the main entrance

Looking to the south from the House across the balustrade flanking one of the twin iron gates

Complex partly because it is both public and private. It was designed to be the house of a great nobleman, when great nobles ruled the country. This means it has something of the palace about it, with its grand staircase and huge ornate rooms intended for state occasions and semi-public gatherings. All the same, the impression it leaves is not that of a palace; it is also a family home with the characteristics of a family home. There are plenty of private-seeming rooms, moderate-sized and intimate, full of pleasant untidiness and the spirit of relaxation; and this spirit can overflow into the big rooms, making them intimate and untidy too. I remember Hatfield as a house where books and newspapers were strewn about the floors, and on the tables of the pillared front hall lay tennis rackets and mackintoshes and old hats.

Even more is the house's personality complex because it is, as it were, an accumulated one. Since it was built, many generations have lived there and each has left its mark according to the taste and habits of each owner and of his period; each has added to it or changed it. So the final impression it makes is not single but diverse and composite, the product of many people and many ages.

The first impression indeed is single. The exterior of the house, though altered in detail, looks pretty much as its original owner must have imagined it. The South Front, designed to be the chief entrance, has a three-sided courtyard with wings of rosy brick faced with stone and a central façade of pale stone elaborately ornamented with crests and trophies and mottoes and above it the pillared cupola of the Clock Tower. Spacious, sumptuous and welcoming, the South Front looks through large iron gates up to a long grassy expanse flanked on each side by an avenue. In contrast, the North Front looks downwards, a great fortress-like façade of brick almost bare of decoration and with its door approached by a steep flight of steps. Majestic and intimidating, it dominates the eminence on which it is placed. East and West Fronts lack the coherent personalities of North and South. The Jacobeans who designed them were scene-painters rather than architects in the fullest sense. Concentrating on great stage spectacles like those provided by the North and South Fronts, they left the East and West as it were to shift for themselves. But, built as these are of the same rose-coloured brick as the rest of the house, relieved by the glittering glass of the broad mullioned windows, and each set high on a balustraded terrace, they assert themselves finely enough. Moreover each has an individual character given it by its surroundings.

The East seems the loftiest since it looks down on two successive terraces; thence the grass slopes away past the sombre mass of the cut yew maze to a piece

From the House: the vista to the east down the terraced approach to the cut yew maze and the New Pond

of water called the New Pond: a misleading and inadequate name, for it is as old as the house and less a pond than a lake, made deliberately picturesque by a boat-house surmounted by an archway of carved and lichened stonework and an island where the overhanging trees gaze for ever, like Narcissus, at their own beauty mirrored in the waters. In the months after Christmas the New Pond sometimes freezes; and I remember how as a boy, skimming around in the early dusk, I would pause on my skates and look up to see the East Front silhouetted against the cold flame of the winter sunset, while the first stars sparkled overhead and there was a nip of frost in the air.

It is in winter that I recall the East Front most vividly. The West Front on the other hand evokes summer memories. Its terrace presides over a quadrangle of pleached limes that smell sweet in the warmth of the July sunshine, enclosing a formal garden thickly planted with flowers and in the middle of it a pool and water-lilies and a sculptured fountain. Over the lime trees rises the dusky red tower of the Banqueting Hall, which is all that remains of the old Palace of Hatfield where the young Princess Elizabeth and her little brother, afterwards King Edward VI, played together four hundred years ago. There is something of the *fête champêtre* about the atmosphere of the West gardens. For me, it calls up Sunday afternoons in the summer with tea spread on two long white-clothed tables in the shade of a mulberry tree, planted, it is said, by James I, and my mother pouring out tea from a silver teapot with an ivory handle.

The character of the inside of the house is varied. Only one thing is the same all over it: a complex, pervading and, to me, infinitely evocative smell compounded of washed stone and varnished panelling and floors polished with beeswax and smoke from generations of wood fires. It meets you the moment you open the door of the South Front and enter the Armoury. This was originally an open arcade. By the beginning of the nineteenth century, however, people were finding it too uncomfortable to walk through in all kinds of weather to get from one side of the house to the other. So the arcade was closed in and the interior redecorated in what was hoped to be an appropriate style. The walls were hung with old English tapestries representing the Four Seasons; and on the panels round them were disposed weapons captured from the Spaniards after the defeat of the Armada in 1588; while along the floor full-sized figures of men, armed cap-à-pie like the ghost of Hamlet's father, hold aloft lanterns, fitted with crimson glass, whose light after nightfall sheds a fiery and melodramatic glow over tapestry and panelling. The general effect suggests the setting of some nineteenth-

The Grand Staircase of Hatfield House, leading to the four great rooms at its centre, originally reserved for state occasions

century dramatization of a novel by Walter Scott rather than the real Jacobean age it was meant to recall. But this gives it a curious individuality; it transports us to the Jacobean age, not as it was, but as it was pictured by the Victorian romantic imagination.

Beyond the Armoury is the Marble Hall, so called for its marble floor. The biggest room in the house, rising two storeys high, it is hung with tapestry, this time seventeenth-century Flemish and portraying in a Baroque florid manner scenes in the love affairs of the god Jupiter. As a child I was specially impressed by one in which jealous Juno, crowned and in red, is depicted as administering a drubbing with her sceptre to Jove's latest conquest, who squalls with open mouth, while a well-trained pair of peacocks, harnessed to a golden chariot, wait docilely for their divine mistress to start on her journey again. At the end of the Marble Hall, beneath a heavily carved gallery, where once the singing boys sang and the minstrels played on lute and recorder, hang four faded eagle-headed Napoleonic banners taken by the Duke of Wellington after Waterloo and presented to the then owner of Hatfield. On the walls below, the pictured countenances of Queen Elizabeth I and Mary Queen of Scots survey the visitor with intent, inscrutable eyes.

The door beneath the Minstrels' Gallery opens on to the Grand Staircase. This is the artistic showpiece of the house, an expression of the Renaissance imagination at its most exuberant. Its wide, shallow steps rise between banisters embroidered all over with fluting and carving and trophies and garlands and masks and little figures – here a cupid, there a gardener with rake and flowerpot – and perched on top of each newel-post a little naked boy holds aloft a ball or a coat of arms, once brilliantly coloured and still touched here and there with faded gold.

The Grand Staircase leads to the four great rooms that occupy the centre of the house, the King James Drawing-room, the Long Gallery, the Winter Dining-room and the Library. These fill the space of the original state rooms, that is to say rooms originally intended to be used only for great occasions – 'for feasts and triumphs', as Bacon puts it in his essay *Of Building* – and especially if the King and Queen and their retinue came to pay the owner of the house a visit. This style of living did not last. Perhaps the Cecil family no longer enjoyed 'feasts and triumphs', perhaps the kings and queens came to stay too seldom for the best rooms in the house to be reserved for their use alone. Whatever the reason, by the nineteenth century the owners of Hatfield had taken over this floor to be used as winter quarters. This meant alterations. The rooms reserved for the Queen were

Hatfield House from the south-east

turned into a library; those for the Prince into a dining-room for winter use; and the Gallery – in the seventeenth century nearly empty of furniture and mainly used for taking a little dignified exercise when the weather was too bad to go out – was filled with chairs and tables and sofas and screens and became, between October and April, the chief sitting-room of the house. But the past was too powerful to be expelled. Each room acquired a new individuality: yet each bears the mark of its history.

James I still inhabits the room which bears his name. His life-size statue in dark bronze stands in a niche of the high chimneypiece of coloured marble; but in spite of this – for he was never a powerful character – he has not managed to make the room his own. It suggests later ages with its doors painted in mock Pompeian style, its elegant gilt Chippendale furniture, its full-length family portraits by Georgian Reynolds and Regency Lawrence and Victorian Richmond and Edwardian Shannon. Ancestral, grandiose and gaudy, the King James Drawing-room is like a saloon in a great house in one of Disraeli's novels, *Coningsby* or *Lothair*. There is a whiff of the Regency about it or of the earlier, brighter years of Queen Victoria's reign.

In the Long Gallery we are back in the Renaissance. The walls, panelled with pilastered oak, are broken twice by big chimneypieces, marbled in paint of a subtle oyster colour, relieved with touches of black and gold. Here too is a Renaissance treasure. In a cupboard in the wall can be seen a jewelled and ena-melled crystal posset set reputed to be the work of Benvenuto Cellini and given by the Spanish Ambassador to Philip and Mary on their wedding in 1554. Beneath it stands the box it came in, made of red tortoiseshell bound with silver. To open it is to get a shock; for, painted inside the lid, is a picture of the severed head of St John the Baptist lying livid and bleeding on a dish as presented to Herod by the daughter of Herodias. The shock takes us back to the period when the treasure was made. Thus, in the sixteenth century, cavalier and court lady, jewelled and exquisite like the posset set, rode into London; while, impaled above them, stared down the bloodstained heads of traitors to the Queen, executed the day before. The Gallery contains other less sensational mementoes of the period: Queen Elizabeth's yellow silk stockings and hat of plaited straw and an illuminated contemporary genealogical table tracing her ancestors back to Adam. Relics of later ages serve as milestones to mark the stages of Hatfield's journey down the path of past time: the oak cradle of Charles I, James II's purse, and the quill pen with which Bismarck and Disraeli signed the Treaty of Berlin.

The Winter Dining-room north of the Gallery is a large featureless apartment

The Marble Hall at Hatfield House

chiefly memorable for some portraits of kings who visited the house: James I with a plain old-womanish countenance and dressed incongruously in vast black balloon breeches and flame-coloured stockings; Charles I by Mytens looking Scottish and obstinate and not nearly so romantic as on the canvases of Van Dyck; George III with crimson cheeks and scarlet uniform depicted, in compliment to his host, as standing in Hatfield Park with the House in the background.

At the west end of the Gallery is the Library, lined from floor to ceiling with books and diffusing a general effect of brown and dark red and wood and leather. The scent of leather – leather binding, leather-covered chairs, leather-topped tables – qualifies, though it does not overpower, the pervading smell of the rest of the house. No period predominates in the Library. The furniture is eighteenth-century, the decoration unobtrusively of the nineteenth; the mosaic portrait of the first Lord Salisbury, set in the chimneypiece, was sent in 1611 as a present from Venice by Sir Henry Wotton, the English Ambassador there. As for the books, they are of all sorts and periods. There are sixteenth-century editions of the classics, seventeenth-century maps and a whole collection of pamphlets dealing with the French Revolution. The books, most of them, seem to have been bought to be

Queen Elizabeth I's openwork garden hat and silk stockings, preserved in the Long Gallery, together with Mary Tudor's crystal posset set, said to have been made by Benvenuto Cellini, a wedding present to her from the Spanish Ambassador

read by someone interested in their subject-matter; and this makes the Library different from the typical nobleman's country-house library, with its typical collection of elegant unread representative classics. Its atmosphere is perceptibly astir with the sense of intellectual curiosity. This contributes yet another distinctive ingredient to the composite flavour of the house.

Next to the Library, and at the turn of the West Wing, is the Chapel. If the Library is different from most country-house libraries, the Chapel is still more different from most country-house chapels. These, most of them, are unobtrusive secular affairs, differing from the other rooms in the house only by the fact that they contain a few ecclesiastical appurtenances: a cross, a bible, some priedieux arranged in lines. Whatever spiritual life they possessed has evaporated now. One cannot imagine anyone praying there. Not so Hatfield Chapel. It looks like a church, complete with a font and an organ and an altar, and like a church still in use: a sacred place set apart and dedicated to the worship of God and to the celebration of his Holy Mysteries. Worshippers there in past ages have left their mark; its appearance expresses, in particular, two phases of English piety. The great window of painted glass portrays – in costumes that combine seventeenth-century fashion with what the designer thought the correct historical dress – incidents in the lives of Old Testament worthies; among them the boy David, wearing a gentle expression and a pretty pink kilt, holds up the huge blind-eyed head of the dead Goliath, and the baby Moses reclines in the bulrushes in front of Pharaoh's palace, a building clearly inspired by the latest thing in French seventeenth-century châteaux. These scenes vividly convey the same strong literal faith, the fervent Bible Christianity which at the same time was producing the English translation of the Bible.

Below the window comes a contrast. The Cecils by 1860 seem to have felt that the sanctuary, as originally designed, did not adequately express their religious sentiment. They therefore replaced it by a white marble altar, surrounded by a reredos of yellow marble and surmounted by a figure of Christ with eyes cast raptly upwards and hands spread out in a gesture of self-dedication. Here in stone we see Victorian piety; here is a visual expression of the revived High Church spirit of the nineteenth century. Taste unfortunately did not revive along with faith; the new sanctuary is not very beautiful. Yet one cannot regret it. It has enriched the atmosphere of the house with yet another element; it helps to reveal it in the perspective of a different and spiritual dimension. Moreover it is evidence of the continuing life of the Chapel. For it does continue. Every Sunday a priest comes up to celebrate the Holy Sacrament; every morning – at least until lately – the sound of the organ has indicated that the household has assembled for morning prayers.

This is not the original organ but one put in with the other improvements in the

nineteenth century. The old gaily painted organ, now in the Armoury, in my childhood adorned the Summer Drawing-room on the ground floor of the East Wing; one of a set of rooms for 'dwelling in' – to quote Bacon again – where the family were supposed to live, when there were no 'feasts and triumphs' or royal visitors to take them upstairs. These rooms however – the Summer Drawing-room, the Yew Room and the Van Dyck Room are chief among them – may be thought spacious and splendid enough for daily existence, with their marble chimneypieces, their window curtains of heavy silk and their panelled walls from which look down at us the faces of earlier ages.

In the Summer Drawing-room and the Van Dyck Room, these are family faces: Elizabethan and Jacobean in the Summer Drawing-room, coiffed and be-ruffed and with high foreheads; in the Van Dyck Room they are Caroline ladies with ringlets and drop ear-rings or gentlemen with flowing locks and falling collars. The Yew Room broadens the perspective to display a whole portrait gallery of sixteenth-century history: Mary Queen of Scots, very young and for once as pretty as she is reported to have been; Leicester in middle age grown fat and puffy and surely no longer the man to attract Queen Elizabeth; a distinguished-looking gentleman, who may or may not be Sir Walter Raleigh, dressed with beautifully restrained good taste in black velvet relieved by a thin chain and narrow sword belt of gold; and a whole series of faces from the Court of the Valois across the Channel, all looking sinister: malignant-eyed Catherine de' Medici, her crazy son Charles IX, Henry Duke of Guise with fierce little eyes and a great scar across his cheek, and his murderer King Henry III, with a small, pale, perverse face and a pearl ear-ring, the perfect Beardsley model born three hundred years before his time. Portraits dominate these rooms; from every wall they watch us with unwinking eyes, at times so intently as to make them seem alive. If one is alone and the faces are Valois faces, the effect can be disquieting.

Beyond the Van Dyck Room the East Wing staircase leads up to the four or five state bedrooms on the first floor. Here again the same two periods leave their traces. This is most to be noted in the two chief rooms: those intended for visiting kings and queens. The King James Bedroom is a seventeenth-century room hung with the same kind of florid tapestry as the Marble Hall, representing the tumultuous amours of Jupiter and with a great canopied bed hung with crimson damask and with a moulding at the back sheathed in yellow silk. In contrast, the Queen's Room bears witness to the fact that it was redecorated for a visit from Queen Victoria in 1847. Nothing could be more Victorian than its bed flounced and fringed with red satin and, on the ledge above the pillows, a gay little crown like

The gallery of the Chapel at Hatfield House, with pictures representing the saints

that worn by the Queen in Thackeray's *The Rose and the Ring*. Above, the ceiling is painted with coats of arms in gay colours like those on a Victorian piece of woolwork.

I have mentioned only a few, although the most important, of the rooms at Hatfield. For the rest, on the same first floor in the other wing of the house are other stately bedchambers, furnished and decorated during the last hundred years, but in imitation of the ancient style; and above them, on all three sides of the court, are bedrooms and dressing-rooms and passages and schoolrooms and nurseries and a great attic originally one, but later divided into rooms for the accommodation of the army of retainers that used to be required to keep such an establishment going at full pitch. The basement five floors below spreads out into as many cavernous and bewildering ramifications as the Kingdom of the Nibelungs; with a kitchen in it, vaulted like a church and as big, and sculleries and pantries and larders and wine cellars and a still room and a servants' hall and a housekeeper's room and a carpenter's shop, and what seems like a whole village of store rooms and lumber rooms.

Hidden among them, an unobtrusive door leads to the Muniment Room where are preserved the Hatfield papers: a collection of documents of past periods, especially the sixteenth and seventeenth centuries, when two successive Cecils were chief ministers of the Crown. These consist of letters both private and official, for in those days there was no Public Record Office and the papers were the property of the minister, if he liked to keep them. The Cecils did. The effect of this decision was formidable: three hundred volumes, including many letters from Queen Elizabeth I to her ministers and favourites, Raleigh and Leicester and Drake and Walsingham and noble Sir Philip Sidney and tragic, foolish Essex; also some from Mary Queen of Scots, among them the only one existing of the fatal letters found in the silver casket which, forged or genuine, were used as chief evidence to convict her of complicity in the murder of Darnley, her husband. Besides these there are letters from foreign potentates, Philip of Spain, Francis I and Henry IV of France and his wife La Reine Margot and her mother Catherine de' Medici. Not all these papers are political; there are some manuscripts of poems among them, some by Ben Jonson and Campion and Dowland; and though there is nothing by Shakespeare himself there is one of the few contemporary references to him. A courtier writes to suggest an entertainment to be offered to Queen Anne of Denmark on a visit to Robert Cecil, First Earl of Salisbury:

> There is no new play that the Queen has not seen; but they have revived an old one called 'Loves Labour Lost' which for wit and mirth will please her exceedingly.

In the Yew Room: the marble fireplace bearing a portrait of the youthful Mary Queen of Scots

There is something strange and ghostly in looking at these papers and still more in handling them. As nothing else does, they seem to put us in direct, almost physical touch with their long-dead authors. Portraits show them to us at second hand and through the eyes of the painter – and who knows if his eyes were to be trusted? But these sallow pages have been touched by their actual hands; they are creased where their fingers have folded them; those same fingers have traced the writing, now faded to a faint brown, by which they uttered their thoughts and feelings at the very instant these passed through their minds; so that as we read we become for a moment their contemporaries, and find ourselves assisting at the drama of their lives while it is still in the process of happening.

The papers in the Muniment Room may stand as a symbol of the spirit of Hatfield; for their express, in the most concentrated form, its outstanding characteristic, its power to stir the sense of history. Other celebrated English mansions are primarily notable as treasure-houses of art or masterpieces of architecture. But Hatfield is not rich in works of art; rather its treasures are memorable historic portraits and unique historic documents. And the house itself has been altered too much and too often to have the unity and consistency of style necessary for it to qualify as an architectural masterpiece. Yet this very fact enhances its value as an image and record of the changing centuries. It is itself a record, a chronicle of England's story written in brick and stone and wood and disturbing the imagination with a sense of momentous historic events and famous historic personalities. The nature of these personalities and the story of their lives form the subject of the following pages.

The Old Palace at Hatfield from the south, showing the clustered lime trees

Overleaf left Queen Elizabeth I in the Ermine Portrait, attributed to Nicholas Hilliard, and right the Rainbow Portrait probably by Isaac Oliver

SINE SOLE
RIS.

Part I

I

ELIZABETH I

THERE IS no question – I must start with Queen Elizabeth. For though this story is the story of the Cecil family, she knew Hatfield before they did and, if it had not been for her, they might not have come there at all. Indeed, their fate and hers were one. Throughout her long reign, her chief minister was always a Cecil – first William, Lord Burghley, then his son Robert – and each identified himself with her in a way that is true of no other monarch and minister in our history. She herself spoke of William Cecil as 'my spirit'. So, equally, could she have spoken of his son: so could they both have spoken of her. Even more accurately; for she was the inspiration of their life's work. As such, she still presides over their house. The portraits of her there show her spirit incarnate. Appropriately they present her simultaneously in two aspects: real and ideal. She is dressed and posed to seem less a human being than the impersonal hieratic image of semi-divine monarchy. In the Ermine Portrait, she stands before us got up like an idol, in a dress stiff with votive gems, the gold sword of state at her elbow and an ermine, emblem of virginity, on her sleeve. The Rainbow Portrait is even heavier with allegorical significance. Her mantle is powdered with eyes and ears to signify that she could see and hear everything; on her arm is a serpent, emblem of wisdom; and she holds in her hand a rainbow, symbol of peace. 'No rainbow without the sun' runs the translation of the Latin motto at the side of the picture; Queen Elizabeth is the sun whose presence alone can give peace to her realm.

But all this panoply of emblem and symbol cannot hide from us the fact that we are in the presence of a real and strongly individual woman, with her pale aquiline high-bred countenance, her long hands and intellectual brow, her hard unwavering glance that seems to see so much and to give so little away. Certainly it has given little away to posterity. No one in history has been more studied than Queen Elizabeth I. Yet writers still disagree about her character, her motives, her capacities. No doubt this is partly because she lived in the sixteenth century.

Cranborne Manor, Dorset, the West Country home of the Cecils

People then were very different from us, with customs and conventions and assumptions unlike ours. But Queen Elizabeth would be mysterious in any age. She wanted to be so. Even when she was not deliberately out to baffle, her mode of expression, with its long involved sentences weighed down with ambiguous qualifying clauses, is as hard to understand as a late novel by Henry James. Nor is her conduct much more intelligible, so unpredictable is it, so changeable and devious; and revealing her as such a paradoxical mixture of the petty and the majestic, the bold and the cautious, the rough and the subtle, the fickle and the purposeful. 'The Queen was sometimes more than a man and in truth sometimes less than a woman,' said Robert Cecil. This sentence is as near as we are likely to get to the final word about her. But only if we recognize that its force lies in its first half, 'The Queen was sometimes more than a man.'

Queen Elizabeth I presided triumphantly over the destinies of England during what was possibly the most crucial phase in its whole history. She was able to do so because she possessed, as few rulers, male or female, have ever done, the wisdom to perceive the right policy for her country and the art to put it into effect; and because she was fired both by a passionate patriotism and by a grand imaginative sense of her role as Regent of God on Earth, to whom she must be answerable for the welfare of her people at the last and dreadful Day of Judgment. It is true that even here the paradoxes of her nature disclose themselves. She loved her country largely because she identified it with herself: and her sense of a divine mission did not prevent her from being uncommonly easy-going alike on points of doctrine and points of morality, if it suited her interest to be so. Yet one has only to read her private prayers and her great speeches to her people to realize that it would be very superficial to think that this meant that her patriotism or her piety was false. Her spirit was as impressive as her talents. When all is said that can be said against her, Queen Elizabeth I, the most famous of English monarchs, deserves her fame.

II

Hatfield was not the scene of her triumphs. All the same it was very important in her life; for it was there that she prepared herself for them. At Hatfield was enacted much of the drama of her youth. This was a drama as tense as *Hamlet*. Indeed the history of Shakespeare's age teaches us that he was a much more realistic author than one might have imagined. To read about Elizabeth's early life is to enter the world of Jacobean tragedy, sensational and spectacular, gorgeous and bloodstained.

Its character was the result of historical circumstances. The sixteenth century in England was a period of revolutionary change, during which a whole long-established political, religious, and economic system was overturned and a medieval country transformed into a modern one. Revolutionary change means chaos or the threat of it. To avoid this, people turn to strong government, in this case to the virtual despotism of a new royal family, the brilliant and formidable family of Tudor, who ruled with the assistance of a new aristocracy, able and forcible as their masters, avid for wealth and power and with little scruple as to how they got them. Indeed, the men and women who governed England during the first half of the sixteenth century, from the King downwards, had some of the characteristics of gangsters. And the world they lived in was in many respects a gangsters' world, violent, lawless and unstable, the scene of a continuous struggle for domination fought by any means, however treacherous and brutal, and often literally to the death.

Modern statesmen sometimes speak of their lives as an ordeal. They might remember that in the reigns of Henry VIII and Edward VI most chief minsters ended by having their heads cut off; while anyone who chanced, by accident of birth, to be eminent enough to be useful as a pawn in the political game played by these ministers ran the risk of being killed along with them. Innocence could not save them, nor age, nor sex. The venerable Countess of Salisbury and the sixteen-year-old Lady Jane Grey both ended their lives on the scaffold: it was thought that they might cause trouble simply by existing. In those days to be important was to be in danger. The very word 'Court' – since the Court was the arena where the struggle for power was fought out – became a synonym for the dangerous and deceptive glories of the world, playing on the ambition of man to lure him to his doom. The poets of the period harp on this. 'Let my son fly the courts of princes,' cries the dying Antonio, husband of the Duchess of Malfi; and, sang Sir Walter Raleigh, 'Go tell the Court it glows and shines like rotten wood.' He had reason to know.

So, very soon, did the young Princess Elizabeth. Almost from the time she was born, her position was precarious. The triumphs of her reign often lead us to forget that for most of her youth the chances were against her becoming Queen. She had rivals with claims to the throne as good as or better than hers. Though she was born a king's daughter, by the time she was three years old her father had killed her mother and declared her to be a bastard. This did not mean that he had turned against her permanently: from time to time he had her to Court and treated her fondly. But his favour was not to be depended on. Indeed, the ageing Henry VIII, with his huge bulk and cruel mouth and cold unpredictable rages, was not the kind of father to give a child a sense of security. After his death, insecurity turned into danger. Henry VIII, in his will, had restored her to the line of succession. From this time on she was a possible candidate for the throne, and as such was flung into the whirlpool of the power struggle. From the age of fourteen,

Henry VIII, and Elizabeth as a princess

Elizabeth might at any moment have found herself in the position of having to defend her character and perhaps her life against those who saw her as an obstacle to their political schemes. Nor, as it turned out, was there anyone she could trust to advise her how best to do this. She had to rely only on herself. It was a strange and terrifying situation for a girl in her teens to find herself in.

However, the future Queen Elizabeth I was equal to it. For eleven years she put on an extraordinary performance in which her qualities of coolness and judgment showed themselves as effectively as ever they were to do in the days of her greatness; her adroitness in avoiding traps, and her self-control. This was the more remarkable in that, now and again, she allowed it to be broken by outbursts of passion that showed she was far from feeling calm underneath. Her position was never safe, and she faced several perilous crises. But she met them in such a way as to survive them all.

III

Several of these crises happened at the old Palace of Hatfield: a spreading college-like building of russet brick that had been planned round a quadrangle and erected in 1496 as a residence for the Bishops of Ely. Henry VIII had taken it over at the Reformation and used it mainly as a country home for his children. In 1533 Princess Elizabeth, three months old, arrived there with a complete household of her own, ruled over by her governess, Lady Bryan. One day her father rode down from London to visit her. It may be presumed, since this was his motive in coming, that he made himself pleasant to her; but the visit was also evidence, had she been old enough to realize it, that his pleasantness was not to be relied on. Mary, his seventeen-year-old daughter by Queen Katherine of Aragon, was also staying at Hatfield, deprived of her royal title. Henry VIII had sent her down there to wait on her little sister as a punishment for refusing to recognize Ann Boleyn as his lawful wife. He had also given orders that, while he was at Hatfield, she was to be confined to her room. However, as he left, she ran up to the roof of the palace, and there, stretching out her hands, she cried out asking his forgiveness. He heard her, looked up, touched his hat in formal recognition. Then he averted his face and rode away.

Within two years Mary was to be avenged. Henry got rid of his second wife, and now it was the three-year-old Elizabeth's turn to lose her title. She was already sufficiently aware of her royal blood to resent this. On hearing the news she paused, and then, 'How haps it?' she said with displeasure. 'Yesterday my Lady Princess, today but my Lady Elizabeth!' Thus early was she brought face to face with the uncertainty of human fortune. A more distressing proof of this was in store for her. She must have been still a child when she learned that her mother had been beheaded by what was in fact the order of her father.

It is a mistake, however, to think of Elizabeth's childhood as all blood and tears. On the contrary it had the advantages as well as the disadvantages of her privileged position. These advantages were great. The century of political revolution was also the century of the English Renaissance. It was an age of discovery and creation, intellectual, artistic, religious; and since the new monarchy and the new nobility were the fountain and centre of all fame and power, the discoverers and creators looked first to them for support.

They found it. Whatever their faults, the new monarchy and the new nobility were not Philistine. They were often highly cultivated; and when they were not plotting to betray their rivals and compass their executions, they occupied themselves in patronizing scholars, founding libraries, collecting works of art and singing madrigals. It became fashionable for a gentleman to be learned. The great ladies of the day also studied history and theology, literature and the ancient languages, and were admired for so doing. Henry VIII himself epitomized this strange blend of the savage and the civilized. The same man who had his wives beheaded and thought it a proper punishment for a rebel to be hung up in chains till he starved to death, could write an able theological treatise and a melodious song. These two last activities were typical not only of the man but of his period. It was the age of the Reformation as well as of the Renaissance. In addition to having minds, the gangsters also had souls, about whose ultimate fate they were deeply concerned. The most crucial intellectual issues of the day were religious, while its emotional life found its most natural echo in the art of music at its most spiritual, in the poignant unearthly strains of Tallis and Taverner. Exquisite and crude, brutal and spiritual – the world of Elizabeth's youth was all four. Once more we think of *Hamlet*. The events of that world are as barbaric and melodramatic as those in the play; but the people engaged in them were, at the same time, fostering a culture as rich and subtle and profound as that of Hamlet himself.

From her childhood Elizabeth was introduced to this culture. When the curtain next rises on the Hatfield scene, she is ten years old, living there with her six-year-old brother, Edward Prince of Wales, and sharing his lessons. These lessons were of an intensive kind. Their aim was to fit the young prince and princess for the exalted state of life to which it had pleased God to call them. This meant what, according to the standards of the day, was the highest, fullest education possible, based primarily on religion and the ancient and modern languages but extending to include history, geography, mathematics, science and music. Edward and Elizabeth were kept hard at it. They got up very early and began the day with prayer and pious reading. Till dinner, which was about midday, they did their lessons; later they separated, he to take part in outdoor exercises, she to practise the lute and viol and, when tired of that, to embroider. On Sundays and holidays both children were taken to listen to sermons. Parker, afterwards Archbishop of Canterbury, preached specially before Elizabeth when she was only seven years old.

So arduous a programme would have been too much for most children. But not for these: they were formidable children. Formidable also were their teachers. Edward and Elizabeth were instructed, not by ordinary professional tutors and governesses, but by scholars of outstanding distinction from the universities: brilliant representatives of the most vital intellectual movements of the time, enthusiastic for the new learning and the new faith. Elizabeth herself had the luck to have as her particular tutor William Grindal, a pupil of Roger Ascham, the most famous educationalist of his time; and later Ascham himself. His theories were intelligent and humane. He was against cramming and against harsh punishments, especially the frequent beatings so popular among schoolmasters of the period; and he believed in studying the individual disposition of each child.

The royal children responded to such methods and such teachers. By the age of seven, Edward wrote admirable Latin verses and delighted in theology. Elizabeth's accomplishments were scarcely less remarkable for her age. At ten, her Latin was excellent and her Italian adequate. A year later she presented her stepmother, Queen Catherine Parr, with a volume, its binding beautifully embroidered by herself in blue and silver, containing a translation, also by herself, from the French of Queen Margaret of Navarre. It was introduced by a covering letter in an exquisite handwriting and included a sentence couched already in the elaborate and metaphorical style of her maturity. 'Even as an instrument of iron or other metal waxeth soon rusty unless it be continually occupied,' she wrote, 'even so shall this wit of mine wax dull and inapt to do or understand anything perfectly, unless it be always occupied with some manner of study.' 'Always' is surely an exaggeration; otherwise these lofty sentiments did express the truth. In these years was kindled, in her strong and active mind, a burning flame of intellectual interest which was to remain alight all her life; so that, even when burdened by the responsibilities of a queen, she still found time to translate from the classics and to turn for help to the stern wisdom of Seneca when, as she put it, 'her soul's quiet was flown away'.

She enjoyed her lessons. But she had other pleasures too: dancing, hunting and hacking through the woods and open country that surrounded the then rural little town of Hatfield. Elizabeth rode well and looked her best on horseback. She was with people she liked, especially her governess, a relation on her mother's side called Katherine, nicknamed Kat, Ashley, a friendly lively woman and very fond of her charge. She was also indiscreet and meddlesome, as Elizabeth was to discover. But this was later on; for the time being these weaknesses did not matter. Finally, and in spite of the difference in their ages, Elizabeth enjoyed the company of her brother. They had much in common, two pale, blond, sharp-featured children, alarmingly collected in manner and with alarmingly precocious interests and intellects. The future Edward VI was a natural puritan: at eight years old he already much enjoyed reading the Proverbs of Solomon, where, he was interested to find, he was warned to 'beware of wanton women'. Elizabeth, though by nature far from puritan, appeared by this time to have been sufficiently influenced, by the company she kept, to take a puritan line. The poem she translated for Catherine Parr was entitled *The Miseries of a Sinful Soul* and was an austere production that compares the strayings of the soul from God to the fornications of an unfaithful wife.

Puritan or not, this was a peaceful period in Elizabeth's childhood. But it was not to last. In November 1546 a message arrived from the Court ordering her to leave Hatfield for another royal residence at Enfield. Soon after she got there, her brother Edward wrote her a letter which showed her how much he missed her. 'Change of place', he said, 'does not vex me so much dearest sister as your going from me . . . I may hope to visit you soon, if nothing happens to me in the meantime.' However, something did happen. Henry VIII died and Edward became King.

Elizabeth was now embarked on a stormier phase of her existence. So indeed was England: with Henry's strong hand removed and a ten-year-old boy as King, the country was for six years a battlefield in which turbulent nobles fought for power. Elizabeth became important as a possible successor to the throne; and, since she was now fourteen years old, she was considered a responsible person and as such likely to be in danger. Within two years she was.

The cause of the trouble was Edward's uncle on his mother's side, Lord High Admiral Thomas Seymour. Seymour's elder brother, the Duke of Somerset, was governing the country as Regent for the young king; but the Admiral was also ambitious for supreme power. He was thirty-eight years old, an artful, reckless, tawny-headed tiger of a man, attractive to women and sharp to make use of his attractions for his own purposes. On Henry VIII's death, he set to work to attract the youthful Elizabeth with a view to marrying her and thus getting himself into the line of succession. He discovered, however, that this might involve him in a prosecution for treason. He therefore transferred his attentions to the widowed Catherine Parr, an old flame of his; so successfully that he married her.

But he had not given up Elizabeth. After her father's death she had been sent to live with Catherine Parr. Seymour took the opportunity to pay her attentions. These were not of a refined kind. He used to burst gaily into her bedroom, bare-legged and in his night-shirt, slapping her genially on the buttocks and sometimes making as if to get into bed with her. Catherine learned of these goings on. She was a jolly romping woman and not particularly shocked by them, but she thought it wiser to render them harmless by taking part in them herself. Together she and Seymour used to advance upon the young princess and tickle her. Catherine's policy did not work; such policies seldom do. Seymour secretly got hold of a key to Elizabeth's room and invaded it before she was up. Elizabeth heard him coming and hid; Seymour waited for her in vain. After this she made a practice of getting up so early that, when Seymour used his key again, he found her sitting at a table

Mildred, Lady Burghley, wife of the 1st Baron, in a painting
at Hatfield House attributed to Hans Eworth

fully dressed and reading. This showed her prudence rather than her true feelings. For she was not unstirred by Seymour's boisterous charms. It was noted that when his name was mentioned, Elizabeth blushed and looked pleased. Some weeks later Catherine Parr, entering a room unannounced, found the couple locked in each other's arms. It is not surprising that after this she arranged for Elizabeth to go and live elsewhere. A few months later Catherine died in childbirth. Seymour had not been so fond of her as to waste time in grief. He was soon absorbed in new plans for power, which again involved marrying Elizabeth.

The next scene staged at Hatfield opens to disclose her in conference with her Treasurer, a fat man called Thomas Parry, just back from London, where he had gone to see Seymour about leasing his house there to the princess. Parry told her that Seymour had asked him a great many questions about her property. Elizabeth demanded the reason for this. 'I do not know,' Parry replied, 'unless he would like to have you also.' He added that Seymour wanted Elizabeth to help him in his plans by making herself pleasant to the Duchess of Somerset. This was a mistake on his part. Elizabeth particularly disliked the Duchess, who had committed the unforgivable sin of treating her without what she considered to be the respect due to a princess. 'I will not do so, and so tell him!' she exclaimed indignantly. Parry went off to discuss the general situation with Kat Ashley. Perhaps she too felt Seymour's virile attractions, for she turned out to be strongly on his side and wanted him to marry Elizabeth. Parry said that Seymour had treated Catherine Parr badly; how would Elizabeth fare? 'Tush,' cried Kat Ashley, 'I know that he will make but too much of her, and she knows that well enough.'

Meanwhile Seymour was taking other steps to realize his ambitions; in particular he thought to put Edward VI off Somerset by telling him that he was kept short of money. 'Ye are a very beggarly king now,' he said; and he offered to lend him forty pounds. Edward took the forty pounds; but remained coldly immune to Seymour's blandishments. As a matter of fact, Seymour's plots were already in process of being discovered. Somerset, though a less ruthless character than his brother, did not hesitate to take strong action against him when he found him threatening his own position. He had Seymour arrested and sent to the Tower of London, for conspiring to marry Princess Elizabeth. Kat Ashley and Parry, suspected of being implicated in this conspiracy, were also taken off to the Tower, where poor Kat found herself confined in an uncomfortable cell with no glass in its window, so that she had to stuff it with straw to keep out the cold. Meanwhile Somerset sent a courtier, Sir William Tyrwhitt, down to Hatfield to try to discover from Elizabeth whether she had agreed to Seymour's proposals. If she

William Cecil, 1st Baron Burghley: a Hatfield painting also probably by Hans Eworth

had, she would be involved in Seymour's treasonable plot and as such liable to the death penalty.

She realized her danger: she had heard too often of too many executions, including that of her mother, to think her own unlikely. It is now that her extraordinary gifts of brain and character first show themselves in action. Outwardly she seemed much upset; at one moment she was raging, at the next in tears. In fact she kept her head. She denied having had anything to do with Seymour and said nothing about his compromising behaviour to her in the past. Tyrwhitt told her that, if she would only confess, all blame would be put on her elders. She continued to deny everything and would not admit that Parry or Kat Ashley were to blame either. Tyrwhitt was baffled. 'I do see it in her face that she is guilty,' he

Edward Seymour, afterwards Lord Protector Somerset, and Edward VI

reported, 'but she hath a very good wit; and nothing is gotten of her but by great policy.' Somerset tried gentler methods. He wrote her a conciliatory letter. Firmly Elizabeth repeated her denials, and she went on to carry the war into the enemy's country by complaining that she heard it was being scandalously rumoured that she was with child by Seymour. Could she be allowed, she asked, to come to Court and demonstrate that this was untrue? She ended with an eloquently phrased profession of injured innocence: 'My conscience beareth me my witness, which I would not for all earthly things offend in anything; for I know I have a soul to save as well as other folk have.'

She was not out of the wood yet. Parry lacked her strength of spirit; weakened by fright and the discomforts of life in the Tower, he blurted out both his recent negotiations with Seymour and also the story of Seymour's earlier relations with Elizabeth. Kat Ashley, confronted with the news of Parry's admissions, broke down and confirmed them. Their double confession was written down, signed, sent to Hatfield and presented to Elizabeth. She read it through, we are told, 'breathless and abashed'. Indeed, it must have been embarrassing to see, written down for strangers to read, the unedifying story of Seymour's bare legs and playful slaps. Yet she finished reading it with relief. Her servants had stood by her on the only point that really mattered: they had said nothing implicating her in Seymour's plots. The crisis was past. Although Somerset believed her to be guilty, she had frustrated every effort to prove her so. All he could do, to show his displeasure, was to send down Tyrwhitt's wife to be her governess in place of Kat Ashley. At this, Elizabeth lost her temper. She 'wept all one night and loured all next day'; and she wrote a letter to Somerset repeating that it would injure her reputation in the eyes of the world to be thought to deserve such strict supervision. 'The people will say that I deserve through my lewd behaviour to have such a one,' she protested. Somerset answered crossly that she thought too highly of herself. She returned to the attack, reminding him that she was the King's sister and that he ought to treat her with more respect. A few months later he yielded enough to let her have Parry and Kat Ashley back again.

It was victory. But Elizabeth had to pay for it. The strain of the struggle had been great on a girl of her age and with her highly strung nervous system. A few days after Tyrwhitt's visit she collapsed and went to bed; throughout the following year she was often ill. But she was not so ill as to be incapable of reflecting on what had happened and drawing some valuable conclusions from it. On the 20th of March 1549 Seymour was executed. Elizabeth heard the news with ironic calm: 'There died a man with much wit and very little judgment,' she commented. Any love for him she had ever cherished was gone, to be replaced by a distrust of the passion of love in general. Born normally susceptible to male charms, she had learned that anyone in her position must be very cautious about yielding to them. For the rest of her life she saw to it that her head ruled her heart.

Seymour's career also provided her with an object lesson of another kind. It taught her that, in the stern battle of sixteenth-century political life, cleverness and personality counted for less than prudence and a sense of reality. From this time on, these were the qualities she had learned to look for in those who served her. Already one man had struck her as noticeably possessed of them: a thin, sober, well-mannered secretary of Somerset called William Cecil, who, some time in 1548, had been sent down to Hatfield to see her on business. Shortly afterwards she appointed him to be her surveyor, that is to say the man in charge of her estates. It was to turn out an appointment of extreme significance.

Finally her experiences had brought home to her the importance of reputation. She must be very careful indeed in the future not to be thought capable of 'lewd demeanour'. In consequence – and this must have been much against her natural inclination – she took to dressing with ostentatious sobriety. When next she went to Court, in contrast to the gorgeous dresses and elaborate hair-styles of the Court ladies, she appeared in a plain dress with her auburn locks dressed severely close to her head. The result was all she could have wished. She attracted a great deal of attention and approval and was welcomed enthusiastically by Edward VI. He called her his dear and sweet sister 'Temperance' and he showed his affection by giving her the Palace of Hatfield as a present.

There she settled down to spend much of the next few years, living a retired life and concentrating on the final stages of her education. Ascham was with her for the first year or so; after he left, she continued working on the lines he had laid down. While they were together, they used to read the Greek Testament and religious writers, ancient and modern. They also made an intensive study of the great classical authors, notably Cicero and Livy, Demosthenes and Sophocles. Ascham entered sympathetically into Elizabeth's difficult situation; he made a point of calling attention to the passages in the classics likely to strengthen her spirit to withstand misfortune; and he encouraged her to prepare herself for the future by reading history. It became her favourite subject, but she also found time to learn Spanish, Flemish and even a little Welsh.

Nor was her education confined to reading. Ascham thought it important for her to be able to express her thoughts readily. Accordingly the two spent hours in intellectual discussion, carried on generally in one or other of the languages she was learning. In all these various activities she put on a dazzling performance. Ascham wrote to a friend: 'Her mind has no womanly weakness, her perseverance is equal to that of a man and her memory keeps alive what it quickly picks up. She talks French and Italian as well as she talks English and has often talked to me readily and well in Latin and moderately in Greek. When she writes Greek and Latin nothing is more beautiful than her handwriting.' Comically anxious that his correspondent should not think that he was exaggerating, out of reverence for royalty, he added: 'I am inventing nothing, there is no need!'

IV

Edward's VI's reign proceeded on its lurid course. Somerset fell and was executed – 'the Duke of Somerset had his head cut off upon Tower Hill between eight and nine this morning', noted the boy king curtly in his diary – and was followed as Protector by his evil and victorious rival, John Dudley, Duke of Northumberland. Then in January 1553 Edward began to exhibit the symptoms of acute pulmonary consumption. He lingered for six months of growing agony. 'Lord God,' he was heard crying, 'deliver me out of this miserable wretched life.' As he breathed his last, a terrific storm broke out, plunging his bedchamber into darkness and filling the air with clap upon deafening clap of thunder. It was thought to be the spirit of the dead Henry VIII protesting from another world against the violation of his will. For Northumberland had played upon Edward's fanatical Protestant feelings to persuade him that the best way to secure the true religion was to break the line of succession, as laid down by his father, and to bestow the crown upon his cousin, Northumberland's daughter-in-law, Lady Jane Grey.

Lady Jane Grey

This reckless plan failed. Most people wanted the rightful heir, Princess Mary; and her friends acted quickly. Within a few weeks Northumberland was defeated and killed, Lady Jane Grey and her husband Lord Guildford Dudley were in the Tower; and Mary was safely on the throne.

During these alarms and excursions, Elizabeth took care to stay quietly in the country. But, when it had become clear that Mary had won, she wrote warmly congratulating her and went up to meet her on her arrival in London. A day or two later, the two sisters made a ceremonial entry into the capital, riding side by side. Though plain and faded, Mary was given a friendly welcome by the populace. But it was the figure beside her that drew all eyes and set the people cheering: the pale young princess with the red-gold hair and piercing glance, sitting superbly on her horse. It is the first account of Elizabeth in which we get a glimpse of her star-quality: that glittering personal magnetism, able to make itself felt by whole crowds, that later enabled her to exercise so compelling and magical an effect on her subjects. 'The Princess Elizabeth is greatly to be feared,' reported the Spanish Ambassador to his Government; 'she has a spirit full of incantation.' Here was another step in Elizabeth's education as a ruler. If she had not realized her spell-binding power before, she must have done so now, and recognized its use as a political weapon.

She was to have need of it. The next year or two were to be the most dangerous of her life. Mary's accession meant that Elizabeth was involved in the bitterest struggle of the age, the religious struggle. Henry VIII had originally broken with Rome for dynastic motives; he also wanted to stop the Pope from claiming the right to interfere with the King's supreme power over his subjects. But, so far as religious doctrine was concerned, Henry was conservative. As has often been pointed out, he was no less ready to burn new-style religious reformers for heresy than to behead old-fashioned Catholics for treason. Despite these strong measures, however, Protestantism grew stronger during his last years. At his death it took over as the official national creed; with the result that, when Mary came to the throne, a substantial part of the English nation was Protestant. A great many people, however, were still Catholic; and still more were passive and uncertain. Mary, a fanatical Catholic, did not therefore find much difficulty in restoring Catholicism as the Church of the country. All the same, England was split over religion as never before.

This put Elizabeth into an extremely delicate position; for, since by her father's will she was now the heir to the throne, all eyes were watching to see what line she took on the split. Any line involved a risk. There was no question, indeed, of openly proclaiming herself a Protestant. If Elizabeth did not conform to her sister's Church, she would certainly lose her place in the succession and most likely her life as well. In fact she did not object to conforming. Though Elizabeth had a strong sense of God as mysteriously directing her fate according to His will, she did not, like Mary or Edward, care much about doctrinal precision. Moreover, in spite of her education, she was not by nature Protestant-minded; she liked hierarchy, ritual and tradition; and so far as the Protestant spirit was against these, she resented it. Like her father, she was against the old religion mainly because it threatened royal supremacy. Yet this very fact also put her against Mary and the Pope. Besides, she knew that if she did back them at all strongly, she would lose the Protestants, that is to say her chief supporters among the people of England.

From Foxe's Book of Martyrs: *the burning of heretics and heretical literature in the 16th century*

She was thus faced with the question: how was she to keep her head on her shoulders and yet retain credit with those she hoped would be her future subjects? She found herself on a political tightrope.

Luckily she was by now an expert tightrope-walker. For five years she contrived to maintain a halfway position, conforming to the outward forms of Catholicism, but in such a way as to persuade the Protestants that she was doing it against her will. In the few private conversations she had with Mary, she protested her loyalty and even managed to shed some tears to prove it; but, away from her, she took every opportunity to increase her own popularity with the public and to suggest that it was she, not Mary, who was the true daughter of Bluff King Hal, the embodiment of the independent spirit of England. This made her liked not only by Protestants but by the average Catholic, for the typical sixteenth-century Englishman, whatever his creed, was aggressively patriotic. For the rest, Elizabeth cultivated an extreme discretion and confided in no one.

*Philip II of Spain, on
a medallion struck to commemorate
his marriage to Mary Tudor*

Mary's first two years were the most risky for Elizabeth. In January 1554 Sir Thomas Wyatt raised a rebellion with the avowed purpose of making her Queen. He was defeated and executed; so also, as a sort of precautionary measure, were the already imprisoned Lady Jane Grey and her husband. Elizabeth, suspected of being a party to the rebellion, was summoned to London; and after a short time she was sent to the Tower with, it might seem, every chance of being executed too. Once more she displayed her courage and her skill. At first she said she was too ill to come to London; when compelled to do so, she made her entry in such a way as to enlist popular sympathy on her side. She had herself carried in, lying in an open litter, clothed in white and looking pale, proud and tragic. She was received with cheers. A few days later, landing at the Traitors' Gate at the Tower of London, she refused to go in and sat down on the steps crying out that she was no traitor; with such spirit that even the guards, sent to arrest her, broke out in sympathetic applause. Once in the Tower, she showed her other and more intellectual gifts. She was examined and cross-examined for hours on end by ministers of the government. But she defended herself so cleverly that in the end it was decided to release her from the Tower and send her to live in the country at Woodstock in Oxfordshire, though under strict guardianship.

She was never to be in such danger again. During these years Mary married Philip of Spain. He did not want Elizabeth to be treated as an enemy. For he was mainly concerned with outwitting Spain's chief enemy on the Continent – France; and France was backing the claims to the throne of England of Mary Queen of Scots, at that time married to the French King's son. Rather than that

Mary Tudor, in a painting by Antonio Moro

this should happen, Philip supported Elizabeth's claims and so wanted to be on good terms with her. He persuaded Mary to treat her sister more mildly.

The result of this change of policy on her part was to bring Elizabeth back to Hatfield. She arrived there early in October 1555. As she drove into the town the bells of the church clashed out in welcome. Her popularity was still growing, largely in consequence of Mary's marriage. The Englishman's love of his country at that time went along with a violent dislike of foreigners. Philip's arrival meant that London was full of Spanish priests and courtiers, to the disgust of its native inhabitants. This disgust began to extend to Mary herself. She did not improve her popularity with her subjects by choosing this moment to start a savage persecution of Protestant heretics. The English were used to seeing people being hanged and executed for treason. Seeing them burned for heresy was a more uncommon experience, and one that they did not like. As Mary's popularity declined, Elizabeth's grew.

She stayed at Hatfield for most of the remaining years of Mary's reign. Though more peaceful than before, these years had their anxieties. The events of the past repeated themselves in less dangerous forms. Once more a plot, the Dudley plot, was discovered; once more Elizabeth's servants were implicated, and poor Kat Ashley found herself in the Tower for another month. But this time Elizabeth herself was left alone. It was intimated to her that she was not suspected; but as a precaution against Elizabeth's getting mixed up in any future conspiracy, Mary sent down Sir Thomas Pope, afterwards founder of Trinity College, Oxford, to watch over her. He turned out an agreeable civilized man, and he and Elizabeth got on well together.

Elizabeth also found herself in difficulties at this time about her possible marriage. As the heir to the throne, she attracted a number of foreign suitors, French, Swedish, Savoyard. Philip encouraged one of them, the Duke of Savoy, as a possible ally against the French. Elizabeth set her face against these proposals. Mary's example had been a warning to her against marrying a foreigner. Demurely she explained that, for the time being, she had decided against marriage: she had a fancy for the holy state of virginity. Apart from these worries, her life at Hatfield was pleasant enough. She was only a captive in the sense that she could not go away without permission. Otherwise she led the normal life of a royal princess in her own palace with her own household and musicians and horses. Her own tutor, too: Ascham was back, helping her to complete her education. Together they studied Plato and the Fathers of the Church; together they discussed history and the principles that should guide a statesman. These discussions were conducted on less unequal terms than in earlier days. Ascham knew more ancient history than she did, but Elizabeth by now had seen history in the making, as he had never done. 'I teach her words and she teaches me things,' he said.

Life at Hatfield had its lighter side too. There is no more talk of Elizabeth's puritan manners and habits. On the contrary, one day we are told of her out stag-hunting, attended by a retinue of twelve ladies, clothed in white satin, and twenty gentlemen in green, and met by fifty archers with scarlet boots and yellow caps, one of whom presented her with a silver-headed arrow wound round with peacock feathers. At Shrovetide 1556 Sir Thomas Pope felt sufficiently friendly towards his royal charge to present her in the Great Hall of Hatfield with a masque paid for by himself, in which twelve minstrels took part, together with forty-six knights and ladies dressed in crimson satin embroidered with gold wreaths and garnished with pearls, all in front of a cloth-of-gold castle decorated with pomegranates. The festivities lasted two days and included also a banquet of seventy dishes and thirty spiced plates – whatever that may mean – followed by a performance of the tragedy of Holofernes.

Mary heard of these jollifications and was displeased. It was one thing for Sir Thomas Pope to treat Elizabeth humanely; it was another to encourage her to get above herself by giving parties for her. Mary wrote to Pope telling him that such follies must stop at once. This did not prevent her from visiting her sister in the following year and being entertained by her with appropriate lavishness. After Mass in the morning, the two sisters watched a bear-baiting, which they much enjoyed. That night after supper, in a room hung for the occasion with a gorgeous set of tapestries, they saw a play acted by the 'Children of Paul's', a company of choristers. When the play was over, one of the company, a boy called Maximilian Poynes, famous for his beautiful voice, sang accompanied on the virginals by Elizabeth herself. The accounts of this visit illustrate vividly the strange contrasts presented by life in those days: first the solemn mystery of the Mass, with its wax lights and splendid vestments and venerable Latin liturgy, followed by the brutal spectacle of a bear and dogs tearing each other's flesh with bloodstained teeth and claws; and then, after nightfall, the courtly company, gathered in the candlelit chamber, to watch the long fingers of the Princess playing on the keys of the virginals, and listen to their frail precise tones as they mingled with the soaring sweetness of the boy's singing.

It was the last time the sisters met. Within less than a year Mary was dying. She died despairing. Everything had gone wrong for her. She was childless; Philip, whom she loved, had gone away and showed no sign of wishing to come back; at the same time he had involved her in a disastrous foreign war, which lost her Calais and left her treasury nearly empty. Moreover, her persecutions had made her people hate her; and, after all, they had proved to be in vain. She had to face the fact that she was to be succeeded by Elizabeth, whom she knew to be at heart a heretic. Already Mary heard that the roads to Hatfield were crowded with important persons, English and foreign, hurrying down to pay court to the future

Queen. The future Queen watched them and waited. A mild afternoon in November found her sitting under an oak tree in the park, reading the Greek Testament. She looked up to see a cavalcade of horsemen approaching; they were the Lords of the Council coming to tell her that she was Queen. At their words she rose and knelt on the grass. '*Domino factum est et mirabile in oculis nostris,*' she said; 'It is the Lord's doing and marvellous in our eyes.'

In the ultimate sense, no doubt, she spoke truly: without the assistance of Providence she could not have survived for twenty-five dangerous years. But it was also true that she herself had done a good deal to help Providence. Elizabeth's precarious progress to the throne was a triumph of coolness and prudence, diplomatic dexterity and histrionic skill. And, for all the many painful moments it must have entailed, it had been worth while. Most born rulers grow up sheltered from the harsher realities of political life, so that, when they come to power, they are ill equipped to deal with them. Not so Queen Elizabeth I: from childhood she had been faced with political reality at its most brutal, and not from a protected position. She knew what it was to be a subject, a suspect, a prisoner. On the other hand she also knew what it was to be a princess: she had the confidence to command and the sense of her queenly role as one who had grown up knowing that in her veins flowed the blood royal of England. Finally her life, for all its drama, had also contained long periods of inaction in which she had time to reflect and observe and draw conclusions as to what were the basic issues of her time, what policies were best able to solve them, and what qualities were most likely to further these policies. Elizabeth's troubled youth was an advantage to her. Nobody ever became a ruler better trained to make a success of it.

She lost no time in laying the foundation of this success. Within a few days of her succession, she had named her chief ministers and held her first Council in the Great Hall of Hatfield. 'The burden that is fallen upon me maketh me amazed,' she declared to her assembled ministers; 'and yet, considering that I am God's creature ordained to obey His appointment, I will yield thereto, desiring from the bottom of my heart that I may have the assistance of His grace to be the Minister of His heavenly will in this office now committed to me.' She realized, however, that there would be no harm in having some human assistance too; and already she had taken steps to obtain it. One of her first acts on becoming Queen was to send for William Cecil and appoint him her principal secretary. Soon after, she left Hatfield. Though she came back for an occasional day's hunting, she was never to live there again.

A 17th-century woodcut of bull- and bear-baiting

2

WILLIAM CECIL
Lord Burghley

WILLIAM CECIL spent even less time at Hatfield than Queen Elizabeth; it was his son Robert who made it the home of the Cecils. Yet William is one of the ghosts who haunt the place. For he and Robert were so closely identified that one cannot talk of one without talking of the other. Robert finished the work that William had started. Any picture of the Cecils of Hatfield and their achievement must include the picture of William.

It is hard, however, to be sure that it is a good likeness. The outer man is clear enough. He stares down at one so many times from the walls of Hatfield: a slight, upright, soberly dressed figure, pale and bearded, with a high forehead and a thoughtful, careworn cast of countenance. His demeanour seems to have been of a piece with his appearance: dignified, discreet and unruffled. His talk, too, was discreet but continuously intelligent, well informed and made racy by a strain of pithy, ironical, worldly wisdom and an occasional stroke of dry academic wit. He was careful to keep this under control. 'I have gained more by my temperance and forebearing than ever I did by my wit,' he once said. The remark is significant; for it bears out the thing people noticed most about him, the overriding impression of dedication, of a man in whom all other interests were kept subordinate to the work which occupied most of his strictly ordered day. Indeed, it is for this work that he is remembered; for what he did as a statesman, not for what he was as a man.

Inevitably this has made it hard for posterity to be sure what the man was like. William Cecil's face was a public face, and a public face is always a mask, hiding the inner man. He confided in no one, had no close friends, 'no inward companion as great men commonly have,' said a contemporary, 'nor did any other know his secrets; some noting it for a fault, but most thinking it a praise and an instance of his wisdom. By trusting none with his secrets, none could reveal them.' We cannot reveal them either. However, the events in his career do disclose some definite

William Cecil, 1st Baron Burghley, in a painting attributed to Marcus Gheeraerts the Younger

facts about his character. They show that though intellectual he was not a contemplative but a man of action, concerned with getting things done. Further, the aims of his actions were twofold. The first was political: William was never content away from the world of affairs, and he was intent to exercise power there. His second aim was dynastic: he desired to perpetuate his name by founding an illustrious family. Throughout his life he pursued these two aims with extreme tenacity. Finally he emerges as a curious blend of the worldly and the religious. On the one hand he was a tough realist, fully aware of the values of material advantages and sharp to learn the arts required to make the most of them. On the other hand, more assiduously even than most men in that religious age, he studied religious subjects and practised religious observances. The astute and hardheaded statesmen, so deeply committed to the affairs of this world, was at the same time aware of the presence and the pressure of the next world. This dual strain divided his spirit. Absorbed in worldly activities, he yet doubted the value of this world's prizes. Division meant melancholy. William Cecil was a sad man.

His upbringing was such as to prepare him for his life's work. He came from a family typical of the new governing classes which rose to power under the Tudors, canny, ambitious, energetic. His grandfather David, the younger son of a poor Welsh squire, left his home – a small grey manor house buried in the remote green hills of the Wales-Hereford border – to follow Henry Tudor in his campaign for the crown. When he became King, Henry rewarded David Cecil by making him a Yeoman of the Guard. This was the foundation of the family fortunes. David also accumulated enough money to buy a property near Stamford in Northamptonshire, where he distinguished himself enough to become Mayor and a Member of Parliament. It was on this foundation his son Richard continued to build. On the one hand he added substantially to the property; on the other he was at pains to keep up the family connection with the Court. He had, as a youth, accompanied Henry VIII to the Field of the Cloth of Gold in the role of a page: later he was made a groom of the Privy Chamber. He supported the King in his breach with the Roman Catholic Church, all the more enthusiastically because it gave him the chance to buy some of the Church's confiscated lands. In general, however, he took care not to meddle in politics.

Meanwhile he married twice. His first wife, Jane Heckington, the daughter of a respected local family and better born than himself, bore him two sons. The elder, William, born in 1520, early showed himself unusually clever and hardworking. After a short period as a Court page and some years at Grantham Grammar School, he went up at the age of fourteen to St John's College,

Robert Cecil, 1st Earl of Salisbury, painted by John de Critz the Elder: at Hatfield House

S:RO, SED SECIO   1608·
                                   ÆTA·48·

Cambridge, the same college that was the centre of the go-ahead intellectual circle which was to provide tutors for Queen Elizabeth. Its mental atmosphere suited William very well. By nature a scholar, he became learned in the classics and also theology. Like his father, he was a firm though moderate Protestant. But there was no question of his going into the Church. From the first he was attracted by political life, and when he left Cambridge he joined the Inns of Court to learn the laws of the land. His years there made a deep impression on him. He left with a peculiar veneration for the law as an expression of the will of society as ordained by God; and he had a consequent horror of anything illegal.

Meanwhile, though always a hard worker – he used to start work punctually at four in the morning – he managed to enjoy himself as a law student. Like Justice Shallow, he liked in later years to recall the gay escapades of his law-student days. One of them shows him as very adroit at extricating himself from any trouble that these might involve him in. It seems that one night, gambling with another student, he lost all his possessions down to his books and bedding. Next day he woke in dismay; but then he had an idea. He made a hole in the wall near the head of his fellow gambler's bed; and in the middle of the night spoke through it. 'O miserable man,' he declaimed in hollow tones, 'repent of thy horrible crimes, consumed in play cozenage and such lewdness . . . or else thou art doomed.' The unhappy victim listened to this apparently supernatural warning sweating with fear. Next day, trembling and falling on his knees before William Cecil, he gave him back his books, his bedding and his money.

The story indicates that at this age at any rate, William's time was not exclusively given up to work. He could relax in other ways too. In later years the French Ambassador is reported to have congratulated him at becoming a father before the age of fourteen. Whether this was true or not, the youthful William could certainly take a risk for love. While still an undergraduate, he got engaged to Mary Cheke, who from a worldly point of view was not a good match. It was true that her brother was a distinguished Greek scholar; but she had no dowry and her mother kept an ale-house. Though William's father opposed the engagement, in 1541 William married Mary Cheke. Two years later she died, leaving him an infant son. He was now twenty-three, with sixty more years of life before him. It is to be noted, however, that this marriage was his last recorded act that could possibly be called imprudent.

In 1545 he married again. This time his choice of bride – though there was no reason to suppose he was not in love – is also evidence of his judgment. Mildred Cooke was the daughter of Sir Anthony Cooke, Governor to the young Prince

A mosaic, in the Library at Hatfield House, of Robert Cecil, 1st Earl of Salisbury

Edward and likely to be a useful connection for William in his future career. She was also fitted to be a companion to him, a favourite pupil of Roger Ascham like Princess Elizabeth, and famous as one of the most learned girls in England. One can believe it from her portrait. With her lofty brow, compressed lips and pale, stern eyes, she looks like the most formidable kind of lady academic. Many found her alarming; which is hardly to be wondered at, seeing that, in addition to talking Greek as easily as English, she was a well-informed and combative arguer for the Protestant cause. But she seems to have had a softer side. She could make herself agreeable to men in a decorous way and she was an admirable wife and mother.

His fortunes continued to prosper. With the help of his father's influence he became a Member of Parliament and a Justice of the Peace; more important, he attracted the favourable attention of Henry VIII. One day on the way to Court he fell into the company of two Irish Catholic priests. The conversation turned on the controversial topic of the Pope's supremacy. Young William argued in Latin with such power and knowledge that his opponents were cowed and silenced. Henry VIII heard of this and sent for William and took him into his service. Nor was Henry the only person to be impressed by him. During the next year or two he made a name for himself with the leading Protestants at Court, especially the Duke of Somerset. When Henry VIII died and Somerset was made Lord Protector, he appointed William to act as his personal Master of Requests. At twenty-seven he was launched on the career that was to lead him to the highest political power.

It was a hazardous journey: the reigns of Edward VI and Mary were to be for William Cecil as much a test and training ground as they were for Elizabeth. Very soon, indeed, his talents were to bring him to a position important enough to be dangerous: sober and pacific, he had shortly to take his chance in the tumultuous and bloodstained arena where lawless ambitious nobles and ruthless religious fanatics battled desperately for power and where a slip might cost him his life. Luckily he was by now well equipped for such an ordeal. William at twenty-seven years old was an extremely sure-footed young man able to adapt himself to work for different persons and factions, and a trained, efficient public servant whom any administration would be pleased to employ.

The next months increased his efficiency by extending his knowledge. England was at war with Scotland; and William accompanied Somerset on the campaign to serve as a judge in courts martial. He cannot have enjoyed it much. He was nearly killed by a stray bullet at the Battle of Pinkie; and in any case he was by nature and conviction profoundly unmilitary. 'He that sets up to live by that profession', he was later to tell his son, 'can hardly be an honest man or a good Christian.' However, he accepted the fact that an army was necessary to protect the state and he took this chance to learn about army organization. Further, the campaign made him realize, as he had not realized before, the extreme importance to England of being good friends with Scotland. Back in England, Somerset showed his sense of William's value by making him his personal secretary. This was not such a piece of luck as might have been thought. Barely a year later, Somerset was driven from power by his rival Warwick and imprisoned in the Tower. William followed him a few months later.

However, his reputation for usefulness soon got him released and established him back at work. He did so well that within two years he was knighted. Meanwhile Somerset too had been released: for a short uneasy period he and Warwick, now Duke of Northumberland, shared the responsibilities of government. William, as one of the few people on good terms with both, did his best to keep them friendly with each other. In vain; in October 1551 Northumberland professed to have discovered evidence that Somerset was conspiring against him. Somerset sent for William and asked him what he should do. William's reply was guarded. 'If you are not guilty, you may be of good courage,' said he; 'if you are I have nothing to say but to lament you.' Innocent or guilty, Somerset's fate was already sealed. By the end of January 1552, his head was off.

William by now was working for Northumberland. This was to prove a more dangerous assignment than working for Somerset. In 1553 Northumberland demanded that his servants should all sign a paper approving his scheme for altering the succession in favour of Lady Jane Grey. This faced William with the most painful decision of his life. Since the succession could only be altered by Act of Parliament, Northumberland's scheme was illegal. It was also contrary to Henry VIII's will. To obey it, therefore, meant offending against the two guiding principles of William's professional life, respect for the law and loyalty to the Royal House of Tudor. On the other hand he knew Northumberland well enough to recognize that to disobey him would cost him his life. William took to going about fully armed and made arrangements for fleeing abroad. However, university training had taught him to refrain from taking action unless he was intellectually convinced that it was right; so, before leaving, he asked the advice of his scholarly brother-in-law, John Cheke. Cheke replied that Socrates in like circumstances had not fled, and he recommended William to read Plato on the subject.

Whether William followed this advice or not we do not know; but he stayed and did not sign. Northumberland insisted; William thought he would certainly be executed. He wrote a letter to his wife declaring that if he had to die it would be for his conscience and to avoid the peril of God's displeasure. But now came a message from Edward VI himself commanding him to sign. He obeyed. Within a short time, however, the country had rejected Northumberland's schemes.

William quickly moved over to Mary's side and sent her a paper explaining his conduct and asking for mercy. Mary granted it readily: she believed his story, for he was, she said, an honest man.

His contemporaries agreed with her. Again and again they praise him as an example of honesty and trustworthiness. Later historians have hesitated to agree with them, especially because of his actions in Edward VI's reign, which they portray as those of a fox, cold and shifty, who changed his allegiance three times in six years to further his ambitions and save his skin.

Certainly his conduct does seem less than heroic. Before condemning it, however, we must remember that a man in his position at that time regarded himself less as a member of a party than as a civil servant whose attitude was to do the best for his country under whatever government happened to be in power. William felt this all the more because, as a prudent law-abiding character pitched into lawless chaos, he saw that his only hope of surviving was to adapt himself to changing circumstances as skilfully as possible. His friends agreed with him about this; so much so that one of them wrote a letter of congratulation on disassociating himself so adroitly from Somerset. 'It were to make an end to amity,' he said, 'if when men fail, their friends should forthwith therefore be troubled.' His contemporaries seem to have looked with equal tolerance on his last-minute support for Lady Jane Grey. As for posterity, it knows too little to be able to judge in the matter. William may have suffered from a sudden loss of nerve, or he may have thought that a message from the King gave an excuse for signing. But certainly his farewell letter to his wife showed that his was not just a cynical time-serving act but did involve a crisis of conscience.

This judgment is borne out by his conduct in Mary's reign. This was skilfully designed to satisfy the rival claims of prudence and principle. Like Elizabeth, William felt no difficulty in attending Mass as a sign of outward conformity. Like most people in his time, he thought it was a sovereign's right to decide the official religion of his subjects. 'The State can never be in safety,' William said, 'where there is toleration of two religions.' On the other hand he knew that his personal religious convictions were too different from those of Mary's government for him to be able to work with it. Though she asked him to stay on, he resigned and retired to the country. He found plenty to do there, running his estates and also adding to his income by investing in foreign trade. Both activities gave him knowledge which was to be of great use to him when he had later to manage the economy of the country. As a relaxation he started building two great houses for himself, one at Burghley near Stamford and one in London.

However, he did not drop his interest in public affairs; and he continued to be on good enough terms with the government to do an occasional job for them. More important, he kept in touch with Princess Elizabeth. It was a very discreet

Burghley House, Stamford: the West Front

touch. By this time both had learned by hard experience that it was vital that their names should not be associated in any way with one or another of the plots that were hatching all the time against Mary's government. But, since William had now been in charge of Elizabeth's estates for years, she must have got to know a great deal about him: and it came as no surprise to anyone when on becoming Queen she appointed him her chief minister. 'This judgment I have of you,' she told him, 'that you will not be corrupted by any manner of gift and that you will be faithful to the State and that, without respect of my private will, you will give me that counsel which you think best.'

II

In this, as in most of her political judgments, Queen Elizabeth I was right. Nor were the qualities she enumerated the only ones that equipped William Cecil to be her chief minister. He had expertise, for one thing; Elizabeth had political flair, but little detailed knowledge of the process of governing. She did not know how the law worked, or trade, or finance, or local government. William had practical experience of all these things. This meant that, when one of these subjects came up, her flair was reinforced and checked by his knowledge. Both were to be needed, and especially when she first became Queen.

To appreciate fully their double achievement, one must realize its extreme difficulty. Elizabeth ascended the throne in circumstances explosive in the highest degree. It was the last crucial stage in the revolution that transformed England from a medieval to a modern country. Henry VII had laid the foundations of a new-style independent nation state. Henry VIII had continued the work and crowned it by breaking with the last check on the King of England's supremacy, the international Catholic Church under the Pope. But his death was followed by eleven miserable years of uncertainty, misgovernment, foreign war and religious strife. Finally, from the last years of Henry VIII onwards, the country's financial position had got worse and worse. Elizabeth arrived in power to find herself encumbered by debt, inflation and a debased coinage.

Things were not made easier for her by the fact that many people thought her a bastard with no right to the throne; moreover her chief rival, Mary Stuart, was already Queen both of Scotland and France. It was true that France was unlikely for the moment to attack England, because she was occupied, so far as foreign affairs were concerned, with resisting the ambitions of Spain, her rival for the position of chief European power. But it was never certain that this conflict would last. At any time the two great Catholic powers might come to terms; and then one or the other of them might take advantage of England's weakness to impose upon her some ruler more committed to Catholicism than Elizabeth. On every side, then, she was threatened with risks – of ruin, of civil and religious war, of foreign domination. Altogether, in 1558, the prospects both for England and for her Queen looked dark and daunting. In fact, they were not so bad as they looked. England had considerable latent resources, and her people were gifted, vital, adventurous. But circumstances were too dangerous for them to reap the advantage of these qualities without exceptional leadership.

However, they got it: from Elizabeth and from William too. For he can also be counted as a leader: he advised her about aims as well as means. The flamboyant princess and the sober civil servant were surprisingly like each other so far as politics were concerned. Both were cool, peace-loving realists born into a fiery, lawless world; and the likeness between them had been increased by the fact that their careers had followed a parallel course. Both had managed by an artful policy of tacking and trimming to preserve their lives and maintain their positions during a period of chaos; both had emerged from the ordeal with similar convictions as to what mattered and what did not matter in the government of their country, a belief in the paramount importance of order, solvency, and unity, and a corresponding horror of disorder and extravagance. Their policy was an expression of these convictions: worldly-wise and realistic, vigilantly in favour of economy and against taking a risk whether for the sake of glory and power or for strict principle, and ready to deceive and delay and change course as they judged best for the good of the country. It was not a heroic type of policy.

Mary Queen of Scots: an engraving made in 1559

Indeed, it is one of the ironies of history that it should be associated with a heroic period; that the glorious England of Shakespeare and Drake and Sidney should turn out to have been ruled by persons who set so little store on mere glory. Yet – and this is another stroke of irony – it was the policy that made glory possible. Only by its means was time given for the country to build up its reserves and recover its morale to a pitch where it was possible and sensible to be heroic.

Overleaf *A map of London published in 1572 and attributed to Joris Hoefnagel*

Clarkenwell

Smythe Fyeld

Suffolke P.   Durisme P.   Somerset Place   Arundell P.

Corte bence

The Corte

Iron bredge

The Temple   Whyt freers

Blak freere   Beruit

Lambeth Marfh

Parys Garden

Steine Chamber

Y' Quenes Bridge

Lamberto

The Slaughter house

Hæc eſt Græcia illa totius Angliæ ciuitas LONDINVM ad flu-
uium Thamefin fita, Cæfari, vt plures exis fumat, Trinobantum
nuncupata, multarum gentium comercio nobilitata, exculta domib. ornata te-
plis, excelfa arcibus, claris ingeniis, viris omnium artium doctrinarumq, gene-
re præstantibus, percelebris. Deniq, omnium rerum copia, atque opum excellentia
mirabilis. Inuehit in eam totius orbis opes ipſe Thamefis, onerarijs nauibus per
fexaginta millia paßuum, ad velem præcito alueo nauigabilis

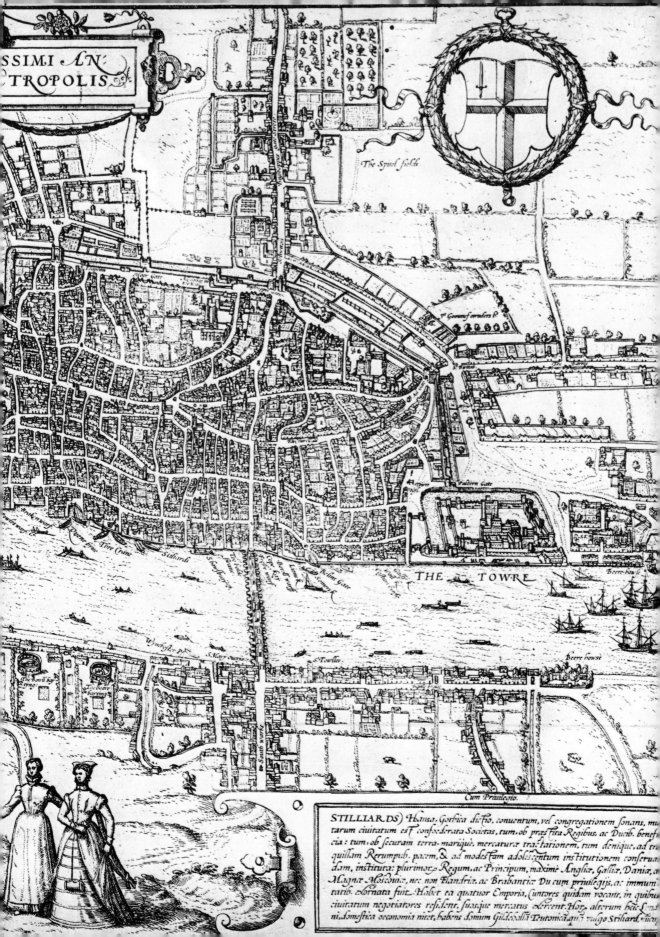

SSIMI AN
TROPOLIS

The Spitel fields

THE TOWRE

Cum Priuilegio.

STILLIARDS) Hansa, Gothica dictio, conuentum, vel congregationem sonans, multarum ciuitatum est confoederata Societas, tum ob praefita Regibus, ac Ducib. beneficia: tum, ob securam terra marique, mercaturæ tractationem, tum denique, ad tranquillam Rerumpub. pacem, & ad modestam adolescentum institutionem conseruandam, instituta: plurimor. Regum, ac Principum, maximè Angliæ, Galliæ, Daniæ, ac Magnæ Moscouiæ, nec non Flandriæ, ac Brabantiæ Ducum priuilegijs, ac immunitatib. Ornata fuit. Habet ea quatuor Emporia, Cuntores quidam vocant, in quibus ciuitatum negotiatores resident, suosque mercatus exercent. Hor. alterum hic Londini, domestica oeconomia nitet, habens domum Gildosallā Teutonicā quā vulgo Stilliard, vocā.

Nor was it a policy without ideal sanctions. Behind its uninspiring exterior lay a far-sighted vision fired by an ardent patriotism which was mixed with a sense of the monarchy as at once the nation's embodiment and a manifestation of God. The Elizabethans were still medieval in that they accepted the order of society, not because they thought it just or convenient from a purely human point of view, but because they thought it was divinely ordered. An Englishman then justified his pride in his country because he believed it peculiarly blessed by heaven; he obeyed his Queen because God had set her to reign over him. For William Cecil this last conviction was the basic abiding principle of his whole career. He told his son, 'Serve God by serving the Queen; for all other service is bondage to the Devil.' Elizabeth, as might be expected, thought this a very proper view to take. It encouraged her all the more to ask his advice. Together they set themselves to devise policies to deal with the English situation in 1558.

Their first object was to make the country a going concern. This meant taking measures to make it solvent and united. William Cecil, as the financial expert, was responsible for making it solvent. He took steps to restore the national finance; to reduce debt, restore the coinage, curb inflation and see that the administration was conducted on a basis of strict economy.

Making the country united was a more formidable task. The chief source of division was religious: the country was apparently split in two. Apparently only; for, though there were fanatics on both sides, the bulk of the population hovered between the two and longed above all for a quiet life. Since there was no question of tolerating two Churches, the best hope for peace was clearly a comprehensive settlement acceptable to the average and attractive to all except the extremists. Such was the Anglican settlement now established by Elizabeth: a Protestant settlement, in that it finally broke with the Pope and the Latin Mass, but a Catholic settlement in that it retained the old order of priests and bishops and phrased its sacramental doctrine in such a way as to admit the belief in the real presence of Christ in the consecrated bread and wine. It was Elizabeth's settlement rather than William's; his religion was more definitely Protestant than hers. But he was a very moderate kind of Protestant; with the general principles of the settlement he was fully in sympathy. Having made the settlement on comprehensive lines, the Government proceeded to enforce its acceptance. They took the view that people might think what they liked, but that if there was to be any peace in England they must be ready outwardly to show signs of agreement.

After taking these steps towards making the country solvent and united, Elizabeth and William Cecil went on to try to make it safe from trouble abroad. They brought Mary's unsuccessful war with France to an end. This involved giving up any claim to Calais. But it was worth it: keeping on with the war meant spending money, which England could not afford. Nor were all the concessions on the English side. The French were supporting the Scottish Queen in her struggle with her Protestant subjects. England now backed up the Protestants. They were victorious, and a peace was signed that turned the French out of Scotland and left England with a friendly Government on her northern frontier. William Cecil had reason to be especially pleased about this. Since his experience in Edward VI's reign, he had been anxious about the Scottish border: it was he who persuaded Elizabeth to back the Protestants. Besides, he was always passionately in favour of peace. 'A reign gaineth more by one year's peace than ten years' war,' he said.

These first years were a triumph for him and his Queen; for in them they succeeded in making England, for the time being at any rate, solvent, orderly and at peace. Now they could settle down to work for their long-term policy, which was to keep off trouble abroad while building up confidence and prosperity at home. They pursued these aims guided by the same policy of mingled balance and firmness which had dictated their first measures. Abroad they played off the great powers against each other by backing each in turn. At home they stuck to a middle course, were lenient to anyone willing to compromise and encouraged anything likely to lead to reconciliation. Having, however, settled for moderation and compromise, they took steps to see that the English people settled for it too. Moderate governments are often weak governments and fail in consequence. Not so the government of Queen Elizabeth I; it enforced its moderation relentlessly. The events of the reign proved that it was right in so doing.

These events are part of the history of England rather than the history of the Cecil family. As such they are not to be told adequately in a book like this. It is enough to say that they represent a line of thought wholly characteristic of William Cecil's outlook. He had always believed in moderation, in order, in peace, in compromise, and very much he believed in balance: balance between parties at home, balance between forms of religious fervour. 'He dissented from papist and puritan,' said a contemporary, 'disliking the superstition of the one and the singularity of the other and often holding out midway between them.' Strong papists did not like this, nor strong puritans. John Knox spoke disapprovingly of William's 'carnal wisdom and worldly policy'. This was a compliment, though not intended as one: most statesmen could do with a little 'carnal wisdom'.

William also believed in the balance of the constitution. His lawyer's training led him to do this. He did not think even the Queen above the law. Her prerogative power had its limits, as he was careful to point out. For the rest, it was his part during the Queen's reign to run the economic and administrative side of government. He looked after taxes, promoted trade, introduced measures to render law and local government more efficient. Yet he was careful to do so in such a way as to create no sense of disturbance. Temperamentally conservative, he realized the tranquillizing effect of custom and habit. He was all for anything that would promote stability and quiet; for this reason, in spite of his dislike of soldiering, he saw to it that the army and navy should be kept ready in case they were needed. Finally, he helped to organize a powerful secret service and spread its activities all over the Continent.

This was a very important part of his work. Throughout the reign a secret service was needed, for throughout the reign the government was in danger. Elizabeth's government was an emergency government, a wartime government, threatened all the time and on every side with overthrow by war or rebellion, or murder, moving from crisis to crisis continuously aware that at any minute all might collapse in chaos and bloodshed. To avoid this the government resorted to the toughest measures; it employed spies and informers and *agents provocateurs* and torture chambers. William was prepared to be very tough if he thought the situation demanded it; extracting confessions by torture, breaking solemnly signed treaties. He did think, however, that desperate measures were only justified by desperate situations. Breaking treaties especially offended his legal conscience. Rulers, he said, should never violate them 'in so open and violent a sort as it shall manifestly appear to the whole world'.

It was this kind of remark that led his enemies to call him a fox. Yet for the most part they did not think badly of him. Mary Queen of Scots herself, though she knew he wanted her killed, said she wished that she had a servant as wise and trustworthy as William Cecil. The Duke of Norfolk, executed by the government in which that servant was chief minister, petitioned Elizabeth before his death that William Cecil should be made guardian of his orphan children; and, when she agreed, 'I thank you', he wrote, 'for your goodness to my poor unfortunate brats that you have christened them with such an adopted father.' William Cecil remained chief minister for forty years, from Elizabeth's accession to the day of his death. This did not mean that his position was secure, still less easy. In the early part of the reign it was always being threatened. Roman Catholics, who looked on him as a great enemy, tried to assassinate him; all the time ambitious rivals thought to oust him from the Queen's favour.

The chief and most dangerous of these was Robert Dudley, Earl of Leicester. He appealed to a strain in Elizabeth to which William had no access: the amorous strain which had responded to her first flame, Lord Seymour. Tall, virile and dashing, with a handsome head and shapely legs, Leicester had already made an impression on Elizabeth when they were both prisoners in the Tower. Immediately

Robert Dudley, Earl of Leicester: a late portrait at Hatfield House attributed to William Segar

after her accession he rode to Hatfield, was warmly received and appointed Minister of the Horse and entered into a violent open flirtation with her which lasted on and off for the next ten or twelve years. The nature of her feelings for him are as much a mystery as most of her feelings. But it is probable that she was as much in love with Leicester as it was possible for her to be. Many people believed that although he was married she seriously considered marrying him herself, if he could be freed from his wife, Amy Robsart.

In 1565 Amy Robsart was found at the bottom of the stairs at Cumnor Hall, Oxford, with her neck broken. Unexpectedly, however, this put an end to the idea of the marriage between Leicester and Elizabeth; for he was suspected of murdering his wife. If Elizabeth was thought to have condoned this, her subjects might turn against her; and Elizabeth cared much more about her subjects' good opinion than for any man. As a matter of fact, it is unlikely that she ever seriously considered marrying anyone. She had the sense to realize that she was far stronger as a virgin queen than as a married one. 'I will have but one mistress in this realm and no master,' she once declared.

Married or single, Leicester retained his position as the Queen's favourite for many years and made use of his position to try to get political power. Incessantly he and his followers intrigued against William Cecil. William, aware of this, was sharp to forestall and circumvent Leicester's plans. He succeeded, partly because he was cool and prudent and dextrous, but still more because ultimately he had Elizabeth on his side.

Ultimately, not immediately; immediately it was often hard to know what side she was on, so often was her purpose hidden beneath a shifting, bewildering smoke-screen of deception and caprice. Three times a day she might alter a decision, and each alteration might be marked by an explosion of temperament, in which she wept and scolded and sometimes even administered a sharp box on the ears to the person who happened to cross her. 'I have found such torment with the Queen's Majesty', William exclaimed on one occasion, 'as an ague hath not in three fits so much abated.' Indeed, he found coping with her in some ways more trouble than defeating his opponents. But cope he did, and very successfully. He gave her his true opinion, as she expected he would; but he did so with tact. He was careful never to disagree with her except in private; in open council he backed her up. Even alone, he did his best to avoid open disagreement. If he saw it coming, he beat a temporary diplomatic retreat. 'Good my Lord,' he advised a younger man, 'overcome her with yielding.' Further, he only asserted his own opinion very strongly when he was sure that she agreed with him. 'I will only love my opinions', he told her, 'if your Majesty loves them.' If he failed to persuade her, he gave in without murmuring. As a servant of the royal monarch he thought it his duty to obey her, once she had made up her mind. 'I do hold and will always, this course in such matters as I differ from her Majesty,' he wrote; 'as long as I may be allowed to give advice, I will not change my opinion by affirming the contrary, for that were to offend God, to whom I am sworn first; but as a servant I will obey her Majesty's commandment, and no wise contrary the same.'

Now and again this meant deferring to her against his better judgment. There were certain subjects the two did not agree about. He would have preferred a more Protestant church settlement; he wanted her to marry so that there should be no trouble about who was to be King after her death; and he disapproved of her having Leicester as a friend, much more a husband. He thought the only reason for her wanting to marry him must be carnal lust, in his view a very unsafe basis for marriage. 'A carnal marriage begins in pleasure and ends in sorrow,' he reflected gloomily. In her heart of hearts Elizabeth may have thought him right in his objections; but the subject was a delicate one in which her emotions were strongly engaged. If William did refer to it, the atmosphere grew alarmingly electric. So long as the flirtation with Leicester lasted, William had to be very careful not to provoke Elizabeth.

Twenty years later he was in greater trouble, this time about the execution of Mary Queen of Scots. William strongly favoured this as absolutely necessary both for the safety of England and of Elizabeth's own life. She was equally against it: she never feared much for her life, and she thought, with some reason, that to execute a crowned Queen was a very bad precedent. When at last, after weeks of hesitation, she did sign Mary's death warrant, the signature was followed by a violent reaction in which she sought to put the blame on everyone except herself and including William. For four whole months he was banished from her presence. It was the most serious quarrel they ever had. What must have made Elizabeth take it especially hard was that it was the one quarrel in which she had been beaten. On their other subjects of disagreement – about the church settlement and about her successor – Elizabeth got her way. William, true to principle, had stated his case; but, since she would not agree, he had yielded.

These differences, however, were few and ultimately unimportant. How could it be otherwise when each agreed with the other fundamentally about policy, as neither agreed with anyone else? With agreement went confidence and admiration. Beneath her changing moods, Elizabeth's trust in William never wavered, and her high opinion of him grew with the years. 'No prince in Europe hath such a counsellor as I have in mine,' she said. He admired her at least as much as she admired him. To start with he had been inclined to disregard her political judgments as coming from a woman. But he soon learned that she was more likely to be right than himself. 'She has so rare gifts,' he said, 'as when her Counsellors had said all they could say she would frame out a wise counsel beyond theirs.'

Indeed, hard-headed middle-aged William Cecil was as much under her spell as any romantic courtier. To him she was a being august and magical, whose infirmities of temper were somehow forgivable. 'Lord be thanked, her blast be not as storms of other princes!' he exclaimed; though he added ruefully, 'they be shrewd sometimes to those she loveth best.'

The mutual feelings of Queen and minister found expression in outward signs. In 1571 Elizabeth created him Lord Burghley and a year later Knight of the Garter and Lord Treasurer, the most honourable position in her government. On his side he showed his love with Renaissance splendour; by entertaining her twelve times magnificently in his country house at Theobalds with masques and pageantry and banqueting at a cost of three thousand pounds per visit. And he presented her with exquisite gifts: a rock-crystal ewer mounted in silver-gilt, an inkstand of silver-gilt and mother of pearl, a set of gold plates curiously enamelled with birds.

III

Serving Queen Elizabeth I might be thought enough work for any man; but William – or Burghley, as we should now call him – had plenty of energy left to spend on the second object of his life, the advancement and elevation of his family. Such an ambition – typical of most rising men in the sixteenth century – is shared so little by anyone living now that it requires an effort on our part to understand it. For one thing we see the life-span of any one family, however ancient, as occupying an infinitely minute space of time compared with the age of the universe, so that to try to perpetuate a family name is futile. Further, advancing one's family's social position does not strike us as a particularly honourable ambition. In theory at any rate, we believe in the equality of man. So did the Elizabethans believe man to be equal in the sight of God: the great they thought were just as likely to go to Hell as the humble. But they thought that, while on earth, everyone had his place in society, and it was right and natural for men to try to raise this place. The Elizabethans believed in what they called 'degree'.

Certainly Burghley believed in it. Himself born a gentleman, he felt it both his duty and his pleasure to raise himself and his children to the rank of noblemen. As usual his belief was qualified both by his faith and his realism. Faith told him that privilege was only justified by merit, and realism told him that nobility was no use unless it rested on a solid economic foundation. The would-be noble must acquire enough wealth to be able to live up to his station in life. To attain these ends Burghley increased his already large property; but he took care not to over-spend and even refused Elizabeth's offer of an earldom on the grounds that it would involve him in too much expense. The result was that, almost alone among the nobles of his time, he was not in debt when he died.

He took an equal care, however, to live in a manner appropriate to the grandee he had now become. He built himself a great house in London as well as his two palatial residences, at Burghley in Northamptonshire and at Theobalds in Hertfordshire; and, very much master in his own house, he saw to it that life in these places should be conducted with appropriate ceremony and decorum. This was of an old-fashioned kind: Burghley was one of the few noblemen of his generation who still maintained the ancient patriarchal custom by which all members of a great household from the greatest downward dined together in the Great Hall of his mansion. This meant a large gathering.

Besides an army of dependants, chaplains, librarians, grooms, efficient orderly servants – there was no place under Burghley's roof for drunken, unruly retainers – he kept open house to a throng of guests: relations, courtiers, men of learning. Burghley specially enjoyed the company of men of learning. The characteristic note of life in his house was intellectual. He was not a sportsman – his only form of exercise was a gentle ride around his grounds on a mule – nor, unlike many of his contemporaries, did he have a taste for poetry or music. He patronized scholars rather than poets – the poets complained loudly about this – and he kept no private company of actors or musicians to sing and play to him during meals. He preferred conversation. But the conversation was of a high level and ranged over a great variety of subjects. Politics were barred; they might lead to indiscretion and in any case Burghley needed mealtimes to be a break in the day from his work. 'Lie thou there, Lord Treasurer,' Burghley would remark humorously, laying down the Treasurer's gown and staff; and then he would turn to relax in talk about science and history and antiquities and theology and the classics.

His library was full of books on the same subjects, together with astronomy and geography. The geography was illustrated by maps: those florid, fanciful maps – they are still to be seen at Hatfield – where a painted savage is depicted standing in Africa, and a turbaned Turk in Turkey, and the seas are alive with gilded galleons and spouting whales and Tritons blowing their wreathèd horns. In the midst of his labours and anxieties Burghley found time to collect a library famous all over England, and to read the books in it, too. He read in bed if he could find no other time, in English and French and Italian and Greek and Latin; Latin especially. He made a habit of keeping a Cicero in his pocket to study in at odd moments.

He had the collector's instinct, extending to many things besides books: pictures, especially portraits of historical interest, coins, gems, gold and silver plate, busts from Rome, statues from Venice. Although indifferent to music and poetry, Burghley had an aesthetic side. Most Elizabethans did. We, living in a Philistine age, may well be staggered by their appetite for the beautiful, their shameless delight in what appealed to their senses and their imagination: July

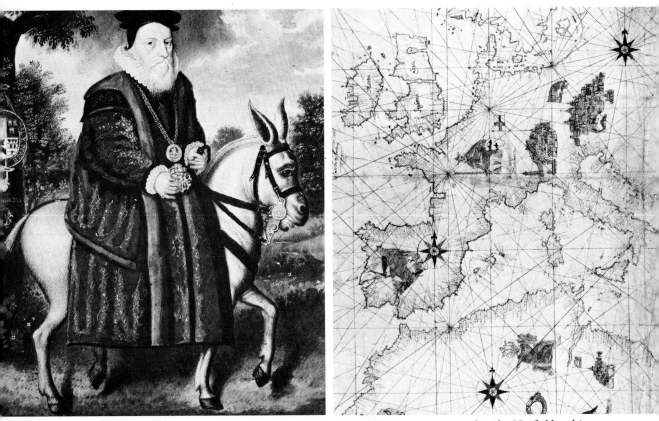

Lord Burghley riding a mule, and a section from one of his maps, preserved in the Hatfield archives

flowers and the smell of amber and striped carnations, jewels and shimmering silks and many-coloured tapestries glinting with gold thread. Sober Burghley, to judge by his possessions, shared this taste. He took an especial interest in the building of his great houses, and sent specially to Italy for the right type of marble for a chimneypiece. As for his garden, it became as famous as his library. His scientific strain led him to fill it with rare plants of interest to botanists. His taste for beauty showed in the planning of his terraces and fountains and avenues, where, for a moment free from the brutalities and tensions of political life, Burghley would walk in the dusk of a summer evening to refresh his tired spirit with the tranquil blossoming of nature and the sweetness that breathed from rose and gillyflower.

He liked his children to be with him when he was at home. His interest in them was personal as well as dynastic. Burghley was a family man, and his children occupied much of his attention. His treatment of them showed his characteristic blend of realism and piety, especially in the manner of their education. He took great pains about this: the subject interested his academic mind – in particular the education of his sons. This was designed to fit them for the great position in life which he had planned for them. Like his own and his Queen's, it was strenuous, starting early and lasting for hours; and though Burghley believed that pupils were more easily led by kindness than by severity – 'Praise openly, reprehend secretly,' he said – he left his sons in no doubt that he expected a great deal from them and would be disappointed if he did not get it. As might be expected, his educational ideal was the same as that of his old fellow student Ascham: the ideal of the whole man, embracing on the one hand the classical and modern languages, science and theology, and on the other writing, fencing, dancing and the graces. Under Burghley's direction this ideal acquired a special stamp once again from his peculiar blend of the worldly and the pious. This appears entertainingly in two contrasting pieces of advice that he wrote for his sons. The first is to his eldest, Thomas, seventeen years old and about to go abroad for a year. It reveals Burghley, the man of faith, at his most austere.

Every morning before leaving his room, he told Thomas, he must kneel and say the Lord's Prayer and the Creed. 'In these prayers you must not think God is served with words which be but the labour of your lips, but you must have your heart free and remember that in prayer you are before the majesty of the Almighty, before the Maker of all to whom all that is in Heaven and Earth is subject; yea, you a simple creature, a piece of clay, a piece of flesh that shall be carrion, one that by no means might presume to speak to God or call him Father, but through the adoption made by Jesus Christ . . . after private prayer every morning where-unto you must bind yourself, and for no manner of business leave it undone, you shall make ready your apparel in cleanly sort, doing that for civility and health and not for pride.' He suggests that Thomas should get a concordance to the Prayer Book and the Bible and make notes in it, 'in such sort as, at your return, I may see how you have observed this precept'. Burghley points out that in one year Thomas might read the Psalms twelve times, the New Testament four times, and the Old Testament once. 'This is all the study I mean you shall bestow in Divinity except listening with attention to preachers.'

Thomas was to end his day with a general confession in which he was to seek forgiveness of his daily wrongdoings. 'If you offend by leaving your ordinary prayers and suchlike, if you offend in eating or drinking too much, if you offend in other ways by attending or minding lewd or filthy tales or enticements of lightness or wantonness of body, you must at evening bring both your thoughts and deeds, as you put off your garments to lay down and cast away those and all suchlike that by the Devil are devised to overwhelm your soul . . . and for ending this matter I commend you to the tuition of Almighty God . . . if you shall please Him and serve Him in fear I shall take comfort of you. Otherwise I shall take you as no blessing of God, but a burden of grief and decay of my age.'

The second piece of advice, written some years later, consisted of ten precepts intended for his second son, Robert, by this time in his late teens. Though they start with a few sentences asserting the supreme importance of religion, they go on to reveal a very different Burghley from the author of his advice to Thomas. Here are some of them, introduced thus: 'I think it fit and agreeable to the affection I bear thee, to help thee with such rules and advertisements for the squaring of thy life, as are rather gained by experience, than much reading; to the end that entering into this exorbitant age, thou mayest be the better prepared to shun those scandalous courses whereunto the world and the lack of experience may easily draw thee.'

1 When it shall please God to bring thee to man's estate, use great providence and circumspection in choosing thy wife; for from thence will spring all thy future good or evil; and it is an action of life, like unto a stratagem of war, wherein a man can err but once. If they estate be good, match thee near home and at leisure; if weak, far off and quickly. Enquire diligently of her disposition, and how her parents have been inclined in their youth; let her not be poor, how generous soever; for a man can buy nothing in the market with gentility; nor choose a base and uncomely creature altogether for wealth; for it will cause contempt in others and loathing in thee; neither make choice of a dwarf, or a fool; for by the one you shall beget a race of pigmies, the other will be thy continual disgrace, and it will irke thee to hear her talk; for thou shalt find it, to thy great grief, that there is nothing more fulsome than a she-fool.

And touching the guiding of thy house, let thy hospitality be moderate, and according to the means of thy estates rather plentiful than sparing, but not costly; for I never knew any man grow poor by keeping an orderly table. But some consume themselves through secret vices, and their hospitality bears the blame. Banish swinish drunkards out of thine house, which is a vice impairing health, consuming much, and makes no show. I never heard praise ascribed to the drunkard, but for the well bearing of his drink, which is better commendation for a brewer's horse or a dray man, than for either a gentleman or a serving man. . . .

2 Bring thy children up in learning and obedience, yet without outward austerity. Praise them openly, reprehend them secretly. Give them good countenance and convenient maintenance according to thy ability; otherwise thy life will seem their bondage and what portion thou shalt leave them at thy death, they will thank death for it, and not thee. And I am persuaded that the foolish cockering of some parents, and the overstern carriage of others, causeth more men and women to take ill courses, than their own vicious inclinations. Marry thy daughters in time, lest they marry themselves. And suffer not the sons to pass the Alps, for they shall learn nothing there but pride, blasphemy, and atheism. And if by travel they get a few broken languages, that shall profit them nothing more than to have one meat served in divers dishes. Neither, by my consent, shalt thou train them up in wars; for he that sets up his rest to live by that

Burghley with his son Robert, both wearing the blue ribbon of the Order of the Garter: a composite portrait painted after the death of Burghley

profession, can hardly be an honest man or a good Christian . . . Besides it is a science no longer in request than use; for soldiers in peace, are like chimneys in summer.

3 Live not in the country without corn and cattle about thee; for he that putteth his hand to the purse for every expense of household, is like him that putteth water in a sieve . . . Be not served with kinsmen, or friends, or men intreated to stay; for they expect much and do little; nor with such as are amorous, for their heads are intoxicated. And keep rather two too few, than one too many. Feed them well, and pay them with the most; and then thou mayest boldly require service at their hands.

81

6 Undertake no suit against a poor man without receiving much wrong; for besides that thou makest him thy compeer, it is a base conquest to triumph where there is so small resistance; neither attempt law against any man before thou be fully resolved that thou hast right on thy side; and then spare not for either money or pains; for a cause or two so followed and obtained, will free thee from suits a greater part of thy life.

7 Be sure to keep some great man thy friend, but trouble him not with trifles; compliment him often with many, yet small gifts, and of little charge; and if thou hast cause to bestow any great gratuity, let it be something which may be daily in sight; otherwise in this ambitious age, thou shalt remain like a hop without a pole, live in obscurity, and be made a football for every insulting companion to spurn at.

8 Towards thy superiors be humble, yet generous, with thine equals familiar, yet respective; towards thine inferiors show much humanity, and some familiarity; as to bow the body, stretch forth the hand, and to uncover the head, with such like popular compliments. The first prepares thy way to advancement, the second makes thee known for a man well bred; the third gains a good report, which once got is easily kept; for high humilities take such deep root in the minds of the multitude, as they are easilier gained by unprofitable courtesies, than by churlish benefits; yet I advise thee not to affect or neglect popularity too much. Seek not to be Essex; shun to be Raleigh.

10 Be not scurrilous in conversation nor satirical in thy jests; the one will make thee unwelcome to all company, the other pull on quarrels, and get thee hatred of thy best friends. Jests, when any of them savour of truth, leave a bitterness in the minds of those which are touched; and, albeit I have already pointed at this inclusively; yet I think it necessary to leave it to thee as a special caution, because I have seen many so prone to quip and gird, as they would rather lose their friend than their jest; and if, perchance, their boiling brain yield a quaint scoff, they will travail to be delivered of it as a woman with child. These nimble fancies are but the froth of wit.

These two contrasting pieces of advice tell us a great deal about Burghley, for they illustrate vividly his division of spirit. In the advice to Thomas we hear the voice of the religious Burghley, harsh with the harshness of one desperately anxious to make his son realize the importance of religion and virtue in a wicked world. In the advice to Robert speaks the worldly Burghley. Drawn from first-hand experience of the wicked world, it is less edifying, with its recommendations not to marry a poor girl whatever her other merits, and its advice as to how most artfully to get on to good terms with a great man. But the precepts to Robert do show how shrewd and observant Burghley was. Moreover, they bring us closer to him than any other record. For myself, they make him more likeable. I like the unselfconscious frankness with which he reveals his worldly side: it shows that he was not always so inhumanly discreet; and they reveal him to be capable of irony. This is a quality uncommon in statesmen in the sixteenth century; or, for that matter, in any other.

Robert profited by his father's wisdom, as his story was to show. Not so Thomas – at least not in his early days. His relation with his father was likely to be awkward; for the English system of primogeniture, so effective in preserving the integrity of large properties, is bad for the relationship between father and eldest son. All too often the father cannot help trying to force his son into what he considers the proper mould for his heir; all too often the son shows himself unwilling or unable to fit into such a mould. Thomas Cecil could not fit into it. He was wonderfully unlike his father: a healthy, lazy, amiable young man with not much brain and intent mainly on girls and sport. Burghley was early aware of his son's deficiencies; though he behaved towards Thomas conscientiously, he had to admit he could not feel affection for him. 'Indeed to this hour,' he said, 'I never showed any fatherly affection to him but in teaching and correcting.' Possibly as a result of this bleak regime, young Thomas did not improve.

As a last resort Burghley sent him at the age of nineteen to learn languages and good manners on the Continent under the care of a tutor, Mr Windebank. Foreign travel proved no more successful than had teaching and correcting. Thomas failed to learn much French and did spend a great deal too much money. 'I see in the end my son will come home like a spending sot and meet to keep a tennis court,' said Burghley tartly. What were his feelings to get a letter announcing that Thomas had broken open his tutor's strong box in order to get more money to spend on his pleasures, also that he was in the process of seducing the daughter of a respectable French family! For once Burghley's calm deserted him. He wrote furiously to Thomas. 'I wish you grace, being commonly reputed by common fame to be a dissolute, slothful and careless young man and especially noted no lover of learning or knowledge.' Clearly this last fact especially depressed the scholarly Burghley. He poured out his distress to Windebank. 'I am hard used to troubles, but none creep so near my heart as does this of my lewd son. I am perplexed what to think. The shame that I shall receive to have so unruly a son grieveth me more than if I had lost him by honest death.'

These words show that Burghley, like other anxious parents, was unnecessarily pessimistic about his son's future. In fact, Thomas did not turn out badly. After two years he returned from abroad, married, and settled down to live a respectable life of public service, the loyal supporter of his famous father and later of his famous younger brother. Burghley appears to have recognized Thomas's improved character. He stopped expecting more of him than he could hope to get and turned his attention to the promising Robert. The fact remained that Thomas was a disappointment to him.

His other children were not. Three of them survived: Anne, Elizabeth and Robert. Though never very demonstrative, Burghley loved them and was deeply concerned for their happiness. Nonetheless, through no fault of their own, the two girls turned out a source of sorrow to him. Elizabeth married Lord Wentworth. The sons of Lord Essex and Lord Buckhurst, greater matches from a worldly point of view, did propose for her; but, for all his worldly ambitions, Burghley thought neither of them was likely to make Elizabeth happy, and he refused them. But life was more uncertain in the sixteenth century and, to his great grief, Elizabeth died within two years of her marriage. Her sister Anne had an even sadder fate. Burghley was especially fond of his 'Tannakin', as he tenderly called her. In 1571, when she was only sixteen, Edward, Seventeenth Earl of Oxford, applied for her hand. On the face of it, it was a splendid match: Oxford was a dazzling figure, high-born, wealthy, beautiful, with a considerable gift for writing poetry and a touch of romantic fantasy. To crown all, he was a special favourite of Queen Elizabeth. All the same Burghley seemed to have had doubts about the marriage, and so even more had Lady Burghley. Oxford was not a type to appeal to a severe puritan. However, advantages in the end outweighed doubts and in December 1571 the wedding was solemnized with glittering pomp in Westminster Abbey.

Within a very short time the doubts of the parents proved more than justified. Lord Oxford turned out a far more unsatisfactory husband than even Lady Burghley could have feared: unreliable, uncontrolled, ill-tempered and wildly extravagant. He shortly began to spend much of his time away from his wife by travelling in Italy. 'Suffer not your son to cross the Alps': so Burghley was to write in his precepts to Robert. He must have been thinking of his son-in-law. In 1575 he got a letter from Italy stating that Lord Oxford had become a drunkard, a homosexual, and a declared atheist. This report was accompanied by detailed accounts of his unseemly amours with his kitchen boys and of his blasphemous jokes about the Holy Trinity. 'No enemy I have can envy me this match,' commented Burghley acidly.

He summoned Lord Oxford back to England and gave him a scolding. Oxford countered by sending his wife back to her family and accusing her – apparently without grounds – of being unfaithful to him while he was abroad. The couple spent the following Christmas with the Burghleys; it must have been an uncomfortable Christmas. For two more years they lived a wretched life, half married, half separated; then Anne died at the age of thirty-three. For seventeen years Burghley had suffered at the thought of poor Tannakin's misfortune. Now, stricken with grief, he followed her to her grave in Westminster Abbey, where she was buried with the same pomp as she had been married.

Lord Oxford's conduct must have been all the more distressing to Burghley because he had been largely responsible for his education. In addition to his other activities, Burghley kept what amounted to a school for young noblemen; some of them his legal wards – he was Master of Wards, a very important position – some of them sent by their parents. The aristocracy of the period often sent their sons to be educated in a great man's household. Burghley liked to accept them, partly because he thought it important that the aristocracy should be properly educated, and partly because he hoped to strengthen Elizabeth's position by building up, among the governing classes of the country, a party trained to devote themselves to her service. The education he provided was run with his usual efficiency: parents felt reassured if they knew their sons were being brought up in a home as orderly and godly as Lord Burghley's. The result was that his house became very much sought after as an educational establishment. Burghley found he could pick and choose, so that it became soon a very exclusive educational establishment indeed, never numbering more than twenty pupils at a time but including among these, at one time or another, some of the greatest fortunes and bluest blood in England; not only Lord Oxford but also the Earl of Surrey, two Earls of Rutland, Shakespeare's Earl of Southampton and he who was to become the tragic and famous Earl of Essex.

The curriculum was on the same lines as that designed for Burghley's own sons. Burghley himself took pains to imbue his charges with his own sense of the incalculable value of learning. He wrote to young Lord Rutland, off to spend some time hunting and enjoying himself at his family home at Belvoir Castle, to keep up his reading: 'Learning will serve you in all ages and in all places and fortunes.' He adds that he approves of Rutland's hunting, but: 'You will when you are weary of hunting, recontinue some exercise of hunting in your book.' There is a touch of schoolmasterly facetiousness in this last phrase; I wonder how much young Lord Rutland liked it. Certainly Burghley failed to acquire any lasting influence on him. When he grew up, Rutland joined the anti-Cecil party in the country. So also did Southampton and Oxford; and Essex actually put himself at its head. Thus, in spite of all his efforts, Burghley did not succeed in turning his pupils into political supporters. From this point of view they were as much a disappointment to him as his son Thomas.

IV

The years passed. Mary Queen of Scots was beheaded; the Spanish sent a fleet to invade England and were catastrophically defeated – 'The great navy of Spain,' wrote Burghley in his jotting-diary, still to be seen at Hatfield, 'driven into ye North Sea and so with great wrack passed homeward.' Queen Elizabeth's reign entered into its final phase. So also did the life of Lord Burghley. For both it was a new kind of phase. The particular dangers and difficulties that had confronted Queen and Minister for so many years had been surmounted. The transition from the old world to the new was pretty well finished; and England was now an orderly nation ruled by a firmly established government.

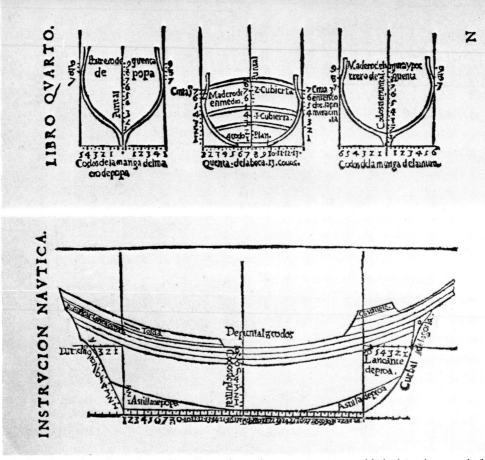

Shipbuilding plans from the earliest Spanish work on navigation, published in the year before the First Armada sailed

This did not mean that there were no longer any questions for a statesman to worry about. Though the danger of invasion was averted, the war still dragged expensively on and the succession to the throne had still to be settled. Moreover, just because they felt safer, people grew somewhat obstreperous. The Commons demanded more power and fewer taxes; the puritans demanded more share in the government of the Church. In addition to his regular work, Burghley had to bring his judgment to bear on these new issues. He found it more of a strain than he would have done in the past. He was now close on seventy, always tired and often ill. Infirmity too had been lately increased by grief. In 1589 Lady Burghley died. Though she played little part in recorded history, she played a major part in home life, occupying her powerful intellect and forceful faith in educating her children in religion, in the management of her huge household and in talking and listening to her husband. Since he had no close friends, he felt her loss acutely. 'I am as lonely as an owl,' he said, and all the more because he was now too tired for much social life. He took to dining in his private chamber alone but for his children, and he did a great deal of his work in bed.

However, there was no question of his giving up his work. Queen Elizabeth would never have let him give it up, and it is unlikely that he wanted to. He was still deeply concerned that the country should continue to be governed in the old ways of prudence and peace and economy. Insofar as he thought such a policy was threatened by new developments, he was against them. The Commons and the puritans should be kept in their place, according to his view; and, in opposition to adventurers, buccaneers and fanatical Protestants, he wanted the war ended on any terms that could be considered decent. Meanwhile he realized that he could not live for ever, and he turned more and more of his attention to the task of ensuring that he should have a trustworthy successor. In fact, he had already found a candidate for the post in the person of his son Robert. If Thomas, the son of undistinguished Mary Cheke, had been a disappointment, Robert, the son of brilliant Mildred Cooke, seemed likely to be the reverse. For the last ten years or so Burghley had trained him to occupy the place his father would vacate, and now was the time to see that he got it. Thus, during his last years but for the first time, the two chief aims of Burghley's life, the political and the dynastic, fused to become one aim; and he mustered all his failing energies to achieve it.

He met with obstacles. History repeated itself. Once more the sober councillor found himself opposed to the handsome, ambitious royal favourite. The new favourite, young Lord Essex, was to prove more troublesome than Leicester had been, for he was even more set on political power. A headstrong firebrand, he came immediately into conflict with the two Cecils, a conflict that was to go on for the rest of the century. But, as in the earlier struggle with Leicester, the result was never really in doubt. The Cecils were always the winners. The reason was partly that the impulsive Essex often made a false step and the sure-footed Cecils never failed to take advantage of this. But it was still more because they had the Queen behind them. However much she seemed to waver, Elizabeth did not lose her judgment; always she knew the difference between an attractive favourite and an efficient minister. Robert rose steadily. By 1596 he was appointed the Queen's Secretary, the most influential post in the government.

Burghley had his heart's desire. But at a cost to himself: the strain of the struggle, in addition to his other work, had left him with his health gone. Sometimes he found himself too ill to go to Court even when he thought his presence was necessary. 'I must keep my chamber,' he lamented to Robert, 'not as a potentate but as an impotent aged man.' Perverse conscientiousness made him tire himself still further by refusing to rest, even when he could. There is a pathetic description of him out in the garden after a hard morning's work and walking up and down under the trees with a book in his hand to prevent himself from falling asleep.

More distressing, the strain had begun to undermine his hitherto unbreakable self-control. He became liable to fits of temper; struck with guilt, he would apologize abjectly after one had passed. This did not, however, stop him from soon giving way to another. It showed the change in him, that he was just as likely to lose his self-control in public as in private. His colleagues noticed that at a council, if anything was said that irritated him, the irritation showed in the various expressions of his face, in the angry tones of his voice, in the way he fidgeted in his chair. A more formidable cause would produce a more formidable reaction. One day, in 1598, the Council were discussing peace terms with Spain. Essex, on the look-out for a chance to distinguish himself as a soldier, spoke up for continuing the war. His words offended against Burghley's most sacred conviction, and a fierce argument followed. At last the old man, speechless with indignation, drew a prayer-book from his pocket, opened it and silently pointed to a passage in the Psalms. 'Men of blood,' it ran, 'shall not live out half their days.'

To us, reading of it with a knowledge of later events, this scene is darkened and made eerie by the shadow of the supernatural. For, two years later and while still in his thirties, Essex was beheaded on Tower Hill. Burghley's words were prophetic. Moreover, they were to give ominous colour to the ancient superstition that dying men have the power to prophesy. Within a few months Burghley was taken desperately ill; ten days later he was dead.

The description of his last days curiously illustrates the difference between ourselves and the Elizabethans. They were at once more ceremonious than us and more natural. The basic, central events of life – birth, marriage, death – took place far more in public than now and were accompanied by elaborate rituals. Throughout his last illness Burghley lay in his great bed in a room generally full of people, loudly bewailing his coming end. He breathed his last with twenty persons – friends, relations, servants – watching him. Before this, foreign diplomats and courtiers had visited him to pay their last respects; important churchmen had prayed at his bedside; and the Queen herself, aged, painted, but still somehow magnetic and 'full of incantation', came more than once to see how he was. Burghley's attendants asked her to bend her head as she entered, lest her high headdress should knock against the top of the doorway. 'For your Master's sake,' she replied humorously, 'but not for the King of Spain.' And, when she had come in, she sat down by the bed, spoke comforting words and fed him with a spoon. Deeply touched, he asked his son afterwards to write and thank her. 'Though she will not be a mother, yet she sheweth herself by feeding me with her own princely hand, to be a careful nurse; and if I may be weaned to feed myself, I shall be more ready to serve her on this earth: if not, I hope to be in Heaven a servitor for her and God's church.'

He did not need to tell her this. Since those distant early days at Hatfield, he had been, she knew well, her one irreplaceable servant, her closest, wisest adviser. For some time she had watched his gradual decline; and though she could still burst out at him as at everyone – 'Froward old fool!' she shouted at one council – yet far more often her affection made her treat him with an extraordinary softness and consideration. She would interrupt a state ceremony to ask if he was comfortable and give him permission to sit in her presence: 'My Lord, we are mindful of you, not for your bad legs but for your good head,' she said with a smile. Now that she realized he was on the point of death, the sense of what she owed to him and what they had endured and achieved together, the knowledge that, of those around her, only he remained who had known her in her youth, and the anticipation of how lonely she would be without him – all joined to well up in a flood of grief. 'I do not want to live longer than I have you with me,' she cried. At her words Burghley's eyes filled with tears.

Meanwhile his surviving children and grandchildren and great-grandchildren were gathered at his home to see him die. Burghley's feeling for his family had grown with the years: the brightest light in the twilight of his old age was the pleasure he took in it, especially its youngest members. A contemporary writes: 'If he could get his table set round with young little children he was then in his kingdom; and it was an exceeding pleasure to hear what sport he would make with them and how aptly and merrily he would talk with them, with such pretty questions and witty answers.' Now with love, and, it may be presumed, with sadness, he said goodbye to them. Yet Burghley was not sorry to die. Age and change had only intensified his basic disenchantment with the world and its prizes; nor had they brought him any compensating detachment. Anxieties, public and private, about war, about Essex, about the succession to the throne oppressed him, if possible, more than ever.

Only at the point of death did he avert his mind from them and concentrate wholly on the faith needed to carry him through the ordeal of his last hours. Lying in his bed, he could be heard murmuring his prayers. 'Lord have mercy,' he would whisper, and then, as the last agony approached, 'Oh, what a heart is this that will not die! Come, Lord Jesus, one drop of death, Lord Jesus!' Those around him asked if they could do anything to ease his sufferings. This last interruption from the world of humanity provoked in him a last flash of human temper. 'Oh, ye torment me,' he gasped. 'Let me die in quiet.' His wish was granted. Still murmuring prayers, he passed into peaceful unconsciousness and died.

Burghley's life-story is a speaking comment on the vanity of earthly glory. Few men have been so successful as he. The two ambitions to which he had dedicated his life had been wholly fulfilled. He had made the Cecils one of the first families in England; in conjunction with his Queen, he had guided the destiny of his country throughout the most glorious reign in her history. 'Yet,' wrote the chaplain who ministered to him in his last hours, 'he had seen and tasted so much of sweet and sour of the world as made him weary to live.'

3
ROBERT CECIL
First Earl of Salisbury

QUEEN ELIZABETH felt Burghley's death at least as much as she expected. For the rest of her life she could hardly hear his name mentioned without turning away her face to hide her tears; nor would she admit that anyone, even his own son, could replace him. In fact she soon began to depend on the son as much as she had done on the father. Rightly: he was the same sort of statesman, equally capable, equally dedicated and with similar aims and methods.

Yet he was a different personality, more complex, more ambiguous. His very appearance suggested this. Possibly because dropped by his nurse when a baby, he had grown up very short, with a crooked back and an awkward way of walking, splaying out his feet. But this dwarf-like figure was surmounted by a head in a high degree refined and intelligent, whose hazel eyes, beneath their delicately arched eyebrows, surveyed the world with a subtle, penetrating gaze. The character of his countenance was reflected in his manners, courteous and modest and noted for a sort of grave, gentle sweetness. His talk, though not so weighty as his father's, was marked by a sharper irony, a more fastidious pleasure in words.

Robert Cecil's public and private character also presented an odd contrast. Robert, the public servant, was prudent, rational, reliable. But about Robert the private individual there was something rasher and less accountable: he was extravagant, a reckless gambler, suspected of many love affairs, and liable to fits of inexplicable depression. Nor did rashness mean openness. The grave sweetness of his manner masked a reserve more impenetrable than his father's, for it was the expression less of discretion than of some basic isolation of spirit. No doubt his crooked back had something to do with this. Deformed people feel themselves to be set apart from others, and especially was this so in the sixteenth century, when, as often as not, they were objects of open suspicion and mockery. Robert Cecil felt himself set apart. He had a sensitive nature, and he was acutely aware of his lack of physical attraction, his inability to shine as a sportsman or swordsman

Robert Cecil, 1st Earl of Salisbury: a portrait at Hatfield House after John de Critz the Elder

like the young nobles who were his schoolfellows. He was further separated from his fellows by his birth. The fact that he was the favourite son of the most powerful man in the kingdom inevitably created a distance between himself and others. He was much too intelligent not to be aware of it.

However, he was also too intelligent not to gain rather than lose by the uncommon circumstances in which fortune had placed him. Burghley, disappointed in his eldest son, had steadily concentrated on Robert, whose unusual fate it was to be brought up from an early age by a Queen's chief minister, to be a Queen's chief minister. His formal schooling followed the same strenuous and scholarly pattern as that of Burghley's wards. But the main part of his education was conducted out of school, in the company of his father and in the inner circle of supreme power, whence he could watch the whole process of government domestic and diplomatic, from, as it were, its hidden central control-room; could hear the crucial problems of the time discussed by the actual men whose job it was to solve them. Finally, all this came to him too in the context of his father's personality, illuminated by his insight and experience and related to the principles that had guided his political life and to his conception of what should be England's future.

Robert made use of these advantages. Bred for brains on both sides, he had an extraordinary quickness in guessing a man's thoughts after hearing only the first words of what he had to say; and he was by nature as hardworking as his father. Moreover, both his intelligence and his industry had surely been intensified by an instinctive wish to compensate for his physical deficiencies by success in other areas of action which involved having power over others. Though more pleasure-loving than Burghley, he was equally ambitious, and for him, too, public affairs were the ruling interest of life.

Already as a boy, sharp-eyed and precocious, he sat watching and drawing conclusions, about political issues and political characters, noting how his father directed the finances and Sir Francis Walsingham ran the Secret Service, wondering why Lord Leicester was loved by the crowd and Sir Walter Raleigh was hated, reflecting on what motives operated most strongly in public life and what qualities made for success in it. Observation and reflection moulded his manner and character, so that, before he was out of his teens, Robert Cecil was better equipped to take part in governing England than most men are at thirty.

His father seemed to have thought so. For when Robert was only eighteen Burghley arranged that he should be chosen as a Member of Parliament. Of course this did not mean what it would mean now: Parliament in those days met only occasionally and for a short time. Even so, Robert was young to be a Member of Parliament, and the experience added to his education. This was not yet finished. During the next few years he went, like his father before him, to Gray's Inn to learn about law, and for a short time to St John's College, Cambridge. At both he behaved with what was always to be a characteristic discretion. The Vice-Chancellor of Cambridge wrote praising him for his 'godly vigilance both at sermons and disputation', and the Watch, the Elizabethan equivalent of the police in London, were pleasantly surprised by Robert's politeness. Most law students then were riotous hooligans with whom the Watch lived in a state of war; but, they said, 'Mr Cecil, the Lord Treasurer's son, passed them by with a courtly salutation.'

After Gray's Inn, came foreign travel. Burghley thought that anyone aspiring to be a statesman should have some first-hand knowledge of foreign languages and foreign institutions, and also some acquaintance with English diplomats overseas. Abroad as at home, Robert observed and reflected, and by the time his education was finished his character and manners had settled into the form they were to maintain for life. Already, at twenty years old, Robert had learned to be subtle and resolute, patient and persistent, tactful and secretive. His grave charm of manner was already noted; beneath it, and not so obvious, was also established an unwavering purpose and a view of mankind free from illusion.

He was to need both qualities in the near future. For now his career was really started, now it was his turn to be plunged into the stormy perilous sea of sixteenth-century court life and sixteenth-century high politics; not quite so dangerous as in Edward VI's reign, but still a sufficiently terrifying region of intrigue and treachery, with the shadow of the block and the Tower looming always over it.

He spent the next few years in still further increasing his political knowledge and laying the foundations of his political future. By the age of twenty-five he was influential enough to be bothered by political suitors asking him for his good offices with Burghley, and was artful enough to know how to deal with them. There is a letter from him to a friend of his called Michael Hicks, asking him to keep one of these suitors quiet by pretending that he had seen a letter from Robert to his father, putting the suitor's case before him. Diplomatic arts of this sort were useful in negotiating the complications of life at a Tudor Court.

They were also invaluable too in helping Robert to a more important achievement. It was at this stage in his career that he got the confidence of his Queen. Introduced to her by his father, he made at once a good impression. Her keen eye perceived that he was a chip, if a misshapen one, of the old Cecil block. She smiled on him and nicknamed him her 'pygmy'. Robert did not like the name; it was touching on a sore spot. 'Though I may not find fault with the name she gave me,' he was to write later, 'yet seem I only not to mislike it because she gives it.' In fact he was too sensible to take it unduly to heart. A displeasing nickname was a small price to pay for the favour of the Queen of England, and in any case his father had always told him that his first obligation would always be to please the Queen. Unless one accepted her whims and words, one had little chance of exert-

Demolition of the Spanish citadel in Antwerp, 1577

ing any influence on her. Accordingly Robert set himself to learn the art of doing so, and with such success that it was not long before he had built himself securely into her favour. She now took to calling him 'Elf' as well as 'Pygmy'. 'Elf' was a prettier name and also one that showed a truer perception of his quality: his lightning swiftness of mind, the delicate charm that exhaled from his small strange figure.

By the autumn of 1586, Queen Elizabeth thought highly enough of Robert to desire him to write a pamphlet for her on a subject of extreme importance, namely her reasons for not wanting to execute Mary Queen of Scots. He protested that he was too young and inexperienced – unlike most Elizabethan worthies, he did not go in for bragging – but he did it, and very well. His reputation was to be further increased by a journey he took to the Netherlands early in 1588, as an unofficial observer, accompanying a diplomatic mission headed by Lord Derby to discuss peace terms with the commander of the Spanish forces there, the Duke of Parma.

Robert had engineered this assignment himself. Burghley had been doubtful about it; but Robert had explained with polite persistence that he thought being present at such an important negotiation would be a great help in his political education. Though himself unofficial, he contrived to make an impression on the official members of the Commission. He was skilful at combining ease and liveliness in conversation with an air of modesty appropriate to his age. The life of the mission in war-shattered Flanders was extremely uncomfortable, spent mainly in chilly inns with no more than an egg and a scrap of herring for supper, and made exhausting by journeys on horseback, sometimes nine hours long and in driving rain. Lord Derby and his colleagues, in particular Lord Cobham, noted with admiration that Robert endured these hardships without a break in his good humour and, though supposed to be sickly, never seemed to be tired. Further, he showed himself so shrewd about the business in hand that he was soon allowed to be present at all negotiations and even got a chance to talk to the Duke of Parma himself. The foreigners were struck by the knowledge and tact of 'this wise little hunchback', as one of them described him. They came to the conclusion that, so far from being a mere observer, he was a confidential envoy of the Queen herself, travelling incognito.

On his side Robert, as when he was a boy at Cecil House, watched and drew his conclusions – about the war and the peace, and the relative power of the armies and the Dutch fisheries and the Flemish economy and also the characters of the persons engaged: the Duke of Parma, M. Garnier his secretary – dressed half like a lawyer and half like a soldier in blue velvet with gold buttons – and Count Maurice of Nassau, whom Robert thought poorly of: 'In my life, I never saw worse behaviour except in one lately come from school,' he said. But, above all individual impressions, Robert was struck by the appalling effect of war. The sight of the Flemish landscape, its ruined towns and devastated fields and droves

The Spanish general Alexander Farnese, Duke of Parma, and right *Maurice of Nassau*

of starving people left him, for the rest of his life, as determinedly peace-minded as his father.

All these thoughts and impressions were poured out in his letters home, interspersed with lighter, more personal passages, about the pleasure he found in the 'hungry air of the seaside' and 'pretty Madame La Motte at Ostend, of discreet and modest behaviour yet not unwilling sometimes to hear herself speak'. In spite of his absorption in politics, he could respond to the pleasures of life. Unlike his father, he liked such sport as he could manage – partridge-netting and hawking – and he enjoyed convivial evenings with conversation enlivened by flights of Elizabethan wit and fancy. He had the taste and talent for words, so common in Shakespeare's time even among those who were not poets; and he had an Elizabethan pleasure in living splendidly amid splendid surroundings. He thought it a real if minor addition to the horrors of war that they involved the Duke of Parma's living in a room with small, mean furniture. 'Peace', reflected young Robert, 'is the mother of all honour and state.'

*A gentleman of the 17th century
with his goshawk*

To the pleasures of sport and conviviality he was soon to add those of wedded love. The records of how this came about are among the few that bring us close to his intimate self, in particular his mixture of caution and swift decision and also his acute sensitiveness about his crooked back. At the Christmas festivities of 1588 there appeared at Court for the first time Elizabeth Brooke, the young daughter of Robert's late companion in Flanders, Lord Cobham. Robert saw her and fell at once in love, so deeply that he made up his mind to try to marry her. But, before he asked her, he wanted to know if she was so repelled by his deformity that she would refuse him. He therefore wrote to a sister-in-law of his to ask her to find out from Elizabeth Brooke if he had a chance. 'The object of mine eye yesternight at supper', he wrote, 'hath taken so deep impression on my heart that every trifling thought increased my affection. I know your inwardness with all parties to be such, as only it lieth in your person to draw from them whether the mislike of my person be such as it may not be qualified by any other circumstance, which, if it be so, as of likelihood it is, I will then lay hand on my mouth . . .' However, all was well. Miss Brooke indicated that she would welcome Robert's addresses.

Getting married was an elaborate and lengthy process in the sixteenth century, at least for people of position. It was April before the couple were formally engaged. The wedding, still further delayed by Lady Burghley's death, took place quietly in August 1589. We know little about the bride. Her epitaph describes her as 'silent, true and chaste'. This is all right so far as it goes, but it does not go very far. She also seems to have been a simple soul, for we find Robert commenting with humorous affection on the fact that she tells everyone what she paid for everything. Perhaps he found this habit of hers especially engaging; it meant that she was refreshingly unlike his own secretive self. At any rate he continued to love her; the marriage was very happy. But it was short-lived. Elizabeth Cecil gave birth to a son and two daughters and died in 1596.

Robert was desolated; his hair literally turned grey with sorrow, and his friends began to fear that he might sink into an incurable melancholy. One of them, Sir Thomas Hoby, called on a visit of condolence, but was so horrified by the sight of Robert Cecil's stricken countenance that he left without daring to say a word to him. However, Robert was too much his father's son for any private sorrow to distract him for long from his dedicated absorption in his profession. He was soon back at work; but he made a vow, that in no circumstances would he marry for three years. In fact, he never married again. He was not by nature a celibate, however, and in later years his name was to be coupled with those of various married ladies: Lady Suffolk, Lady Derby, Lady Anne Clifford. Indeed, his enemies accused him of being very unchaste. There is no evidence to prove that they were right; moreover enemies in those days were given to making groundless accusations of this kind. But it does look as if any loves he may have had were light loves, and that no woman ever took his dead wife's place in his life.

All this is to anticipate. In 1589 he was twenty-six years old, newly married, happy, hopeful and on the threshold of political power. He took his first insecure step across it a year later. In April 1590 died Sir Francis Walsingham, leaving vacant the office of Chief Secretary to the Queen. The principal secretary was, after the Lord Treasurer, the chief minister in the government and in some ways even more influential. He supervised all the main areas of government, all the ground now covered by the Home Office, the Foreign Office and the Ministry of Defence, as well as what was at that time the most active and efficient Secret Service in Europe. Further, and even more important, the Secretary acted as intermediary between the Queen and the Chief Council of State, the Privy Council. Thus, more than any other minister, the Secretary had the chance to get the ear of the Queen and to press his views upon her. It is no wonder that Burghley had long wanted Robert to be Secretary. With himself as Lord Treasurer, the 'Wise Fox' could then be pretty sure of being in control of government policy.

Unluckily Walsingham had died before Robert could be considered experienced enough for such a big job. On the other hand there was no obvious rival candidate. Burghley therefore persuaded the Queen as a temporary measure to let him take over the Secretaryship himself. In practice this meant that he delegated much of the work to Robert, who thus got the chance to learn it and to show other people, and especially the Queen, that he was likely to be the right man to have the appointment. Burghley made no secret that this was what he wanted. In May 1591 Elizabeth visited him at his country house at Theobalds, where she was as usual entertained at a cost of several thousand pounds with ceremonies and banquets and theatrical performances, one of which included some pointed jokes about 'Mr Secretary Cecil' and what a help such a person might be to Her Majesty. Robert called further attention to himself by appearing dressed as a hermit to welcome the Queen in a flattering speech. Elizabeth did not take offence at these broad hints. She continued to smile upon her 'Elf', and at the end of her visit she knighted him. Three months later she paid him a greater compliment by appointing him, young as he was, a member of the exclusive and supreme Privy Council.

Robert had now got his foot inside the door; in the next few years it was a question of edging himself bit by bit further inside. He was launched on his career, a career which meant a lifetime of back-breaking, unremitting toil. For, in addition to his regular work as unofficial Secretary, he was often finding extra tasks thrust upon him. These included work in Parliament, where, in the session of 1593, he appeared as Minister representing the Crown and opened the debate about supplies. He also took an active part in other business, notably in a Bill to relieve the poor and suffering, especially soldiers who had suffered in the wars. The effect of these activities was to make Robert interested in the whole subject of poor relief. He gave a good deal of thought to it during the next years. The measures for the relief of the poor and old, passed in 1597 and afterwards, were the result of his ideas and passed under his auspices.

Meanwhile he waited patiently and watchfully for any opportunity that might help him to rise. It was an anxious time for him because there were other men ambitious to become the Queen's chief adviser – in particular Raleigh and Essex. Each had supporters; the rising generation, as well as being less submissive than their fathers, were also more aggressive and romantic. The spirit of young England in the 1590s, half heroic knight-errant, half tough buccaneer, thirsted for risk and adventure and battle and glory. They thought it ignoble to seek peace with the devil-dogs of Spain, or to make money by cautious regular trading rather than by snatching treasure from the New World in a campaign of splendid piracy on the high seas. What right, they said, had Spain to the New World and its treasures? Should the English not go out to capture and colonize it and its El Dorado, the fabled city of gold?

Such feelings led many young men to turn to find leaders in the picturesque and warlike figures of Raleigh and Essex rather than in Robert Cecil, prudent, peaceful and relatively law-abiding. From the first, then, Robert had these rivals to contend with. In the event, Raleigh turned out to be not very formidable. He was too arrogant to be popular, and moreover he put himself out of the running with the Queen by getting himself imprisoned in the Tower of London as a punishment for seducing a Maid of Honour and then secretly marrying her. In any case Essex had the advantage of being already the reigning favourite. His tragic story was to be the subject of the drama that occupied the stage of English history during the last years of Queen Elizabeth's reign.

This was largely a personal drama in which the chief figures were Essex and the Queen, not Robert Cecil. But Essex's ambitions made it also a political drama; and here Robert did play an unobtrusive but decisive part. If he had had his way, it would have been a reconciling part. Did he like Essex? In later years he claimed that he did; and he may well have been susceptible to Essex's considerable personal charm. On the other hand, the high-born, handsome Essex was the type of man to stir Robert's sense of physical and social inferiority. Whatever his private feelings may have been, he thought it sensible to be on good terms with Essex. He made gestures of friendship towards him and even helped him to make up some of the tiffs which marked his stormy relationship with the Queen.

Ultimately these efforts of Robert's were in vain; inevitably he was driven into a settled opposition. Essex could never be persuaded to accept the role of personal favourite so long as a Cecil remained the Queen's chief political adviser. Essex wanted to be a favourite in order to get power. Robert, steely-handed inside his delicate velvet glove, had to resist. The ambitions of the two men made conflict between them certain. The issue of this conflict, it must be repeated, was never ultimately in doubt. It was in the hands of the Queen, who, whatever she may have felt for Essex as a man, had no opinion of him as a statesman.

But the struggle was made tense and dramatic, while it lasted, by Essex's personality. Strength of personality was Essex's outstanding characteristic: his power to assume the centre of the stage, to dominate any scene in which he found himself. His appearance had something to do with this, his magnificent handsomeness, at once so male and so aristocratic, with his tall, slim, broad-shouldered figure and athletic grace and winning smile, all enhanced by the charm of glowing youth and by what especially appealed to the Elizabethans, both high and low, the glamour of an ancient lineage. For Essex, unlike his rivals, traced his descent from the old nobility. The impact of this exterior was reinforced by the fact that it was the expression of a nature at once fiery and magnetic, with a glitter about it which enabled him to draw the crowds wherever he went, and even to dazzle subsequent historians. For, like Mary Queen of Scots, Essex has managed to impose himself on posterity as a figure of romance. All the more because, again like her, he had the luck to have his head cut off: a spectacular death is a great help towards a romantic reputation. Essex would not have been a hero of romance, if he had lived to die of old age.

For, looked at detachedly, there is not much to admire in him. He was not one of the great Elizabethans so far as talents were concerned; nor in character either. He had his qualities: he was generous and brave, in an impulsive, fitful kind of way. He was also spoiled, vain, headstrong, and without any kind of self-control. If he did not get his way, he would either relapse into a fit of sulks or burst out in an explosion of temper. More often than not, too, his way was the wrong way, for Essex – it was his most fatal defect – had no sense of reality. Bemused by some shimmering dream of personal glory, he misjudged the national situation, the economic situation, the military situation; he failed to understand Queen Elizabeth, or Robert Cecil, or himself. Robert Cecil on the other hand judged and understood all these things pretty well.

Essex's merits and defects made themselves apparent early in his career. He appeared at Court for the first time as a youth of nineteen years in 1587. He immediately scored a dramatic success with Queen Elizabeth, fifty-four years old and at an age when a woman is beginning to be aware of the approach of old age, and is therefore acutely susceptible to the exhilarating, rejuvenating charm of one who looked the very figure of youth. Further, he was the nephew of Leicester, the one man she had been near to loving in the days of her youth, and he recalled those days to her mind. Essex on his side was young enough to be flattered and interested by the attentions of an older woman; and how much more when this particular older woman was his Queen and the cleverest woman

Robert Devereux, 2nd Earl of Essex, by William Segar

101

alive as well! A violent flirtation flared up between them, adorned with all the elaborate airs and graces thought appropriate to a relationship between Gloriana and an admirer, conducted with enthusiasm on both sides and in public. 'There is nobody near her', wrote an observer, 'but my Lord of Essex; and at night my Lord is at cards or one game or another, so that he cometh not to his lodging till the birds sing in the morning.'

Such nights brought tangible rewards. Essex was made Master of the Horse and Knight of the Garter. His head was easily turned, and his faults now began to show themselves. He grew violently jealous of any man to whom the Queen showed attention. He fought a duel with Sir Charles Blount because at a tournament he wore a favour she had given him, and was just prevented from fighting another with Raleigh on a similar pretext. A little later, moved by dreams of military glory, he flung off without permission to join an expedition against Portugal. The Queen summoned him back and gave him a scolding; but soon he was more in favour than ever. By 1590 his restless spirit had matured enough to entertain more serious ambitions to power.

Two new characters now appear in this story to encourage those ambitions: the brothers Anthony and Francis Bacon. They were Robert Cecil's cousins, for their mother, Anne Cooke, was Lady Burghley's sister. Like Lady Burghley, she was learned and intellectual. So were her sons. Francis, the younger, was much more: a man of versatile genius, philosophical, scientific, literary. Up to the time that he appears in our story, however, his gifts had not done him much good. Not content with a life of study and contemplation, he wanted to triumph as a man of affairs as well as of thought; he passionately desired power and glory.

At first he had hoped to get them through the influence of his uncle Burghley. But Burghley, either because he mistrusted Francis Bacon's character or feared him as a rival to his own son Robert, did nothing for him. By 1590 Bacon was over thirty and no higher up the ladder than he had been at twenty-five. Frustration was exacerbated by financial worry, for he had more than an ordinary share of the Renaissance love of splendid living and had spent so lavishly on books and works of art and gorgeous entertainment and handsome youths that he was now deeply in debt. The time had come when something simply had to be done to mend his fortunes. Since the Cecils were clearly not going to help him, Bacon turned his eyes – 'lively hazel eyes like a viper's', said John Aubrey – towards their rival. Could he not better himself by serving the cause of Essex? It struck him that Essex's personality and position and his own brains and knowledge ought to prove an irresistible combination. To further his purpose, he joined forces with his elder brother Anthony, also ambitious and needy. Together the two brothers presented themselves to Essex, Anthony as the possible organizer of a private information service concerned with foreign affairs and Francis as a general political adviser. Essex showed himself willing enough to make use of them, with the result that from now on his campaign to oust the Cecils in favour of himself was put on a more purposeful and professional footing.

It did not turn out to be effective. Essex and Bacon were a less successful combination than had been expected. For one thing Bacon, like many intellectual persons, lacked political instinct. Here Robert Cecil was more than a match for him. Just because Bacon was so clever, he trusted too much to the conclusions of his conscious intellect. He had none of Robert Cecil's intuitive perception of the right moment to act or to refrain from action, his capacity justly to estimate the relative strength of the forces operating in public life. More fatal still, Essex was temperamentally incapable of profiting by Bacon's advice. Bacon's schemes demanded patience, persistence and subtlety; Essex was incurably impatient, unsubtle, changeable. Moreover, enamoured of the idea of military glory and the popularity that went with it, he was always liable to leave the Court to take part in some would-be heroic adventure, while the Cecils stayed immovably at the centre of power. The result was a series of engagements in which Essex always overplayed his hand, so that after some delay and trouble the Cecils emerged victorious.

The occasion of each engagement was a vacancy in the administration. Bacon saw that, if Essex was to defeat the Cecils, he must have supporters in key positions. On their side, the Cecils tried to stop this from happening. The first round in the fight was, as we have seen, about who should succeed Walsingham as Secretary. In the event Robert did not get the post; but neither did the candidate suggested by Essex. Since Burghley temporarily took over the work, the result can be counted as a victory for the Cecils. The next clash came in 1594, as to who should be Attorney General, the chief law officer of the government. Essex proposed Bacon; the Cecils countered by proposing Sir Edward Coke, a distinguished lawyer. Essex threw himself into the battle with a rash violence which the artful Robert took care to encourage.

One day the two found themselves together in a coach. 'My Lord,' said Robert, 'the Queen has resolved that ere five days pass, without any further delay to make an Attorney General. I pray your Lordship to let me know who you will favour.' Essex answered that everyone knew that he wanted Bacon. 'Good Lord!' Robert exclaimed, 'I wonder your Lordship should go about to spend your strength in so unlikely and so impossible a matter. Give me one only precedent for the appointment of so raw a youth to that place of such moment.' 'I could name', replied Essex pointedly, 'a younger than Francis Bacon, of less learning and of no greater experience, who is suing and shoving with all force and for an office of far greater importance than the Attorneyship.' Robert replied, 'I well know that your Lordship means me, and I admit that both my years and experience are small. Yet, weigh the scale which I studied in and that great wisdom and learning of my schoolmaster . . . If at least your Lordship had spoken of the Solicitorship, that might be of easier digestion to her Majesty.' Essex lost his temper. 'Digest me no digestions!' he shouted. 'The Attorneyship for Francis is that I must have; and in that will I spend all my power, might, authority and amity, and with tooth and nail defend and procure the same for him against whomsoever.' It is to be presumed that Robert Cecil saw to it that the Queen heard about this conversation and the little attention Essex appeared to pay to her wishes in the matter. A few months later Coke was made Attorney General.

In 1595 the post of Solicitor General, second chief law officer of the Crown, fell vacant. Essex was by now resigned enough to try to get it for Bacon; and this time he was helped by Bacon's masterful mother, who went herself to see her nephew Robert on behalf of her son. Robert explained that the Queen had not yet made up her mind on the subject. 'Experience', he said humorously, 'teaches that Her Majesty's nature is not to resolve but to delay', and then added that he thought his father would manage to get some job or other for Francis. Lady Bacon received this suggestion sceptically. 'Some think', she said, 'that if my Lord had been in earnest it had been done.' She went on to compare Francis's failure with Robert's success; was he not already Secretary in fact, if not in name? Robert judged this was time to speak out. 'As for that,' he said, 'as long as none is placed, I watch still; though I may think myself as hardly used as my cousin. And I tell you plainly, Madam, I disdain to seem to be thought that I doubted of the place, and so would I wish my cousin Francis to do. It may be Her Majesty was too much pressed at the first, which she liketh not.' These last words show how much better Robert Cecil understood his royal mistress than Essex or Bacon did. In fact, anxious to keep on reasonably good terms with Essex, he had been in favour of Bacon's becoming Solicitor General. A few months later, however, the Queen appointed someone else.

The last round in this particular phase of the Essex–Cecil fight took place in 1596. It was a bad year for the country. The expensive war had left the government poor; crops had failed so that the people were hungry, and in December four Spanish galleons raided the Cornish coast and burned Penzance. It was felt that something must be done to enrich the Treasury and to hit back at the Spanish fleet. Accordingly in July a fleet, led by Essex and Raleigh, set out to capture the Spanish port of Cadiz and some treasure ships at that time in its harbour. It was a triumphant success. The English swept into Cadiz harbour and Essex, flinging his hat into the sea with a splendid gesture, leapt on to land at the head of his men and captured the town. This was just the kind of exploit he had always dreamed of performing; and it met with the kind of reception he had dreamed of, too.

Sir Francis Bacon of the 'lively viper's eyes', and a map showing Cadiz occupied in 1596 by English ships

He returned to find himself met everywhere by cheering crowds, the popular hero of England.

At last the way seemed open to his highest ambition. But was it? While he was abroad, Robert Cecil had moved forward silently to achieve his long-sought objective. The Queen had appointed him officially her Chief Secretary. Worse still for Essex, the capture of Cadiz turned out to be in one important respect a hollow victory. While he had been capturing the town the Spanish Admiral had heroically sunk many of the treasure ships, and much of what treasure was left had been plundered by the English sailors. Only a small proportion of what should have been her due got to the Queen. There was a painful session about this at the Council, in which Robert Cecil, in his new capacity as Secretary, pointed out these facts to Essex. 'I was more braved by your little cousin than ever I was by any man in my life,' wrote Essex furiously to Anthony Bacon. Anthony Bacon and the rest of Essex's supporters were as angry as he was. 'Robertus Diabolus', Robert the Devil – so they nicknamed Robert Cecil. In fact it was the Queen, not the Cecils, who had been primarily responsible for Essex's disappointment. Any personal affection for him had not altered her conviction, borne of a lifelong experience, that not he but Robert Cecil was the kind of minister she needed.

The next year or two were calm politically but darkened for Robert by personal grief. It was now that his wife died; and, soon after, Burghley began to grow so ill that it was clear that he would not live much longer. Robert saw that all was done to keep him alive; but the prospect of his father's death filled him with foreboding. It was likely to be a blow officially as well as a personal loss, for it would leave him alone to confront his opponents without his chief supporter and adviser. For this reason he felt reluctant when, at the beginning of 1598, Elizabeth sent him abroad on a mission to King Henry IV of France. France was considering making peace with Spain, and Elizabeth, as an ally, wanted to discover what Henry's intentions in the matter really were. Also – which was an equally important question to her – she wanted to persuade him to repay some money she had lent him.

Robert, small, crooked and modestly attended, did not make much impression on his first appearance as English Ambassador at the French Court. But soon his

Henry IV of France

agreeability and intelligence got him on easy terms with the King, who invited him to go wolf-hunting, introduced him to Madame his sister and to his mistress, Gabrielle d'Estrées, and took him for private walks in the garden, where he talked to him in a manner genial, informal and cynical. Robert was unseduced by these attentions. He thought Gabrielle d'Estrées pretty, but was critical of the King's sister, whom he described as 'well-painted, ill-dressed and strangely jewelled'. As for the King, Robert did not trust his geniality in the least and found his hunting invitations merely irritating. 'The King', he writes, 'has sent tonight to my lodging to court me and entreated me that I will go tomorrow a-hunting with him to kill a wolf and play the good fellow and not be melancholy. I have absolutely denied him and made him a sullen answer and desired him that he would give me leave to attend him about those affairs for which I was sent, being at no time fit for hunting and much less now.' He turned out to be right to distrust Henry. After three months of hanging about, Robert came back to England with the French debt still unpaid; a little later Henry made a separate treaty with Spain that showed no consideration for the interest of his English allies.

Burghley died a few months after Robert's return. His death was a turning-point in Robert's life. For, though for some time past he had done much of the chief minister's work, he had shared responsibility for it with Burghley. Now the responsibility was his alone: he, not Burghley, was now Queen Elizabeth's 'spirit'. From her point of view this did not mean any great change. Robert was as much her dedicated servant as his father and shared the same point of view. He too saw the good of his country as best achieved by a policy of tough moderation, a balancing middle-way course, to be pursued flexibly but with resolution. These general aims had now to be reinterpreted to fit a changed situation. Burghley had realized this. A little before his death he summoned Robert to him for a last solemn interview. Robert related it in later days: 'Having then his body wearied with sickness, his mind mightily perplexed with the State besides his old age which of itself is a most great cross, he called me to him almost weeping. "Son," said he, "thou art young and perhaps thy father's care and thy own good behaviour may move thy prince to impose a part of that heavy weight which I have all my time carried upon thy weak shoulders; which, if it happen, upon my blessing I charge thee that these three things thou have before thy eyes: the first, tend in all thy actions in the state to shun foreign wars and seditions; labour, with thy prince's honour, to reconcile her to all her enemies so far as may stand with honour and safety; thirdly, have regard to the tottering commonwealth after thy mistress' death to invest the true and lawful successor." '[1]

---

[1] The words of Robert Cecil given here are reported to us at second hand. But they are so much in character that they may well be judged authentic.

In these words Burghley, as it were, formally hands over to his successor and suggests how best to carry on the work to which he had given up his life. For him this work had been constructive; for Robert, it was to be preservative. Burghley had been mainly concerned to help Queen Elizabeth to establish a united orderly England with its national comprehensive Church under a strong monarchy. Robert had now to secure this new England against anything that might threaten its stability. This for Burghley meant a reasonable peace with Spain, and the avoidance of any future foreign entanglements, as likely to lead to war. Finally and most important, the new England must be made safe for posterity, which meant, now that the Queen was growing old, that Robert must do all he could to arrange who should be her successor. Burghley remembered all too well the civil chaos and lawless violence that had followed the death of Edward VI when the succession had been left uncertain. Robert listened to his dying father, agreed with him and followed his advice. From now, peace with Spain and the settlement of the succession were the two aims to which his policy was first of all directed.

II

Meanwhile Essex was getting more difficult than ever. Disappointment, after what seemed to have been the glorious triumph of Cadiz, had left him irritable and frustrated. He began to think his ambitions were never going to be realized. Restlessly he indulged in dreams of glory, on warship or battlefield; and fitfully he tried to bring them about. He did manage to lead an expedition against Spain in the Azores in 1597; but this proved a failure; he also took an active part against making peace with Spain and, as we have seen, quarrelled with Burghley about it. Failure made him yet more quarrelsome. This, a few months later, was to involve him in a dispute at once comic and disastrous.

The occasion, as so often in English history, was the Irish question. Ireland, always in a state of unrest, had lately been growing more so under the leadership of a new, effective rebel chieftain, O'Neill, Earl of Tyrone. The government, to reimpose order, decided to appoint a new Lord Deputy. A small Council was held at which the Queen proposed Sir William Knowlys. Essex argued in favour of Sir George Carew. Elizabeth overruled him. Essex once again lost his temper and offensively and deliberately turned his back on her. He should have known better than to treat Queen Elizabeth I like this. She boxed his ears. Beside himself with rage, he put his hand to his sword and would have drawn it had not other

The King James Drawing-room, Hatfield House

councillors sprung forward and stopped him. He rushed out of the palace swearing furiously. A friend recommended him to apologize. Essex answered hotly, 'I have been content to do Her Majesty the service of a clerk but can never serve her as a villein or a slave!' Elizabeth, who still cherished a weakness for him, relented enough for things to be patched up temporarily. But the incident was in fact a milestone on Essex's journey to disaster. His half-drawn sword, and still more his mutinous words, had evidenced a line of thought that, if pursued, would threaten the security of the throne. Essex did pursue it. Next year the curtain rose on the last act in his tragedy.

Once again Ireland was the cause of catastrophe. By the summer of 1598 the situation had become so bad there that the English government made up its mind to send out a military expedition. Here, thought Essex, was another chance to triumph as a soldier; and he persuaded the government to appoint him commander. He set out with an unprecedented number of men and supplies to help him, and orders to attack Tyrone's forces, which were gathered in Ulster, as quickly as possible. One would have thought that these were orders after Essex's heart. But unaccountably he failed to obey them. Instead, moody and inert, he wasted his resources in ineffective little campaigns in southern Ireland.

It was not till after six months that he went north. There he met with a final *débâcle*; no triumph, no battle even – only a meeting with Tyrone on horseback in the middle of a river, when, it was whispered, Essex conceded most of his enemy's demands in return for a promise of help if Essex decided to invade England and rout his enemies there. Whether this was true or not, Essex had certainly begun considering imposing his will on the Queen by force. However, his mind veered this way and that; and now, suddenly swept away by an impulse, he deserted his army and dashed off to England to try whether his personal charm could still soften Elizabeth's heart. He burst into her private apartments to find her dressing and, it can be presumed, looking fully her age and not her best. She was equal to the situation, welcomed him pleasantly and apparently without surprise. He left her feeling relieved and hopeful. Meanwhile she sent for Robert Cecil. That afternoon Essex presented himself before the Council to be confronted with a very different Queen Elizabeth. After icily questioning him about his conduct in Ireland, she dismissed him. Soon afterwards he got orders that he was to be confined to his house for an indefinite period. Queen and favourite never saw each other again.

Six months later, it was announced that Essex was to be brought before the Court of the Star Chamber. Then, a day or two before it was to take place, the

James I: a painting at Hatfield House attributed to John de Critz the Elder, after Van Somer

trial was cancelled. This cancellation, it afterwards transpired, was the work of Robert Cecil. Though inevitably opposed to Essex's political aspirations, he was unwilling to quarrel with him; nor did he desire his complete downfall. He still thought the best policy would be for Essex, like Leicester before him, to be the Queen's favourite but not her minister. Apart from anything else, Essex was popular with the people. Why, thought Robert, antagonize the people by crushing him? Accordingly he used his influence to stop the trial.

His action only put off the evil day. Essex himself made the evil day inevitable. Failure only drove him to wilder dreams; could he not arrange that his army, left in Ireland, should come over and rescue him? And perhaps an army from Scotland, too? The young King James VI might send troops in return for a certain promise of succession to the English throne. In secret Essex began to correspond with James, probably to this effect. He justified this extreme cause on the ground of self-preservation. He was growing paranoiac as well as ambitious; he saw himself surrounded by enemies bent on destroying him, and at the head of them was Robert Cecil. Just because he was his most formidable rival, Essex fancied Robert was his most active enemy, who was plotting – and had for years been plotting – to compass his destruction. From this time Robert Cecil became the object of Essex's obsessive fear and hatred. He was encouraged in this by his supporters, who also did all they could to work up the civilians of London against Robert. They represented him as a mean-spirited, jumped-up hunchback, an odious contrast to that open-handed, nobly-born friend of the people, the Earl of Essex. Their words bore some fruit. Apprentice boys sang offensive rhymes about Robert in the streets: one morning early in 1600 passers-by saw, scrawled on the door of Cecil's house, these words: 'Here lies the Toad.'

Cecil appeared indifferent to these attacks; but they cannot have made him friendly to the man ultimately responsible for them. In any case more powerful and practical reasons were now turning him against Essex. At long last he had come to the conclusion that there was no dealing with him; also he had got to know that Essex was now toying with the idea of active rebellion. It was now only a question of time before the government would be forced to take extreme action against him. Robert Cecil had to be sure, of course, that the Queen would back extreme action. But this was not difficult. Through his spies he had found out about Essex's letters to King James of Scotland; and he saw that the Queen got to know about them, too. This was decisive. In her last years the question of

Nonesuch Palace, Surrey, where the 2nd Earl of Essex, returning discomfited from Ireland, flung himself at the feet of Elizabeth I, and below a view of London engraved by J. C. Visscher about 1616

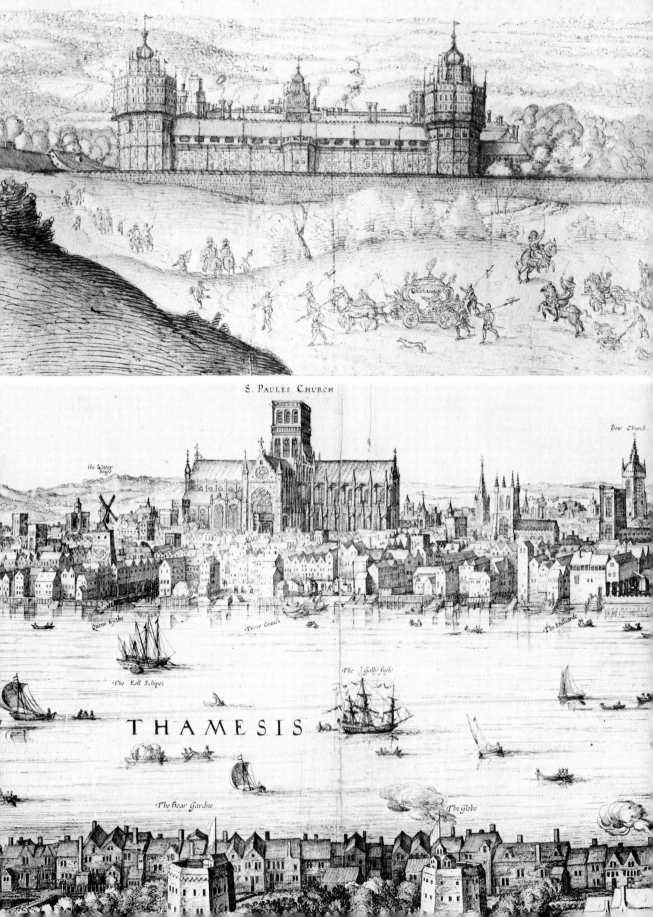

S. PAVLES CHVRCH

Bow Church

the Water
house

Church Crede

Quene hythe

Three Cranes

The Stilliard

The Eell Schipes

The Gally fuste

THAMESIS

The Bear Gardne

The Globe

her successor had become the sorest possible point to Elizabeth, the very mention of which sent her into a rage. To speak of it to her seemed like deliberately proclaiming her coming death. To intrigue with her successor was a kind of treason. Such treason had a peculiar horror about it, when committed by a man on whom she had lavished so much affection and whom already she had forgiven so much. By his letters to James, Essex had wounded Elizabeth in the tenderest fibres of her being; and she did not forgive him again.

In the last month of 1600 events began to move confusedly to their climax. Excluded from Court and surrounded by a rabble of discontented hangers-on – shady adventurers, hot-headed fellow nobles – Essex, in a condition of growing and hysterical desperation, brooded and raged and listened to tales of plots against himself. His plight was made worse by financial trouble. He had by now so much overspent himself that he was dependent almost wholly on a right, given to him in the past by the Queen, to a rake-off from the sale of sweet wines. Now, in October 1600, she refused to renew it. The prospect of financial ruin, in addition to all his other troubles, drove Essex to openly treasonable courses. On the 3rd of February he and his fellow conspirators decided on a scheme by which some were to seize the Court and the Queen while others took control of the City. However, before this startling scheme could be put into action, Robert Cecil, who had been watching the progress of the whole affair, now decided that the time had come to strike. With cool competence he took action to forestall Essex's plans. He saw that the Court was protected and sent his brother Lord Burghley down to the City to proclaim Essex a traitor and warn the City authorities against him. After a day of futile alarums and excursions, Essex found himself in the Tower of London. A week later he was in Westminster Hall on trial for his life.

The Court and the trial were marked by a dramatic scene which cast an unexpected light on the personality of Robert Cecil. At the start of the proceedings Essex, handsome, haggard and in black, struck an attitude of calm defiance. But, as the evidence against him piled up, he began to lose his nerve and tried to defend himself by making wild accusations against his enemies and in particular Robert Cecil. Cecil, not himself, Essex claimed, was the traitor: he had heard for a fact that Cecil had declared the Infanta of Spain, England's national enemy, to be the rightful heir to the English throne.

Robert Cecil was not visible in Court: characteristically he had chosen to attend the trial concealed behind a curtain. But, at Essex's words, the curtains parted and he stepped forth. Beneath the vaulted and immemorial ceiling of the great hall, and with every eye in the vast crowd assembled there fixed on them, the magnificent, tempestuous figure of Essex confronted the small, pale, crooked figure of Robert Cecil. But it was a Robert Cecil for once bereft of his usual gentle composure. Falling on his knees, he addressed his accuser in a flood of passionate words.

'The difference between you and me is great,' he cried, 'for I speak in the person of an honest man and you, my Lord, in the person of a traitor. For wit I give you the pre-eminence – you have it abundantly. For nobility also, I give you place – I am not noble, yet a gentleman. I am no swordsman – there also you have the odds. But I have innocence, truth of conscience, and honesty to defend me against the scandal of slanderous tongues and aspiring hearts; and I protest before God·I have loved your person and justified your virtues; and I appeal to God and the Queen that I told Her Majesty your afflictions would make you a fit servant for her. And had I not seen your ambitious affections inclined to usurpation, I could have gone on my knees to Her Majesty to have done you good; but you have a sheep's garment to show, and in appearance are humble and religious: but, God be thanked, we know you! . . . I stand for loyalty, which I never lost; you stand for treachery, wherewith your heart is possessed; and you charge me with high things, wherein I defy you to the uttermost. You, my good lords, Counsellors of State, have had many conferences, and I do confess I have said the King of Scots is a competitor, and the King of Spain is a competitor, and you I have said are a competitor; you would depose the Queen, you would be king of England, and call a Parliament. Ah! my Lord, were it but your own case, the loss had been the less; but you have drawn a number of noble persons and gentlemen of birth and quality into your net of rebellion, and their bloods will cry vengeance against you. For my part I vow to God I wish my soul was in heaven and my body at rest, so this had never been.'

'I thank you, Mr Secretary', answered Essex bitterly, 'for my humbling – that you in the rust of your bravery come to make oration against me here today.'

'My Lord,' said Robert Cecil, 'I humbly thank God that you did not take me for a fit companion for you and your humours; for if you had, you would have drawn me to betray my Sovereign as you have done. But I would have you name the Counsellor you speak of. Name him, name him!' he cried with growing emotion, 'name him if you dare – I defy you!'

Essex said that young Lord Southampton, also on trial, had reported the story to him. Cecil implored Southampton to give the name of his source. Southampton said it was Sir William Knollys, Comptroller of the Queen's Household. Robert Cecil demanded that Knollys be brought to Court; in spite of his agitation, he kept his head enough to remember to ask the messenger not to tell Knollys why he had been sent for, so that he would have no time to prepare an evasive answer. As it turned out, Knollys, when he came, completely exonerated Cecil. The Secretary, he said, had once talked to him unfavourably about a book which claimed that the Infanta should succeed to the throne of England. 'But these words were reported to me in another sense,' stammered Essex in horrified confusion. Robert Cecil refused to accept this excuse. All his suppressed indignation both at Essex's hostility to himself and at what he thought the weakness of his warlike policy burst out. 'Your malice,' he said, 'whereby you seek to work me into hatred amongst all men, has flown from no other course than for my affection for peace for the good of the country and your own inflamed heart for war.' The outburst lasted only a moment. Then the habit of a lifetime's self-control reasserted itself. He went on in gentler tones, 'I beseech God to forgive you for this open wrong done unto me as I do openly forgive you from the bottom of my heart.'

'I also have to forgive you,' said Essex. This was too much for Robert, who thought, reasonably enough, that he had done nothing needing Essex's forgiveness. He broke out, 'Upon my soul and conscience, you are a traitor!' Essex retorted that, though he might be legally a traitor, he was not one in conscience. 'You do well to deny that last,' said Cecil implacably. 'As you have showed yourself a rebellious traitor, so you shall die an impudent traitor.'

It was a momentous and revealing episode. Shaken to his depth by the deadly danger in which he suddenly found himself – for, if Essex's story was believed, the Queen would judge him to be as much a traitor as Essex himself – Robert Cecil's iron reserve had broken down to disclose the tumult of contending motives and impulses which seethed within him: his pride and his sense of inferiority physical and social, his old affection for Essex and his new-found bitterness against him, his horror of rebellion, his hatred of war, his devotion to his Queen and finally the thin, strong strand of Christian belief and Christian moral feeling implanted in him by his early education.

The incident destroyed any vestige of hope Essex may still have entertained. He heard the dreadful sentence of death calmly; but two days later, under pressure of the strenuous ministrations of his puritan chaplain, he broke down and asked some of the leading Ministers of the Crown, including Robert Cecil, to come to the Tower that he might ask their forgiveness. An unedifying scene followed in which Essex alternately wallowed in abject confessions of guilt and strove to excuse himself by putting the blame on other people, including his own sister. 'It is the custom of the English to betray each other,' commented the French Ambassador caustically when told of the scene. Robert Cecil accepted Essex's apology; but prudently saw to it that he set down both the confession and his accusations in writing.

Essex and four other persons were executed, but by the standards of the time the rebellion was punished mildly. Cecil's influence was on the side of mercy; though ruthless enough when he thought it necessary for the security of the state, he was neither cruel nor vindictive. Alas, this did him little good with the people

Queen Elizabeth I with some of her courtiers: effigies at Hatfield House

of England. Feeling against him was violently inflamed by Essex's death. Essex was now looked on as a martyr as well as a hero; and, since Elizabeth, even in age, still retained some of her magical power over the hearts of her subjects, the blame for Essex's death fell chiefly on Cecil. The crowd shouted at him in the streets. 'Robin with the bloody breast!' they called out, and 'What are the Cecils? Are they better than pen-gents?' Angrily they asked by what evil and unnatural practices this low-born hunchback had got the better of that princely, open-handed warrior, the Earl of Essex. Even in Cecil's household, men were found to echo these accusations. One of his servants was heard to say of him, 'It is an unwholesome thing to meet a man in the morning who hath a wry neck, a crooked back and a splay foot.' By night, alley and lighted tavern rang with a new song:

> Little Cecil trips up and down;
> He rules both Court and Crown,
> With his brother Burghley clown
> In his great fox-furrèd gown.
> With the long proclamation
> He swore he saved the town.
> Is it not likely?

The shock given by Essex's death soon passed, but not the dislike felt for Robert Cecil. He had never been a popular figure. Though he could exercise a strong charm on an individual and in the intimacy of a private room, on any larger group he made a doubtful impression. This was partly due to his deformity and his secretiveness, but still more to the fact that he did not fit in with any accepted pattern of character. His complex nature, glinting forth through his mask of apparent gentleness, baffled people and made them feel uneasy; all the more because events showed it to be combined with such a formidable capacity quietly to eliminate his opponents. Robert regretted his unpopularity; but from an early age he had learned to discount other people's opinions. 'He that will be impatient of slander', he said crisply, 'must procure himself a chair out of this world's circle.'

All the same his sense of unpopularity tended to increase his feeling of isolation. This had grown with his greatness. The peak of power is a lonely place. For Robert Cecil it was especially lonely because by a cruel stroke of fate he had, by the time he had reached it, lost the two persons with whom he seemed to have been most intimate, his wife and his father. Nor, though he loved his children and especially his son William, was he ever to find anyone to take their place in his confidence. It is no wonder that the melancholy strain in him grew stronger. The mature Robert Cecil, like the mature Burghley, was a sad man. Sadder perhaps, because his melancholy was more obsessive. He might try to distract it by means of work, or gambling, or hawking, or building, or gardening. But it was never long before the shadow would steal over his spirit once more. 'My nature is now composed of so ominous a spirit', he wrote to a friend, 'as I no sooner see afar off the probability of new privations or misfortunes . . . but I do yield to my genius, no other reckoning than to assure it, that whatsoever can wound me will betide me.'

In fact, even with Essex safely beheaded, Robert Cecil still had reason to feel low-spirited. The sheer weight of work he had to do was enough to depress him. 'God knows I labour like a packhorse,' he complained. He had to keep an eye on the whole area of government here and abroad and to represent the administration in the House of Commons when Parliament met, as it did in 1601. It was a new-style cantankerous House of Commons violently protesting against the taxes. Robert found dealing with it a strain on his temper, and showed it. But, in spite of some sharp exchanges, he retained the good opinion of Members of Parliament. They recognized that, like Burghley, he respected their ancient and legal rights. 'I would have all men to know thus much, that there is no jesting with the Court of Parliament,' he declared to them. Robert Cecil was no more a democrat than Shakespeare himself; like him he believed in 'degree': 'England never came to harm', he said, 'from gentlemen or men of worth. Some Jack Cade or Jack Straw or such rascals are those that have endangered the Kingdom.' But equally he disbelieved in illegal rule whether by noblemen or by a monarch. No one was so high as to be above the law.

In his belief in law, Robert was a direct disciple of his father. Burghley had thought that the country would never be safe so long as Mary Queen of Scots was alive, but he would not hear of her being assassinated: she must be condemned in a Court of Law after a proper trial. Robert reacted in the same way when somebody suggested assassinating Tyrone. He said vehemently, 'I would rather serve my country in any other kind than stain my conscience with blood, which, shed by a lawful cause, was an acceptable service to God; but, spilt by indirect means, would cry for vengeance from above.'

Robert Cecil's work was not confined to his official activities. He had all the time to keep his eyes open to protect his position against unofficial attack; to guard against competitors for power, notably Walter Raleigh. The relations between these two remarkable men present a curious study. At moments they seemed to have been on terms of personal friendship. Yet intellectually and temperamentally there was a wide gulf between the adventurous, arrogant Raleigh, with his dreams of colonial empire and his daring religious speculations, and Robert Cecil, cautious, realistic, religiously orthodox and looking sceptically on colonial dreams of any kind. Politically the gulf was yet wider. Not only were they rivals for the Queen's favour, but Raleigh, like Essex, wanted that favour to further the kind of risky warlike policy which was fundamentally opposed to the Cecil tradition of what was best for England. Political views soon proved stronger than personal feelings. To oppose Essex they had formed an uneasy alliance. But, once Essex was defeated, the alliance began to break up and Robert grew more and more concerned to check Raleigh's schemes.

His final problem was to cope with the Queen. 'The Queen is now wholly directed by the Secretary who governs all things as his father did,' said a contemporary. It was not true of Robert any more than it had been of Burghley. So long as there was breath in her body, there was no question of anyone except herself directing Queen Elizabeth I.

For Robert, his relations with his royal mistress formed the most delicate part of his job. Even more delicate than they had been for his father; for Burghley had started in the advantageous position of an older man advising a young woman. Robert was a younger man advising an old woman, and one armed with the authority of long experience and the irritability of advancing years. However, he proved to be just as successful as Burghley. Basically his method was the same. But his manner was different. Burghley addressed Elizabeth affectionately but with comparative restraint; Robert gave her the full Gloriana treatment, employed the same flamboyant flattery as did her courtier favourites. Though he was approaching middle age and she was old, he would refer to her as a nymph and comment with rapture on the 'crystalline beams of her eyes'. In spite of his efforts, she sometimes lost her temper with him: 'She reviled me notably for I know not what,' he complained on one such occasion. In general, however, he was successful in diverting storms and became especially adroit at conducting business with her in such a way as to avoid occasions of trouble. If he had to bring her a controversial Bill to sign, he used to start talking about some subject which he knew interested her; and then, when the discussion was at its height, slip the Bill in front of her so that she did not notice what she was signing.

All the same, if he thought it necessary, he spoke displeasing truths to her as firmly as Burghley had done. He could not help being a little proud of this: 'But for myself, I know not one man in this kingdom that will bestow six words of argument to reply, if she deny it,' he said. He was able to do this because she trusted his judgment; not only because she knew him to be disinterested, but because she realized that, like his father, he agreed with her about the ultimate ends of policy in a way that no other minister or favourite did. Robert believed in her as much as she did in him. For all the trouble he had from her vanity and tantrums, he had learned from experience to share Burghley's profound admiration for her political insight; and Burghley's love for her, too. Robert's compliments, though phrased so extravagantly, were not insincere in the sense that they were false to his feeling. Even in her wrinkled, painted old age, Elizabeth still kept some of her magical power to inspire devotion. She inspired it in Robert Cecil. 'I never saw anyone about the Queen', said one of his friends, 'that loved her better and was less mindful of future fortune than he did.'

This is an exaggeration. The events of the next year or two showed that Robert Cecil was far from unmindful of his future fortune. But they also showed that he always put his concern for it second to his concern for the Queen's interest. All the same, these events – Robert's main preoccupation at this time – did involve a subject that he could not discuss with her, namely who was to be her successor. Burghley had been quite right in stressing this question in his last charge to his son. It was the crucial issue of the time. There was still a risk of the sort of trouble that had arisen after Edward VI's death. No safe future could exist for the new England till it was settled who was to be the next monarch. Should it be King James of Scotland or the Infanta of Castile or Lady Arbella Stuart? All three had claims, all three had supporters. Robert had no doubt he wanted King James. As chief minister, therefore, he must take steps to ensure that his candidate was successful, and without a contest: everything must be fixed beforehand so that it should pass off quietly. Further, the process must be his doing and leave him in

Sir Walter Raleigh and his son

1602

Sr Walter Raleigh Knight Lord Warden of
the Stanneries   of the
        & of the Isle of Jarsey & her Mᵗⁱᵉ Lieute
nant general of the Counties of Devonshyre & Cornwall

power. It was necessary to ensure the future of the country; it was also necessary to ensure the future of Robert Cecil.

It was clear that the sooner he got in touch with James the better. He started trying to do so, soon after Essex's death. Two things made negotiation tricky. In the first place, he knew James was prejudiced against him; for Essex had represented him to James as a strong supporter of the Infanta. Secondly, he must keep the negotiation secret from Elizabeth; if she knew of it, all was lost. Her reason for refusing to name her heir was, as usual with her, a complex mixture. She judged that a proclaimed heir to the throne would be a centre of unrest; all discontented persons would gather round him with an eye to the future. Here she was right and Robert Cecil agreed with her. For this reason he wanted the succession settled, but secretly. Not so Elizabeth: the prospect of her death filled her with an obsessive, irrational horror which led to an uncontrollable shrinking from the thought of any subject, such as the choice of her successor, that forced her to face it. 'The name of my successor is like the tolling of my own death bell,' she cried; 'I can by no means endure a shroud to be held before my eyes while I am living.' There was no doubt that, if she discovered that Robert was actually making arrangements with James as to what was to be done after her death, she might dismiss him from her service.

To make arrangements for James's safe succession to the Crown without Elizabeth finding out, and to do so in such a way as to secure his own position in the new reign – such was the dangerous and delicate operation Robert Cecil set himself to perform. Luckily he had the qualifications for it, the tact and persistence and the steady nerve.

The first thing was to find the right intermediary with whom to open negotiations with James. Two presented themselves: Lord Huntly and the Master of Gray. Robert judged neither suitable. Lord Huntly was entangled in Catholic intrigue, and the Master of Gray was a handsome, wily diplomat more agreeable than trustworthy. Moreover, the Master of Gray does not seem to have known how to treat Robert Cecil with proper respect; for, some years later, he was heard spreading the rumour that they had first met in a brothel. With displeasure, Robert denied this accusation. 'Though I may have had my frailties, as have all sons of Adam,' he said, 'yet have I ever scorned that opprobrious base course of life.' It is fair to Robert to say that what we know of the two men inclines us to believe him rather than the Master of Gray. In any case, a more acceptable intermediary soon offered himself in the person of Lord Mar, a Scottish peer on an official mission to London. With him matters were soon settled; a code of names was chosen which Robert Cecil and King James were to use when writing to each other; and also secret routes by which letters were to be conveyed between Scotland and England. Robert opened the correspondence; his letter and those that followed were couched in extraordinary high-flown language, almost as difficult to understand as Elizabeth's own. However, they were dexterously designed to win James's confidence without implying any disloyalty to Elizabeth. They left no doubt that Robert would do all he could to see that James became King, but that his first duty was still to his Queen. He also indicated politely but definitely that he expected to be kept in power after James came to the throne.

James was greatly impressed by these letters, especially as Robert had been careful to sprinkle them freely with classical and Biblical allusions; for James fancied himself both as a scholar and a theologian. For nearly two years the correspondence continued its long-winded, pedantic and artful course. Artful, that is to say, on Robert's side; James would never be much of a diplomat. At last the desired end was reached: Robert had convinced James that he was the right man for him, the most powerful, the most trustworthy. But it had needed all his skill to achieve this end. Up to the last minute there was also a chance that things might go wrong. James might say or do something indiscreet; or he might be diverted from the right path by hostile influence. For other groups were trying to nobble him; notably one headed by Raleigh, now estranged from Robert and on fire with ambition. Robert skilfully managed to put James off Raleigh. He warned James against him on the grounds that he was both a rebel and a heretic: the two most damaging accusations possible in the eyes of one who was both piously orthodox and a believer in the Divine Right of Kings. For more details about Raleigh he referred James to Lord Henry Howard, a clever nobleman with a bad reputation for mischief-making and a known enemy of Raleigh. Even in the tough-minded seventeenth century it was embarrassing for a respectable statesman to be associated with Howard. Robert Cecil seems to have felt this; for in a paper of his, in which he speaks of 'worthy Henry Howard', he has as an afterthought crossed out the word 'worthy'.

Finally, there was always the risk that the Queen might discover the negotiation. One day she nearly did. She was driving with Cecil in a coach, when a messenger rode up with a packet of letters from Scotland: Robert was sure it contained one to him from James. The Queen asked for the packet. However, he was equal to the occasion. He knew that she had a horror of bad smells, and, before she took it in her hand, he intervened as if to cut the string for her politely, and then – 'Faugh!' he exclaimed, 'it smells vilely!' She shrank back disgusted; by the time she had recovered herself, he had contrived to slip James's letter into his pocket. Such incidents were a strain; and even if all worked out as planned, the future was dark and anxious. For who knew what the new reign might bring? 'I do confess I am sorry to meddle or participate,' he wrote, 'being one that can take no great pleasure in the present, wherein you best keep but pain and peril; nor do desire to live until the future when I think I have made a great purchase,

Sir John Harington about 1583

if my innocency may be so happy as to escape an undeserved ruin.' The memory of how much he had always been misunderstood and misrepresented added a streak of bitterness to the depression that hung like a shadow over his tired spirit. His tired body, too: the pressure of work and worry combined began to affect his always fragile health. In the winter of 1602 Robert Cecil became more ill than he had been for thirty years.

Meanwhile the great event, the prospect of which had been the cause of all his hopes and fears and schemes and strains, was looming close. During the rest of 1602, Elizabeth showed that she had not yet quite lost her old vitality. She still played the virginals, and danced at a Court Ball and in the spring rode out maying in the woods; and she still had enough high spirits to enjoy teasing her courtiers. One evening she saw young Lady Derby wearing a miniature in a gold case round her neck. Thinking it was the picture of some lover, Elizabeth took it from her and opened it to find a picture of Lady Derby's uncle, Robert Cecil. Amused, she tied it to her shoe and paraded round the room. Robert, practised in playing up to her moods, immediately composed a poem on the incident which he later had set to music and sung to her.

But the time for these scenes of Court comedy were soon to close and the curtain to rise on a tragic spectacle. Soon after the beginning of 1603 Elizabeth grew very ill; and, though she lingered for three months, it was clear she was dying. Forced at last to face the onset of death which she had so long evaded, her spirit underwent a dramatic change. She showed no fear, she was always brave; but her zest for living completely forsook her. She would not go to bed; hour after hour, throughout the short winter days and long winter nights, she lay on cushions, staring with fixed, fading eyes silently at the fire. On the rare occasions when she did speak, it was only in some brief, concentrated phrase to give voice to the haunted desolation that filled her heart. Once she said to her Maid of Honour Lady Scroop, 'I saw one night my own body exceedingly lean and fearful in the light of the fire. Are you wont to see such sights in the night?' And to Sir John Harington, her godson, who thought to raise her spirits by telling her a joke, 'When thou doth feel creeping time at thy gate, these fooleries will please thee less.'

Robert Cecil was often with her; as she grew worse, he told her that she must go to bed to reassure her subjects that all was being done to maintain her strength. Her answer showed that the spirit of the old Elizabeth was not yet quite extinguished. 'The word "must" is not to be used to princes,' she said superbly. 'Little man, little man, if your father had lived, you durst not had said so: but ye know I must die and that makes thee so presumptuous.' In the end she yielded and went to bed. Her going was a sign that at last she accepted her death. She told her servants, 'I wish not to live any longer, but desire to die.' Now, as Burghley had done, she recognized the ultimate vanity of earthly glory. The Archbishop of Canterbury, summoned to pray at her bedside, alluded to her greatness as a Queen. She interrupted him: 'My Lord, the crown which I have borne so long has given enough of vanity in my time. I beseech you not to augment it, when I am so near death.'

Ladies of the Court in the funeral procession of Queen Elizabeth I

There was one more duty she had to perform, however, before she could turn her back completely on this world. On the 22nd of March Robert Cecil, the Lord Keeper and the Lord Admiral gathered round her bed, the lords on each side and Robert at the foot. The Lord Admiral asked her to name her successor. Enigmatic to the last, but with a final flicker of her ancient fire, 'I tell you my seat hath been the seat of kings,' she whispered; 'I will have no rascal to succeed me; and who should succeed me but a king?' Mystified, the two lords looked uncertainly at each other; Robert Cecil spoke up to ask whom she meant. 'Who,' she answered, 'but our cousin of Scotland?' She paused, then added, 'I pray you, trouble me no more.' They had to trouble her once more, however: it was thought necessary to confirm her words in the presence of more witnesses. Next afternoon a larger and more representative body presented themselves, but only to find her incapable of speech. Once more Robert took the initiative and asked her to give them some sign that King James was in fact her choice. With a final effort of her nearly spent forces, Elizabeth lifted her hands slowly above her head and brought her fingers together in the form of a crown. She died soon after midnight.

The news was brought to Robert Cecil, waiting expectant in another room of the great dim palace. Immediately he summoned the Council. Next morning, at half past ten, on a green outside Whitehall and heralded by trumpets, he read aloud a proclamation – it had been drafted by him beforehand in readiness for the event – declaring James I King of England. Soon, all over the country, people were listening to the same proclamation. It was received everywhere unopposed. 'The King's ship', wrote Robert, 'has come into the right harbour without cross of wave or tide that could overturn a cock-boat.' If so, it was because he had been the steersman.

III

James I's peaceful accession to the throne of England was the most important event in Robert Cecil's political life and the crowning achievement in his career. Through Robert's dexterity and decisiveness, James was safely on the throne before the people of England had fully realized that Queen Elizabeth was dead. The most critical step in the process of transition was over. But, if it was to prove worth taking, Robert Cecil had to ensure that the new government carried on the old policy, that it pursued the long-term aims established by Burghley and the late Queen; and with himself in charge. Obviously the first thing to do was to get into good personal relations with the King.

Hatfield House: the North Front

Accordingly Robert went north to catch him on his way down from Scotland. He met him at York. It was an occasion that must have called forth all his faculty of lightning adaptability; for nothing could have been more of a contrast to Queen Elizabeth than the thirty-eight-year-old James I, an awkward, ugly figure dressed in a shabby doublet heavily quilted to protect him from an assassin's dagger, with a straggly beard, a slobbering tongue too big for his mouth, who shambled about fiddling with his codpiece and, throughout the interview, was always leaning against something or someone to support a weight too heavy for his weak, knock-kneed legs. His talk was as unkingly as his looks: a garrulous stream in which out-of-the-way learning and long-winded theories mingled incongruously with homely endearments and jocular familiarities, all uttered in a broad Scottish accent. However, the interview went well; as it ended, 'Though you be but a little man,' said James facetiously, 'we shall surely load your shoulders with business.'

James's good impression was confirmed in May when he paid a three-day visit to Theobalds. Its mere appearance impressed him: Burghley and Robert Cecil had let the Renaissance strain in their imagination have full rein there, and James, coming from the bleak castles of Scotland, was awed and dazzled by this fairy palace of a place, with its courts and fountains and elaborate gardens and the turrets of rosy brick, surmounted by gilded weather-vanes and a loggia on whose walls was depicted in brilliant colour the history of England, and a great green hall lined with artificial trees, complete with bark and birds' nests, and a ceiling adorned with a sun that was moved by machinery, and stars which, after dark, shone and twinkled. More important, James was impressed by the personality of his host, the effect he gave of knowledge, efficiency and authority. By the time the King left, Robert was firmly established as chief minister; and permanently. He lived eight years more. During that time the 'Great Little Secretary', as he was nicknamed, was indisputably the most powerful man in England. The policy of the government at home and abroad was his policy.

Yet he was never to feel confident, much less cheerful. Though barely forty, he looked far more; grey-headed, lined, ravaged. The outer man was a mirror of the inner. Robert Cecil in James I's reign was worried as he had never been in Queen Elizabeth I's. Almost at once he began to regret her. He wrote to Sir John Harington, 'I wish I now waited in her presence . . . I am pushed from the shores of comfort and know not where the waves and the winds of a Court will bear me. I know it bringeth little comfort on earth; and he is, I reckon, no wise man that looketh this way to heaven . . .' His forebodings were justified, for his situation

The Chapel, Hatfield House

as chief minister was uneasy as Burghley's had never been. The foundation on which his sense of security rested had disappeared: Elizabeth's death meant the end of that forty-five-year unbroken relation between Monarch and Minister which had enabled the Queen and the Cecils to guide the country safely through so many storms. It is unlikely that any new king could have continued it.

The title page to the works of James I

Certainly James I could not. He had his merits: he was clever, learned, pacific and, on the whole, well-meaning. But his cleverness and his learning were of a donnish theoretical kind, showing little grasp of reality; and his character had been fatally damaged by early experience. Born awkward, timid and physically feeble, he had passed his childhood, lonely and unloved, amid treachery and brutal violence, had seen men murdered in his presence, and himself had been kidnapped, betrayed and threatened with assassination by one or other of the high-born Scottish thugs who had set themselves up as his guardians. His youth had been even more of an ordeal than Elizabeth's and, unlike her, he lacked the acuteness and strength of character to profit by it. On the contrary, it broke his nerve. He grew up

James I as a boy, painted probably by Arnold Bronkhorst

quirky and fearful, all too easily influenced by anyone who took the trouble to make up to him; and, to compensate for his sense of physical inferiority, over-confident in his intellectual powers. The same sense of inferiority had endued him with an unfortunate propensity to fall a sentimental victim to the charms of handsome and strong-looking young men.

Altogether James I, though a pathetic figure and not without a curious like-ability for the amateur of human oddity, was, as a king, deplorable: unreliable and undignified, silly with the peculiar silliness of the clever, turned easily from his course by fear or flattery, yet with a grossly inflated idea of his royal authority. For it was the final disastrous effect of James's sense of inferiority that, in order to make up for the feeling that he was personally inadequate, he exaggerated the rights of his position. James it was who first asserted the doctrine of Divine Right in virtue of which the King claimed to override all other legal rights. Robert Cecil was bound to find relations with such a man difficult. But he managed them with his usual adroitness. He took most of the heavy work of government off the King's shoulders; but, by the admiration he professed for James's wisdom, he avoided any appearance of dominating him. Robert had learned by experience that, however different from each other monarchs may be, they all liked flattery, and from the first he flattered James as outrageously as he had flattered Elizabeth. Once, when addressing an assembly in the King's presence, he described him not just as the wisest of kings but also as the wisest of men and the living image of an angel messenger from Heaven.

James accepted such tributes as his due. But he was not without shrewdness, and it is to be doubted if he thought them sincere. Indeed, the relations between the two men were never to be comfortable. When all was said and done, and in spite of Robert's tact, James must secretly have resented being dependent on him. Moreover, Robert Cecil was not the sort of man he could ever have felt comfort-able with. He was altogether too reserved and refined and mysterious and good-mannered. Nor did he share James's insatiable Scottish appetite for theological discussion or his addiction to coarse, homely jokings and gossipings. James did his best to get on familiar terms with Robert Cecil. He told him he need not kneel when first addressing him, as he used to do when first addressing Elizabeth, and he nicknamed Robert his 'little beagle': beagles were dogs with very short legs. But he felt easier when Robert was not there.

So did Robert Cecil. Accustomed to royal whims, he played up readily enough to James's gestures of friendship. Past were the days when he minded jokes about his size. He was willing enough to allude to himself as 'beagle' in his letters to James. Yet there was a gulf between the two that no nickname could bridge. Robert Cecil soon got to know the King well enough to perceive James's lack of sense and judgment and the fact that he had a wholly different political outlook from his own. He felt a painful contrast between past and present. Robert had not forgotten Elizabeth's weaknesses – it was now that he coined the phrase 'she was sometimes more than a man, sometimes less than a woman' – but he remembered with longing the cold, strong brilliance of her political insight, her thrilling, if intermittent, grandeur of spirit; and above all the fact that, however capricious she might seem, she pursued steadily the same ultimate political aims as he did. It was well worth while kneeling in her presence to get this kind of reassurance. 'I wish to God that I spoke still on my knees!' he sighed.

It was not only the King's personality that made Robert Cecil feel like this. It was also the atmosphere of his Court and of the new era that opened with his succession. The changes apparent in the last years of Elizabeth were intensified under James. To us, who know them by the poems and plays and houses they left behind them, the Elizabethan and the Jacobean ages do not seem so different from one another; for they were expressions of the same culture. Indeed, it was in the Jacobean age that this culture reached its peak; in the tragedies of Shakespeare, the comedies of Ben Jonson, the speculations of Bacon, the buildings of Inigo Jones. But the Jacobean age infused this culture with a new and disturbing spirit; to turn to it from the Elizabethans is like turning from a dazzling, windswept noonday to a sombre, stifling torchlit night. The uncertainties of the new reign and the reaction against the heroic struggles of the previous age led in some people to a mood of pessimistic Hamlet-like disillusionment, in others to a feverish appetite for wealth and pleasure and, in most, to a slackening of moral standards. Elizabeth's Court had not been a place of austere virtue. It was a Renaissance Court, alive with intrigue and danger and magnificence. It was also a centre of intelligence and power; and, though its manners could be rough by later standards, its inhabitants were too much in awe of the Queen not to observe a certain decorum.

It was different at the Court of James I: James was not the man to impose a sense of decorum on anyone, for he had none himself. Nor could his Queen, the festive and brainless Anne of Denmark, make up for her husband's deficiencies in this respect. Moreover, coming as both did from grim and penurious Scotland, they were dazzled by the seemingly limitless opportunities for a life of ease and pleasure offered by wealthy England; and they were encouraged to make the most of them by the mob of hangers-on from Scotland and elsewhere who soon began to flock round them. James I's Court was a Renaissance Court in a darker sense than Elizabeth's had been. Since it was the centre of power, distinguished people still gathered there; and it presented a splendid spectacle, with its gorgeous costumes and sumptuous banquets and exquisite entertainments designed by Inigo Jones, with words by Ben Jonson, and music by Nicholas Lanier. But it was corrupt as well as splendid: the festivities were the occasions for every kind of amour, normal and less normal, and the blue-blooded performers in the entertainments, both male and female, were sometimes too drunk to stand up. Further, from time to time, there arose to the glittering surface of Court life hints of a sinister underworld – of procurers and blackmailers and hired assassins and practitioners of black magic – with which some of the leading Court personalities had secret dealings.

Anne of Denmark, the wife of James I,
in masque costume, by Isaac Oliver

Robert Cecil was not altogether unaffected by the changed atmosphere of the world. He was more extravagant than his father and less scrupulous. Times were changing: Robert was not so strict as to refuse to change a little along with them. Basically, however, he remained a man of the past, an Elizabethan living in a Jacobean world, and he was not at home at James's Court. Its habits offended against his prudence, his taste and his realism. For how could the King of England retain the respect of his subjects if he and his friends behaved in this unseemly fashion? No wonder Robert Cecil felt that he was pushed from the shores of comfort to the winds and waves of a stormy ocean!

However, the government of England was for the time being in his hands, to be carried on as he thought best. This, broadly speaking, was on the same lines as for the last forty years: a moderate middle-way policy, but strictly enforced. This, as Burghley had suggested in his last charge to his son, meant ending the war with Spain. Robert Cecil made this a priority. In the first place, he thought the war dangerously expensive. Secondly, it no longer served the policy of balance. The central fact of the European situation was still the struggle between France and Spain. It had always been the Cecil policy to oppose whichever of these two seemed dominant. Formerly this had been Spain; now Robert thought it looked more like France. Better, then, to relax the effort against Spain. Not many of his countrymen agreed with Robert about this. For them Spain was the official national enemy, the champion of the Scarlet Woman of Rome, the unrighteous claimant to the wealth of the New World, whom all good men should unite to overcome. Robert himself wanted peace with Spain only if he could get it on good terms. However, the information he got from abroad made him think that at last he was likely to get good terms. He was also helped by the fact that the King hated war.

But now came a hitch. Before he could start negotiations with Spain, there arrived in England a French envoy called de Rosny with an offer of alliance with France. Since he got no change out of Robert Cecil – 'a man who is all mystery', so he described him to his government – he proceeded adroitly to put his proposals before James, who was sufficiently converted to summon Robert to his presence and scold him for not accepting the French offer. But now luck intervened to help Robert in the shape of secret information leading to the discovery of two plots against the government. The facts about these plots – the Bye Plot and the Main Plot – are obscure; for, once they had been betrayed, anyone involved in them was so concerned to put the blame on someone else that it was impossible to believe what he said. It did emerge, however, that a number of important persons were accused of being implicated, including Robert's brother-in-law, George Brooke; Lord Cobham, the Warden of the Cinque Ports; and Walter Raleigh himself; and that the aims of the plotters were to oust the Cecils, kidnap the King and compel him to do their will, even if this entailed threatening his life. Robert Cecil reported all this to the King, whose youthful experience had made him pathologically afraid of plots. He turned to Robert as to his saviour, and was so frightened and so grateful to him that he was willing to agree to any proposals he might put forward, including the treaty with Spain.

The story of the Main Plot adds another chapter to the curious chronicle of Robert Cecil's relations with Raleigh. James's accession had contributed to widen the breach between them. For, in consequence of Robert's representation, James at once showed himself hostile to Raleigh. At their first meeting he received him coldly and showed his displeasure further by greeting him with an atrocious Shakespeare-style pun: 'I have heard but rawly of you,' he said. A few days later he dismissed him from his post as Captain of the Guard. The effect of this was to throw the ambitious Raleigh into the ranks of the disaffected and disappointed, then humming with wild talk of conspiracy and rebellion.

It seems unlikely that Raleigh did more than listen to such talk. But both his words and his behaviour were indiscreet. Robert Cecil, who now looked on him both as a rival and the advocate of a thoroughly dangerous policy, took advantage of this indiscretion. One evening Raleigh, still at Court, was walking on the terrace of Windsor Castle when Robert approached him with a message summoning him to the Council. He obeyed and was immediately arrested on a charge of treason. The result of a treason trial in those days was a foregone conclusion; and, though Raleigh protested his innocence, he was treated by the Attorney-General Coke, who was prosecuting him, as if he was an already convicted traitor. Robert Cecil, though presumably responsible for Raleigh's arrest, felt himself bound several times to rebuke Coke and intervene to get Raleigh a fair trial. When he was sentenced to death, Robert Cecil was seen to be in tears. Later, largely it was thought by Cecil's influence, Raleigh was reprieved and imprisoned. During the years that followed Raleigh always spoke as if he liked and admired him.

Of course the signs of goodwill may have been, on the part of both men, insincere gestures concealing a strong dislike. But, seen in the context of the long story of their relationship, the signs indicated something more complex: a clash between private and personal impulses common in that violent and unstable age. Their early friendship, as shown in their correspondence, looks like genuine friendship. But, on the dangerous public stage where they acted out their lives, private sentiment gave way to the pressure of ambition or political conviction. Since Robert saw Raleigh both as a rival and a danger to the state, he worked ruthlessly to render him powerless. Raleigh on his side worked equally ruthlessly to compass Robert's downfall; for he could imagine no other means of regaining power. However, some personal regard for each other still remained; and, once he was sure he had won, Robert Cecil did what he could to soften Raleigh's lot. Raleigh recognized his goodwill and impulsively responded to it. 'I failed both in friendship and in judgment,' he wrote to him from the Tower; 'this is all I can now say for myself: vouchsafe to esteem me as a man raised from the dead . . . who will acknowledge your Lordship with a love without mask or cover.'

Robert Cecil was free now to settle down to the task of negotiating peace with Spain. This involved hard bargaining. It also meant the opening of a more peaceful period, which lasted for the rest of Robert's life and in which he was able steadily to pursue his policy of international balance and commercial expansion. Thus he had attained his second political objective. He had also got some private advantages in the process. In 1603 the King had created him Lord Cecil; now, as a reward for his part in the peace treaty, he raised him a step in the peerage to become Viscount Cranborne. In 1605 he was to create him Earl of Salisbury. Further, and of more practical use, from now on the Spanish government paid him a pension of one thousand pounds per year. It was a sign of the times that he accepted it. In principle he was against corrupt practices. Even his enemies never accused him of letting his actions be influenced by corrupt motives. Indeed, pension or no pension, he was never to hesitate from acting against Spain if he thought it for the interest of his country. But the change in moral atmosphere in the reign of James I meant that people were growing more lax in money matters, and it had become an accepted custom for foreign governments to try to keep the rulers of England in a good humour by, as it were, offering them an annual present. The rulers of England saw no reason to refuse the present.

At home meanwhile, for the next two years, Cecil was occupied in maintaining order and unity. This meant first of all maintaining the Elizabethan religious settlement, threatened on the one side by puritans who disliked it as still tainted with popery, and on the other by the Roman Catholics who looked to the new King, as the son of a Roman Catholic mother, to relax the laws against them. Both parties were to be disappointed, for James I, who fancied himself as a theologian, opposed both. He had suffered far too much as a boy under the Scottish Presbyterian Church to want to encourage anything like it in England; and, though he felt kindly towards individual Roman Catholics, his religious studies had led him wholly to reject their doctrines. He made his opinions clear, with the result that early in his reign he had already managed to alienate extreme factions in both parties.

Robert Cecil, as chief minister, felt the religious situation to be potentially dangerous. Again one has to remember that the early seventeenth century still presented itself, to people living then, as a period of acute crisis during which at any moment revolutionary changes might take place. Abroad they were taking place. The Counter-Reformation was sweeping over the Continent, while in Scotland and the north generally there were movements to erase all traces of the ancient Church. Robert Cecil perceived that there were a number of Englishmen who would like England to follow one or other of these foreign examples. These Englishmen were enemies of the Anglican settlement and, as such, enemies of that national unity which was his first political aim, as it had been Burghley's and Elizabeth's. He, like them, held that the English Church should be comprehensive enough to include many shades of opinion, but that it should be the only Church permitted to exist.

He believed in a single national Church to which all must conform. But he was content that the formality should be fairly formal – no more than an occasional attendance at an English church service. He had learned from experience that to demand more would be looked on as persecution; and persecution, he said, created martyrs. Martyrs always made trouble. Perhaps also, he thought, people who attended an English service as a matter of form might be converted to a sincere belief. For, although less interested in theology than his father and less strict morally, Robert was not irreligious. There was a spiritual strain woven into the fabric of his complex nature, and it had been strengthened by education: it was from religious as well as from political reasons that he wanted the Anglican Church to maintain its position. He made it clear to the puritans that they must not tamper with the services. Roman Catholics he saw as a greater danger; they were triumphing all over Europe, and in England they included some powerful persons. Already the Bye and Main Plots had shown that some of these were ready to rebel against the established order; and, although the laws against Catholics had been more strictly enforced since these plots, the Roman Catholics remained strong. Robert felt more drastic measures were necessary. But how should he find occasion for imposing them?

Once more a plot came to his help: the most famous plot in English history. It was on a November evening in 1605 that Lord Monteagle, a young peer, sitting down to dinner, was handed an anonymous letter warning him not to attend the coming opening of Parliament. He took it to Lord Salisbury, as he now was, who in his turn took it to James I. Either or both of them – Robert was content to let James think it was himself – took the letter to imply a conspiracy to blow up Parliament. Accordingly they sent people to search the Parliamentary cellars. There they found Guy Fawkes and his barrels of gunpowder. The conspirators were soon rounded up, tried and executed. Salisbury took an active part in examining the prisoners. Detachedly he admired the way that some of the accused bravely kept silent under torture. But the plot confirmed his fear of popish rebellion, and he thought this so great a danger that for once he was not in favour of mild punishment. The conspirators were condemned to be hung, drawn and quartered. Afterwards Salisbury took the opportunity to bring new measures to weaken the Roman Catholics. He wanted to make sure that in no circumstances would they ever again think it worth while to start a rebellion.

Guy Fawkes with his fellow conspirators: a 17th-century engraving

James made no effort to check him in this. As before, his fear of being murdered had stifled any inclination he had to oppose Salisbury's will. Altogether the Gunpowder Plot had happened so conveniently for Salisbury that it has been suggested that he had made use of agents to start it himself. There is no evidence to support this startling suggestion, and a great deal to make it unlikely. It is not impossible, however, that he had, through his efficient spy system, already got wind that some kind of Roman Catholic plot was in preparation; and that he had let it mature, the better to crush it completely when the right time came.

IV

The year or two following the Gunpowder Plot were the most untroubled of Robert's later life, with the result that he was better able to give some of his attention to his personal affairs. He was deeply concerned about his children: his son William, his daughters Frances and Catherine. He had taken on Burghley's belief in the institution of the family and also his dynastic aspirations. These last were kept in check by his good sense. A stranger wrote him a letter offering to send him a genealogical table purporting to trace the descent of the Cecils from the ancient Princes of Wales. Robert Cecil was not impressed; he scrawled on the bottom of the page, 'I desire none of these vain toys nor to hear of such absurdities.' However, like his father, he did want his family to be eminent, and he set to work to train up his eldest son to be a statesman like himself.

Fawkes and the others brutally executed

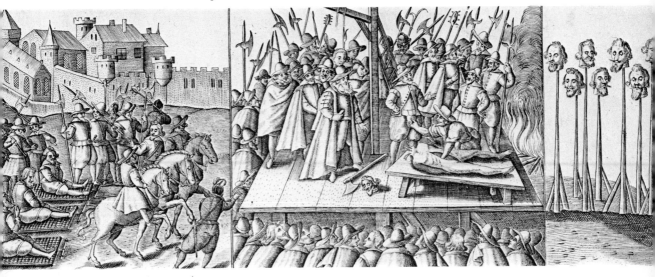

He met with a similar disappointment. Young William turned out to be no more qualified by nature to rule England than his uncle Thomas had been. The same story repeated itself, though with variations. William did not go in for sowing wild oats as Thomas had done; and Robert was a less formidable father than Burghley. His rebukes were relatively gentle; for, unlike Burghley, he loved his son with a special and tender affection. However, his plans for his education were equally unsuccessful. At first he was worried that William was not growing enough; he was all too well aware of the jokes he might have to endure if he were to be short like himself. This fear proved groundless. William grew up plain and horse-faced, but sufficiently tall. Mentally he was less satisfactory. He was an attractive little boy, to judge from a letter he wrote when nine years old to no less a person than Walter Raleigh. At this time Robert Cecil, still friendly with Raleigh, had sent his son to spend the summer with the Raleigh children in Dorset. 'Sir Walter,' the letter read, 'we must all exclaim and cry out because you will not come down. You being absent, we are like soldiers that when their captain is absent they know not what to do; you are so busy with idle matters. Sir Walter, I will be plain with you, I pray you leave all idle matters and come down to us.' Attractive children, alas! all too often turn into dull men; and, long before he became a man, it was clear that William Cecil was very dull: docile and affectionate but slow, muddle-headed and interested only in horses and the activities associated with them.

This was not for want of teaching. From the earliest years Robert was concerned that William should be put through the same sort of high-powered course of study as he himself had been. So that he should get the benefit of the best teachers and the most stimulating intellectual atmosphere, William was sent at the age of eleven – this was not uncommon in the seventeenth century – to St John's College, Cambridge, to be under the care of a private tutor, Roger Morrell, who was ordered to send home a report every day of his pupil's progress. Morrell, reasonably enough, protested that this was too often; he thought his protest especially justified because, in his view, Robert Cecil himself impeded progress. For, in order that his son should get to know the great world and be known by it, he was in the habit of sending for him from time to time to come and show himself at Court. Things got worse after James I came to the throne, for then the Court was often established near Cambridge when the King came to hunt at Royston. William was now able to get a day's hunting with the excuse that he had to pay his respects to the King.

The result was that Morrell's reports about his intellectual progress were soon

Sir Walter Raleigh's study at his home, Sherborne Castle in Dorset

so bad that Robert Cecil decided to put his foot down. He therefore gave orders that William and Morrell – Morrell apparently went hunting, too – must talk Latin, not English, even in the heat of the hunt. As might be expected, Morrell found it impossible to put this desperate remedy into practice. 'The sound of Latin', he said, 'was so harsh mid the cry of dogs that it came not oft.' Soon Robert forbad William to hunt at all or even keep a hound as a pet. He also wrote him a sharp reproof about his letters home: 'Your letters are without date from any place or time, which makes me doubt whether you be at Royston at some horse race or at Cambridge. Your name is not written and therefore I have written it underneath as I would have it. I have also sent you a piece of paper folded as gentlemen use to write their letters, whereas yours are like those that come out of a grammar school.'

Sharp words were followed by a moment of compunction. Robert wrote to Morrell suggesting that perhaps William had progressed so little because he had been taught in too dry a fashion. Whatever the reason, William's education at sixteen seemed a lost cause, and Robert saw no point in keeping him at Cambridge. Once more he wrote to Morrell to give in caustic words his final judgment on the results of his son's university education: 'He cannot speak six words in Latin, out of which language I did expect you and he would not seldom have discoursed. In any part of story without book he is not able to show memory of four lines, neither is his manner of repeating anything like to those whom tutors teach to speak distinct and ornate. For his logic, a month would beget more knowledge than he hath, in one of no greater capacity. If you say that his mind had affected other pleasant studies, either the mathematics, languages, or that he hath given himself to music, or any other gentleman-like quality, then must I answer you that I find no such thing. So as I conclude that either the fault is in my suffering him to be out of the University, or in your neglecting him in the University.'

He still felt that he must do what he could to fit William, even if he was stupid, for his future position in life; and, once more following his father, he sent him abroad to learn foreign languages. Unlike Burghley, however, he allowed his son plenty of money; and, though he wrote him a letter of moral advice as to conduct abroad, he was obviously anxious not to seem hard or unloving. 'However', he writes, 'you may find in this letter plain-ness, and fatherly admonition, you may promise yourself that all proceeds from care and love, and that I free you from any fault for lack of duty towards me. And therefore, let nothing trouble your mind that I write, though you make use of my counsel and direction; for if I may know anything you desire or want for your ease and comfort while you are abroad, be not afraid to ask it of your loving father, that prays to God to bless you.'

The hunt: a woodcut from The Noble Art of Venerie, *1611*

Meanwhile, it was immediately important to establish William's future on a sure foundation. Before he went, therefore, Robert took two important steps with this in mind. Henry, Prince of Wales was the same age as William, and already the two boys knew each other. It would be wise, Robert thought, to take advantage of this to get William the promise of a place in the Prince's service. He therefore wrote to the Queen, who sent a friendly answer. So far so good.

Robert's second act was bolder and more surprising. He arranged for William to be married. A safe position at Court in those days depended largely on having influential friends. This was best achieved by marrying into an influential family. Robert judged William had better get married as soon as possible, and decided he could not do better than choose a wife from the Howard family. On the one hand, the Howards – and especially Thomas, Earl of Suffolk – had always been friendly to himself; on the other, they were connected by marriage with the Essex family, who for obvious reasons had always been hostile to him. This marriage might lead to a desired reconciliation. He therefore made proposals that William should marry Lord Suffolk's daughter Catherine. The docile William did not object; nor – and this was more important – did Lord Suffolk. Accordingly, in the summer of 1600, William was fetched back from Paris for a few days and married quietly to Catherine. After the wedding he left his bride and returned to Paris. A child marriage of this kind, made for political reasons and when the bride and bridegroom did not know each other, might seem bound for disaster. In fact, this one lasted sixty years, and was blessed by five sons and three daughters; and, so far as we know, it was happy.

Two years later Robert saw to it that his older daughter Frances also made a good marriage, to the eldest son of Lord Cumberland. We know little else about her; and less about her sister Catherine, except that, like her father, she was slightly deformed. This fact led to his writing a letter which, like that about his hesitation before proposing to Elizabeth Brooke, is one of the few documents we have in which the curtain of his reserve lifts to disclose him more intimately. Once again he is writing to his sister-in-law: Catherine is going to Court and her father is worried about how she will be treated there. 'I know it is the fashion of the Court and London to laugh at all deformities,' he wrote; 'I would be exceeding glad that somewhat was done to cover the poor girl's infirmities before such ladies and others as will find her out, should see her in such ill case as she is.' This letter, written in the midst of all his work as chief minister, shows how fond he was of his daughter, and how much he had suffered from his own deformity when young. It also reveals the Court ladies of the time as a barbarous lot.

This fact about them was differently and comically brought home to Salisbury in July 1606. Christian, King of Denmark, was at that time in England visiting his sister Queen Anne. Lord Salisbury asked both kings and their retinues to stay with him at Theobalds, where he entertained them with his customary magnificence. The entertainment culminated in a banquet followed by a masque, in which several Court ladies took part, on the subject of the Queen of Sheba's visit to King Solomon. Unluckily everyone did himself so well at the banquet that when the time came for the masque the actors were in no fit state to perform, nor the audience to witness the performance. First of all a lady who represented the Queen of Sheba, advancing up the steps to present the King of Denmark with some refreshments, tripped up, deluging him with cream, wine, jellies and spices. Enlivened with drink himself, the King took this in good part; and, after being hastily cleaned up, he rose to lead the Queen of Sheba out to dance. It proved a disastrous move: both fell down and had to be taken off to bed. James I remained to receive the homage of some ladies representing the Virtues. Alas! they were no better able to offer it than the Queen of Sheba. Faith, Hope and Charity staggered forward in turn, but each found herself unable to speak and had to retire to an outward hall, where they were heard being violently sick. They were followed first by Victory, vaguely waving a golden sword, who suddenly stumbled over and went to sleep, and finally by Peace, who arrived fighting drunk and thwacking everyone she encountered with her emblematic olive branch. Poor Lord Salisbury's reflections on his party are not recorded. He had spent more than a thousand pounds on it.

Ben Jonson, who wrote masques for
Anne of Denmark: a portrait possibly
after Abraham Blyenberch

His family feeling was not confined to his children. He was fond of his niece and his half-brother Thomas, now Earl of Exeter. After an inauspicious start, Thomas had turned out a likeable character. He might well have been jealous of a brother younger than himself, who had done so much better in the world than he had. On the contrary, he gloried in Robert Cecil's success. Once Robert, in one of his strange fits of despondency, said he was afraid that Thomas did not really love him. Thomas replied, 'Let this letter be kept as a witness against me if you shall not find in me towards you a love void of envy, of mistrust, and as glad of your honour and merit as a dear brother ought be. For I am not partial, but confess that God hath bestowed rarer gifts of mind upon you than upon me.'

Outside his family, Robert seems to have had few friends. Apart from his reserve, the pressure of his work left him without time or energy to make them. Further, though his public position meant that he had to keep some sort of open house, he does not seem to have had much taste for society. Otherwise he spent his spare time hawking and hunting or in literary and artistic pleasures, adding to his collection of gems and tapestries and books – 'A book is more to me than gold,' he said – and in listening to music. Unlike his father, he maintained a company of musicians and singing boys. For him, as for so many Englishmen in that tense and dangerous age, music had a unique power to tranquillize the spirit.

> In sweet music is such art,
> Killing care and grief of heart
> Fall asleep or, hearing, die.

So wrote Shakespeare; so felt Robert Cecil. The strains of lute and viol, the angelic serenity of the boys' voices, made him forget for a moment the plots and the torture-chambers and the intrigues of rival statesmen and the vagaries of foolish kings. He took a paternal interest in the future of his musicians, and arranged that the boys were trained for some trade that enabled them to earn a living after their voices had broken. Robert was generous to relatives, friends, dependants, and lent lavishly, even to men unlikely to pay him back and to enemies like his cousin, Francis Bacon. Maturity had not made him more careful about money. One of the most unexpected features of his character is that, prudent in everything else, he was recklessly extravagant in his private spending, and all his life was a gambler. He still sometimes lost hundreds of pounds at a sitting.

But his biggest expenditure was on building. It occupied a special place in his activities, and was by far his greatest interest outside politics. In this he was a man of his age. Most of the new nobility in those days, including Burghley, had gone in for building on a large scale. The fact that they did so was a sign of changed times. The medieval noble lived in a castle fortified to protect him from attack. The Tudor monarchy, by imposing civil order on the country, had done away with the need for this. Instead the nobles built themselves homes for peaceful and agreeable living. The most conspicuous achievement of the new taste for building was the great houses built by the great nobles. These were half homes and half palaces. There were practical reasons for this. Their owners were local princes with courts which were the centre of local power and culture and social life. They needed suitable buildings for such functions. Further, the Tudors had continued the practice of going on royal progresses, by means of which the King got to know his subjects by travelling round the country with his retinue. He expected the magnate of each district to put him and his retinue up. This could not be done adequately unless the magnate possessed a sort of palace to do it in, containing apartments designed for the purpose.

There were also spiritual and psychological reasons for building these houses: it was a means by which the great nobleman expressed his sense of his position. Burghley, wrote a contemporary, had built Burghley House to be the 'mansion of his Barony', to mark, that is to say, the place in the social and political scale that his family had now attained. The spirit of that period was sacramental. It believed that an inward and spiritual truth should be expressed in an outward and physical symbol. Their mode of life was full of ritual. The lover fell on his knees, the mourner hung his walls with black, the gentleman and the yeoman wore clothes that denoted their position in society as ordained by God. For God had ordained a society in which each man had his place; and it was right that this place should be shown in the way he dressed. Also in his dwelling; it was right that a man's greatness should appear in the scale of house he lived in.

Two other motives operated to encourage the taste for building. One was a desire for posthumous fame. For the Renaissance man, it was the sign of a superior spirit to wish to be remembered after death; and there was no better way to achieve this than by building. The other motive was to add to the sum of beauty in the world. Beauty then was not looked on as an extra luxury, an amenity to be cultivated by those who liked that kind of thing. It had a spiritual meaning: combining as it did the celestial qualities of order, harmony, grace, it was an embodiment of that Divine Perfection to which the soul should aspire and, as such, was an attribute of every worthy work of man. Art owed its value to the fact that it was such an embodiment. At that period domestic architecture in England rose to be a fine art. The same creative imagination that inspired *The Faerie Queen* and *The Tempest* and Byrd's *Great Service* showed itself also in Hardwick Hall and Audley End.

In one respect, however, the great houses of the period differed from its literary and musical masterpieces. They were seldom the expression of a single man. We often do not know the names of those who designed these great houses. In fact, several persons generally had a hand in it; and, since architecture was a popular gentleman's hobby, one of these persons was often the man who commissioned the house. Robert Cecil was such a person. Building was his favourite recreation because it was creative, a form of self-expression. His most memorable form, as it has turned out; for, though he has permanently influenced the course of England's history, he is not remembered as a personality, in the way that Oliver Cromwell is, for instance, or Wolsey. In the houses he built, however, he is still mysteriously alive. Far more than any other records he has left, do these houses reveal the sensitiveness and imagination which lay hidden beneath his sober exterior. The ghost that most haunts the imagination of the visitor, walking through the galleries of Hatfield, is that of the small, pale courtly figure of its originator.

He started his building career in the last years of Elizabeth's reign with a house in Chelsea. This turned out to be not big enough for his needs. The year 1602 saw the beginning of a magnificent mansion, Salisbury House, just south of the Strand. Meanwhile, he had inherited Theobalds after his father's death, and was

Salisbury House on the bank of the Thames, from a drawing by Wenzel Hollar

engaged in adding to it till it became a masterpiece of architectural fantasy and one of the show places of England. But 1607 saw him embarked on a different kind of building, in the shape of Briton's Burse, an ornate structure housing a sort of combined shopping and financial centre, erected on some property he had acquired, also in the Strand district, and was developing as a commerical proposition. Some years before, he had bought land in Dorset, including a hunting lodge of the medieval English kings at Cranborne. He now set to work to turn this into a small modern country-house. On the bare, grey, fortified medieval walls he imposed tall lattice windows, sculptured Italian loggias and Jacobean chimneys of russet brick; and all these without any apparent regard for symmetry or harmony of style. The result, however, is a subtler, richer harmony. Robert Cecil and his builders between them have combined these diverse elements to produce a house that is as delicate an expression of the lyrical and romantic strains in the Elizabethan imagination as *A Midsummer Night's Dream* itself.

Cranborne is Salisbury's most exquisite architectural bequest to posterity. But the most important is Hatfield. In 1607 James I, who coveted Theobalds as a hunting centre, indicated that he would like to have it; and he offered to exchange properties spread over twelve counties and including the palace at Hatfield,

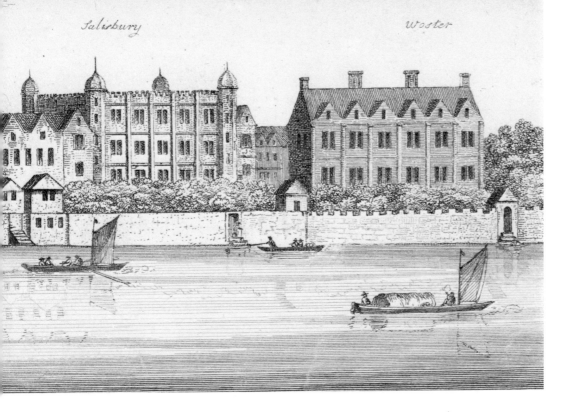

where the youthful Elizabeth had first appointed a Cecil to be her Minister. Salisbury agreed. On the 27th of May he invited James I for a last visit to Theobalds, where he entertained him with yet another masque – this time more soberly conducted – in which the spirit of the place, discovered on a darkened stage and in lines specially composed by Ben Jonson, welcomed her new master and said farewell to her old, who

> Now in the twilight of sere age
> Begins to seek a habitation new.

With enthusiasm he threw himself into the task of refashioning his new habitation. There was no question of making do with the existing palace. From now on Salisbury gave any time he could spare from his political work to planning and building a new one, on the grandest possible scale. Begun towards the end of 1607, it took five years to build and cost over thirty-eight thousand pounds, the equivalent of half a million now. It was planned in collaboration. The main designer seems to have been Robert Lemynge, but his plans were modified by the advice of Simon Basil, the official Surveyor of the King's Works; of Thomas Wilson, Salisbury's man of affairs, who concerned himself mainly with the question of cost; possibly of young Inigo Jones; and naturally of Salisbury himself, who, in addition to choosing the site, kept the whole process of design and construction under his eye, making suggestions and proposing alterations. The materials came from all over the place; local wood and brick was combined with stone from Oxfordshire and Kent and Normandy and marble from Italy. So too did the craftsmen include English John Burke, who carved the trophies and garlands on the grand staircase; French Maximilian Colt, the maker of Queen Elizabeth's tomb in Westminster Abbey, and sculptor at Hatfield of the statue of James I in the Grand Drawing-room; and Dutch Martin van Bentheim, who made the painted window for the Chapel.

The spreading acres of garden were, if possible, even more elaborate and lavish than the House. They were at once a gorgeous spectacle – lawns and blossoming orchards and a shining lake and foaming fountains and statues and terraces, from which flights of steps, lined with gilded figures of lions, descended to parterres of many-coloured flowers – and also a horticultural treasury, famed for its unique

John Tradescant the Elder, maker of gardens, and a gardener carved on the Grand Staircase, Hatfield House

collection of rare plants. Like the House, the gardens were the work of several hands. In charge was a man with the strange name of Mountain Jennings; but Du Caux, another foreigner, was responsible for the fountains and lake, and a distinguished botanist, John Tradescant, for the rare plants. Salisbury, hopeful about the ability of such plants to survive in the English climate, sent Tradescant abroad, whence he returned bringing figs, oleanders and myrtles. Even more optimistically, Salisbury established a vineyard in the Park, employing for the purpose two specially engaged French gardeners and planting thirty thousand vines.

These glories were short-lived. The vineyard has disappeared now, and all but a few fragments of the original garden. So also has vanished a whole constellation of gatehouses and pavilions and turreted lodges, gay with carved gables and gilded cupolas, which surrounded the House and through which the visitor moved, as it were, in a glittering crescendo up to the sumptuous entrance. Altogether, as originally conceived, house and entrance and garden embodied an extraordinary conception, an extended dazzling flight of visual fantasy, in which diverse elements – natural and artificial, English and exotic, stately and fantastic – united to realize a romantic daydream of the Earthly Paradise.

V

Salisbury must have needed to take refuge in such a daydream from time to time. His own life was becoming far from a paradise. Its final phase was opening, and it was to be a troubled one. He was appallingly overworked, for one thing. People said they could hardly get to see him for the press of persons waiting in his anteroom for an interview. Nor was he in a state to stand overwork. His health was deteriorating. He was often in pain and liable suddenly to be forced to take to his bed in a fit of unexplained illness; and he looked older than ever. There were mental as well as physical causes for this. The lull following the Gunpowder Plot was over. From 1607 Salisbury was in political trouble.

Not that he was less powerful. In April James I appointed him Lord Treasurer as well as Chief Secretary. For the only time in English history the two most important positions in the government were held by one person. But in fact Salisbury's position was not so strong as it looked: his influence with the King was threatened. It is true that James, more and more bored with the routine business of government, left more and more to his chief minister. But this meant that the gulf between the two had begun to widen. James spent his time away from Salisbury, hunting, discoursing, overeating, in the company of those he found congenial; and these were persons unlike Salisbury. Rather, they were hostile rivals, often Scottish, who longed to oust him from power and take his place.

In 1607 their influence was strengthened by the appearance on the scene of a new figure, Robert Carr, a Scottish squire, blond, blooming and twenty-one years old. His youthful handsomeness was of just the type to kindle James's amorous fires. He first noticed him taking part in a Court joust and fell immediately head over ears in love. Soon he appeared everywhere with him, his arm around his neck; within a few months he had knighted him, appointed him a Gentleman of the Bed Chamber and showered him with gifts of land, money, jewels and fine clothes. Carr belonged to the Scottish anti-Cecil faction. His rise to favour meant that this faction had for the first time got a foot in the inner citadel of power. From now on Salisbury found James harder and harder to manage.

Nor was this his only political worry. Far worse was the government's financial situation. Ever since he had come to the throne, James's expenditure had been growing by leaps and bounds till it was far bigger than his income. This was not altogether his fault. In those days the King was expected to pay all the day-to-day expenses of the government. These had been lately increasing; at the same time the value of money was getting less. But both James and his Queen were extravagant. They poured out wealth on feasts and entertainments and clothes and sport; and on favourites. Carr's jewels and fine clothes added substantially to the royal expenses. The result was that when Salisbury became Lord Treasurer he was faced with a financial crisis. The King, he discovered, was living at the rate of eighty thousand pounds a year over his income and was already nearly a million pounds in debt.

It was clear that tough measures were needed. Salisbury took them. First of all he went through the royal accounts and recommended drastic economies, and saw to it that some at least were enforced. Once James asked for twenty thousand pounds to give to Carr. Salisbury realized that words would never persuade him that this was impossible. He therefore took him into a room in his house in which was a table covered with twenty thousand pounds' worth of silver coins. James asked what it was. Salisbury explained. Shaking with agitation, James stammered out that for the time being three thousand pounds would be enough. Economies alone, however, could not make the King solvent. Salisbury looked about for means of making money. He sold Crown properties, collected old debts, revised ancient dues that had fallen into abeyance. In two years he had paid off much of the King's debts.

However, he realized that the same difficulties were bound to occur unless some new system for financing King and government were devised. Salisbury

Robert Carr, later Earl of Somerset: a portrait after John Hoskins

set about devising one. In 1610 Parliament met and he came forward with a scheme to be known later as the Great Contract. By this the Crown was to offer to give up a large number of irksome and ancient dues and impositions in return for a permanent grant from Parliament of two hundred thousand pounds a year. The Commons listened and a few days later came forward with proposals of their own less favourable to the King.

After this the bargaining began. Debates went on for several months; in all of this Salisbury took a leading part. His original speech introducing the Great Contract was remembered as a masterpiece of the art of parliamentary speaking, lucid, lively, persuasive. His later speeches were equally impressive. Even now one can enjoy their easy, epigrammatic phrasing. 'The worst kings make the best laws,' he said at one point: 'Richard III the Tyrant, and Henry IV the Usurper.' Through his words his spirit gleams out cool, incisive, sensible, hostile to any hint of fanaticism and with that profound belief in the rule of law which he had learned from his father. He vigilantly opposed any attempt by the Commons to extend their rights beyond what was lawful; but equally he insisted that the King must respect the rights of Parliament. Indeed, while he refers to James I himself in his usual flattering terms, he is not unduly respectful about dead kings. Though his family owed their rise largely to King Henry VIII, he said of him, 'I love not to look upon anything that Henry VIII did, for he was the child of lust and a man of iniquity.' Salisbury conducted negotiations so adroitly that, when Parliament rose in July, it looked as if he was going to get the Great Contract accepted.

However, when in November Parliament met once more, each party to the bargain had begun to think again. The Commons feared that if they gave the King so much money he would never need to summon them; and the King, encouraged by the Scottish Party, took the view that he was not getting enough and asked loudly for more. Salisbury fought desperately to save the situation; but in vain. The Great Contract was dropped.

He was deeply disappointed. 'The vexations of the last Parliament can only be compared to the plague of Job,' he said; if anyone chanced to refer to the Great Contract in his presence he became noticeably out of temper. This was unlike him, but hardly to be wondered at. It was the first great failure of his life, and it was over a question of supreme importance. Indeed, it meant the end of the Elizabethan triumph, the defeat of the policy to which he and his father had dedicated their lives. The aim of that policy was peace and stability. This depended on the government's being solvent. If it was not, it had to go to Parliament for money; and Parliament would refuse to give it except on terms which the King would refuse to grant. The result would be conflict.

The Great Contract was an outstanding example of the kind of flexible middle-of-the-road measure by which the Cecils had successfully adapted existing situations to maintain stability and continuity. The King and Parliament, by turning it down, were heading straight for the clash which was to end in the Civil War and the execution of Charles I. It is possible that, if they had listened to Salisbury, there would have been no war and Charles I would have kept his head on his shoulders. Certainly the Great Contract offered the best chance the Stuarts ever got of averting these unfortunate events; and, even though he failed to put it through, Salisbury deserves credit for proposing it. All the more because personally he was liable to lose money by the proposal; he drew a substantial part of his income from the antique institutions which the Great Contract would have abolished. The fact that it was his idea to give this money up is proof that he was not, as his enemies alleged, a man determined to enrich himself at the expense of the people of England.

They did allege it, however. At no time a popular figure, he now became more unpopular. The common people still looked on him as the crafty crookback who had outwitted their hero Essex; the gentry regarded him jealously as a man of the past, obstinately clinging to office in spite of failure. Carr and his friends began actively to try to oust him; for Carr now aspired to political power and was encouraged by James I, who, unlike Elizabeth, never seems to have realized that a handsome favourite is not the same thing as a capable statesman. Courtiers followed their master. Men who formerly professed themselves Salisbury's friends drifted away to hover round Carr, while Carr's own manner to Salisbury was marked by a new and displeasing insolence. People began to say that Salisbury's long period of power was at last on the wane. Who knows if they were right? James I was still dependent on his chief minister; and that chief minister had in the past shown himself remarkably successful at eliminating possible rivals. Perhaps he could do it again!

We shall never know; for fate intervened to leave the question doubtful. In February 1612 Salisbury was taken very ill; the doctors examined him and diagnosed a tumour in the abdomen. During the next weeks he recovered enough to enjoy walking in his garden, bright with the fresh green of a fine March. But April brought a collapse; less than a month later he was dead. He spent much of this month journeying to and from Bath, where he had been advised to go by a doctor to try if the waters would do him any good. His chaplain kept a detailed record of the journeys, so that we get to know him then as never before. Up to then – except in two instances, his letter about his marriage and his outburst at Essex's trial – Salisbury moves before our mental eye like a figure too distant for us to see his face. Now, just before his death, it is as if a spotlight is turned on him, by which we see his countenance close to and at a moment when the final crisis of his existence has broken down his reserve. Faced by the prospect of imminent

155

death, the great little Secretary stands revealed, not as the unruffled, unobtrusive public servant which he appeared to the world, but as a tormented spirit.

Indeed, his was a tragic predicament. He had to face the fact that, for all its apparent success, his life looked like turning out a failure. He had dedicated himself, at a cost of many years of hard labour, to maintaining the balanced settlement in Church and State established by his father and Queen Elizabeth. Now new forces had arisen that were threatening to destroy the very foundations on which that settlement rested. Furthermore, grief at his failure had begun to be darkened by fear: fear engendered by a sense of sin.

Fully to enter into this, we must adjust ourselves to look at human life in that religious perspective in which it presented itself to men in the seventeenth century. For people nowadays, whatever creed they profess, life in this world occupies the centre of their attention. But seventeenth-century men, pious and worldly alike, took it for granted that life in this world was the prelude to an eternity of bliss or torment according to how far they had obeyed God's commandments. It is therefore not odd that, when they saw death approaching, many people became uneasy. If they were statesmen, they were likely to be very uneasy indeed. It was impossible to be a successful statesman in the seventeenth century without sometimes being devious or ruthless or unscrupulous. Salisbury was no more guilty than many in these respects. But he was guilty enough to feel disturbed when he came to contrast his career with the good life as preached in the Gospels. Their message, as taught to him by his powerful and pious mother, had burned itself into the deepest fibres of his being. Throughout his life there were moments when he suffered from the sense that his way of living was at odds with it. Already he had prefaced his Will with a detailed declaration of his faith, because, he said, he knew that statesmen were often thought irreligious. Now, with his earthly hopes in ruins and himself on the point of death, he turned to survey his past against the sublime and terrifying background of the Divine Justice, and he shrank back in conscience-stricken dismay.

The journey from London to Bath took five days; for the heavy, springless coaches, jolting over the rough roads, had to travel very slowly to avoid causing the sick Salisbury unnecessary suffering. Yet his mind was feverishly alive. He travelled with a retinue of servants and three companions: Bowles, his chaplain, and two old friends, Sir Walter Cope and Michael Hicks. To them he poured out, with an extraordinary lack of inhibition, the flux of thought and emotion that ebbed and flowed within him. At one moment he dwelt on his approaching end: he was ready for it, he said, he was sure he would not live to return from Bath. At another he spoke passionately of his love for his son, William; he would gladly die for him, he proclaimed, and he gave orders that he should not come to see him; it would make the prospect of parting from him too painful. Then, his mind reverting to his own condition, he began to pray aloud to God and, oblivious of the fact that he was not alone, to confess to Him each particular sin.

Hicks, the old companion of Salisbury's convivial moments, found all this painful and unnecessary; surely there was no need to bother himself with thoughts of God yet! He wrote off to a former festive friend of Salisbury's called Sir Hugh Beeston, asking him to join the party at Bath to cheer him up with light conversation and, if he felt up to it, with a little gambling. Salisbury was in no state to win a game of skill. 'We shall be sure to get four or five pounds a piece from him,' he said facetiously; 'if this should fail, yet it is hard luck if you wring not one fiddling suit or other from him or at least some velvet cloak not much the worse for wearing.' Alas! Beeston never got a chance to win so much as a worse-for-wear velvet cloak; Salisbury was far too ill, and far too distressed. The strain of illness began to tell on his nerves. If one of his servants was late, he would be seized by a fit of uncontrollable irritation, to be followed by a remorseful apology. 'God knows it is my pain and weakness,' he cried.

He arrived at Bath on the 3rd of May, but after a day or two it was clear that the waters were not going to do him any good. As he grew worse, he strove to withdraw his mind from concern with this world; he told himself that God was helping him to do this by making his illness a long one. Yet the thought that he needed his help in this way began to suggest a new anxiety to his sick spirit. 'One thing troubles me,' he told the chaplain, 'that I could not have come to this resolution, if God had not afflicted me.' The chaplain explained that this was nothing to worry about; Christ had described himself as the shepherd who, unsought for, came to search for his sheep. Salisbury snatched at this comfort. 'That sheep am I,' he repeated again and again, 'that sheep am I!'

Conviction of God's mercy mingled with the uneasiness brought on by suffering to change his mood. 'Ease and Pleasure', he told Cope, 'quake to hear of Death; but my life, full of cares and miseries, desireth to be dissolved.' These words reveal a turning-point in the course of his feeling about his death: resignation had changed into longing, longing was soon to change into unearthly rapture. Suddenly it seemed as if he saw Heaven opening in vision and the light of God's love shining down to draw him upwards. One night his servants heard him praying. He turned and said to them, 'Do you hear me? Know that, if God now takes my soul out of my body, I am prepared.' Next afternoon he said goodbye to them; and then, resting himself on his crutches and lifting his eyes and stretching out his hands with a smile of ectasy, he cried out, 'Oh, Lord Jesus! Now, sweet Jesus. Oh, Lord Jesus, now let me come unto thee! . . . Thy Will be done. I am saved, I am saved!' 'Here', his chaplain relates, 'the tears ran down his cheeks stopping his speech so that for a great while there was nothing but a mournful silence.'

Inevitably Salisbury's spirit could not maintain itself at this pitch of spiritual elevation; but it stayed serene. An old friend, Sir John Harington, also at Bath for his health, came to see him. 'Sir John,' said Salisbury humorously, 'now does one cripple come to visit another'; and then, in graver tones, 'Death is the centre to whom we all do move – some diameter-wise, some circularly, but all men must fall to the centre. I know not, Sir John, which of us two is nearest, yet I think myself . . . and now, Sir John, what good have you found by the Bath?'

More good than Salisbury had himself found, so it appeared. For next day he collapsed. William was told and, disobeying his father's orders, came to Bath. Salisbury could not hide his delight. Both were in tears when they met; then he broke out, 'Oh, my son, God bless thee.' He went on to give William some last words of advice and warning. They are interesting for the light they throw on himself; on what had tormented his own conscience, on his horror of violence, and his reverence for what was hallowed by law and tradition. 'My good son,' he said, 'embrace true religion, live honestly and virtuously, loyal to thy Prince and faithful to thy wife. Take heed by all means of blood, whether in public or private quarrel.' As he ceased speaking, he was for a moment overcome with emotion. Then he told the chaplain he wished to take the sacrament; and, partaking of the body and blood of Christ, implicit in the consecrated bread and wine, he found his soul mysteriously strengthened. He lived for a few days more, his mind sometimes wandering. In a lucid interval he grew restless and said that, after all, he did want to be taken home. Once more the slow cavalcade took the road. By the time it reached Marlborough, Salisbury was too ill to go further. He died there on the 24th of May without sigh or struggle and clasping his chaplain's hand.

He was buried at Hatfield; by his own wish privately and quietly. 'I desire', he had said, 'to go without noise or vanity out of this vale of misery, as a man that has long been satiated with terrestrial glory.' He had, three years earlier, approved a design for a tomb which was erected after his death in Hatfield church. It is in the allegorical manner of the high Renaissance, and is a visible image of his moral situation as it presented itself to him in his last years. On a slab of black marble supported at each corner by white figures representing the cardinal virtues of Justice, Prudence, Temperance and Fortitude, lies the figure of the dead man clad in his Lord Treasurer's robes and with his actual Treasurer's staff in his hand. Beneath the slab a rough pallet props up his skeleton, macabre witness to the condition to which all mortal greatness must in the end come; and awaiting the verdict to be delivered on him by his Creator on the final Day of Judgment.

The tomb of Robert Cecil, 1st Earl of Salisbury, in Hatfield Church

The verdict of his contemporaries was given sooner. It was extremely un-favourable. Now that he was dead, and there was no need to fear his displeasure, all the hostility that had been accumulating against him during these last years burst out in a torrent of abuse. It came from noble and simple, Catholics and Protestants, townsmen and countrymen. Even the people of Hatfield complained that he had filched some woods from them to add to his estate. This was the least of the misdeeds alleged against him. He was accused of cheating the King, the Church, the Parliament; of oppressing the poor and twisting the law to suit his purpose and to add to his fortune. It was also said – with no justification whatever – that he had died of venereal disease. Once again the alleys of London rang with the sound of voices chanting libellous rhymes about him:

> Here lies, thrown for the worms to eat,
> Little bossive Robin that was so great.
> Not Robin Goodfellow or Robin Hood
> But Robin th'encloser of Hatfield Wood,
> Who seemed as sent from Ugly Fate
> To spoil the Prince and rot the State,
> Owning a mind of dismal ends
> As trap for foes and tricks for friends.
> But now in Hatfield lies the Fox
> Who stank while he lived and died of the Pox.

The figure conjured up by this rhyme is strikingly unlike the conscience-ridden, hypersensitive soul whom we have watched praying and agonizing at Bath a week or two before.

VI

Robert Lord Salisbury's death ends the first phase in the story of the Cecils of Hatfield. Historically it is its most important phase. No subsequent member of the family was to influence the course of English history as he and his father had done. Yet the figure they cut in most history books is a trifle dim: they emerge from their pages as hardly more than trustworthy, efficient civil servants. It must be admitted that they do not appeal to the imagination in the way that some of their contemporaries do. Set beside Raleigh and Sidney, Drake and Marlowe, Bacon and Donne, they look rather like a pair of inconspicuous rooks who have strayed into an aviary populated by eagles and birds of paradise.

However, closer inspection reveals them as remarkable rooks. For, together with Queen Elizabeth – the three cannot be separated – they represent the political wisdom of the age; and this was a remarkable wisdom. Events proved it. So long as they were in full power, England was well governed. When, under James I, their power began to weaken, England grew less well governed. When the last of them disappeared and the Stuarts disastrously took over, England was on the high road to financial chaos and civil war. Moreover, the period of the Cecil ascendancy was a crucial period during which was successfully accomplished the transformation of England from a medieval to a modern nation, and a settlement was established in Church and State which, after the storms of the seventeenth century had blown over, formed a stable foundation on which was built the subsequent greatness of the country.

Nor was this an easy achievement. During the sixteenth century, England was in a state of chronic crisis which again and again might have exploded into anarchy unless dexterously handled. Luckily it had rulers who handled it with commanding skill. William had studied history to some purpose. He, and Robert too, saw further and deeper into the political situation than did their rivals, and so had a much better idea of the right way to deal with it. On the surface this was not an inspiring way, but rather a continuous, cautious process of adaptation and compromise, with little in it to stir the heart of the adventurous and the idealistic. But it was the wisest way. Jealous, clever, viper-eyed Francis Bacon said of his cousin Robert, 'He was no fit councillor to make affairs better, yet he was fit to stop them from getting worse.'

Meant disparagingly, this in fact was praise. While keeping their far-sighted objective always in view, William and Robert judged that the best way to reach it was by avoiding each peril as it arose rather than by pursuing some plan laid down in accordance with preconceived ideological principles. They realized that plans to make affairs better all too often ended in making them worse. So did faith in ideological principles. 'Men must be saved in this world by their *want* of faith,' says the wise Halifax. William and Robert Cecil would have agreed with him. But they would have laid stress on the word 'this'. In the other world of God's eternity, they believed faith to be the necessary condition of salvation. The mixture of the religious and the worldly, so typical of their period, was in them especially noticeable; for in both each strain was so genuine. Indeed, the outstanding single impression left on the mind after studying their story is of this mixture, of the paradoxical contrast between the tough sceptical spirit in which they conducted public affairs and the anxious unquestioning conviction which inspired their devotional lives. It is a contrast that adds to their mystery. For, in spite of all that I can learn about them, my Elizabethan forbears remain for me mysterious: beings from an alien world gazing down from the panelled walls of Hatfield in attitudes as formalized as those of a figure on a court card, and with pale, shut, enigmatic faces.

Part II
I
DECLINE

In 1612 Hatfield House was finished; grandly its courts and gilded turrets and terraced gardens spread themselves beneath the changing Hertfordshire sky. But the man who had planned them all was dead, and more than two hundred years were to pass before the place was to be inhabited again by personalities adequate to its magnificence. Not that it was ever empty. For those who can see ghosts, there should be plenty from the intervening period to be observed, soundlessly pacing the halls and grounds of Hatfield. But they are, most of them, dull ghosts. It shows in their faces. William, Lord Burghley, and Robert, Lord Salisbury, if not handsome, looked intellectual and refined; their descendants for the next five generations seldom looked refined and never intellectual.

Nor were they. The history of the Cecils raises baffling questions for believers in inherited talent. Two generations of able, energetic men were succeeded by two more of great distinction, notable for acute political insight. Then – was it the result of Robert Cecil's marrying simple-minded Elizabeth Brooke? – came an abrupt change. Robert's successors were undistinguished men conspicuously lacking in political insight. Indeed, this lack was the only thing that makes their life-stories at all entertaining. The Second, Third and Fourth Earls of Salisbury showed themselves comically unequal to the high position in which the exertions of their forefathers had placed them. Unluckily for them they were born in particularly tricky times for any man in a high position.

Throughout the seventeenth century England was locked in more or less mortal combat about whether King or Parliament should hold the ultimate power in the country. The Salisburys, as members of the governing aristocracy, had to decide which side to take in the fight. Nervous and muddle-headed, the Second and Third Earls wobbled between the two, though with a bias towards the Parliament. The Fourth Earl, reversing the process, plumped for the King. But unfortunately the King at that moment happened to be James II, perhaps the most

James Cecil, 6th Earl of Salisbury, painted by Rosalba Carriera in Venice, 1733

inept monarch ever to occupy the throne of England. He was, however, no more inept than the Fourth Earl of Salisbury, whose political activities in favour of his royal master were ineffective and even ridiculous. Still, they showed that he felt that such activities were part of the duties imposed on him by his station. These seventeenth-century Lords Salisbury were not equal to upholding the family tradition; but it did retain some influence over them. They still aspired to be statesmen. It was not till the beginning of the eighteenth century that the Salisburys gave up any attempt to concern themselves with those interests that had made their ancestors great.

The Second Earl meddled ineffectively in politics on and off throughout his long life; he is a classical example of the dangers of having a distinguished father. All poor Mr Morrell's efforts had been in vain: the tall well-meaning boy had grown into a tall well-meaning man, bony, reddish and horse-faced, who should have spent his life as a country gentleman, occupied in those field sports for which alone he showed any talent. But education and social position had imbued him with the idea that he ought to be a statesman. At the same time – perhaps from an unspoken sense of his inadequacy as compared with his great father – he had no confidence in his political judgment. Unable to make up his mind, he tended always to follow the line of least resistance and to submit to any strong and victorious leader. When faced with a choice between two strong personalities, he dithered. 'He was a man of no words,' wrote Clarendon, 'except in hunting and hawking in which he only knew how to behave himself; in matters of state and council he always concurred in what was proposed for the King and Council and repaired all those transgressions by concurring in all that was proposed against him, as soon as any such propositions were made.'

He got off to a difficult start. His father's death was soon followed by that of Henry, Prince of Wales. William had lost the two persons to whom in his weakness he might have looked to give him a lead. Moreover, his father had left large debts. William sold property to pay them; but then settled down to live as expensively as his father had done. He kept open house to Court and county and, when his eldest daughter was born, arranged that Lady Salisbury received congratulations on the event in a room newly hung with white satin embroidered with pearls and gold-and-silver thread, at the cost of fourteen thousand pounds. Salisbury also entertained James I several times magnificently at Hatfield. The manners and morals of his courtiers do not seem to have improved since the old days at Theobalds: after they left, it was discovered that they had gone off with some valuable pieces of plate.

If the purpose of Lord Salisbury's entertainments was to win the King's favour, it was unsuccessful. William applied for several important appointments, including that of Gentleman of the Bed Chamber, but failed to get any of them. This was thought to be owing to the influence of Queen Anne, who disliked the Cecil family, giving as her reason that she thought that in any position close to the Royal Family they were likely to have a bad influence on her children. This was an unconvincing line to take, considering that she did not object to her children being close to Robert Carr, whose relations with her own husband were a cause of scandal, and who had recently been mixed up in a peculiarly sinister murder case.

The accession of Charles I in 1629 led to a change for the better in the Salisbury fortunes. Queen Henrietta Maria came to stay at Hatfield; and during the period between 1630 and 1639, when Charles was trying to rule without Parliament, he employed Lord Salisbury several times to help him to collect the Ship Money tax and to organize the local military forces. It looked as if Salisbury approved of Charles's efforts to become an autocrat. In reality his conduct was only a sign of his readiness to give in to apparent strength. For in 1639, when Charles's efforts failed and the English people began to divide themselves into those who backed the King and those who backed the Parliament, the Earl took up an uncertain and a middle position. The Commons even came to think of him as an ally; for at one moment they suggested that he should be made Lord Treasurer.

There was a good reason and a bad reason for his line of action. The good reason was that it was right: Charles I's Divine Right policy was against the best interests of the country. Moreover, in opposing it, Salisbury was returning to the Cecil tradition. In spite of their reverence for Queen Elizabeth, Burghley and his son had always insisted that she held her rights under the ancient laws of England and that these never admitted that the monarch had an unlimited power. If they had been alive in 1641, Burghley and Robert could not have supported the King.

Salisbury's bad reason for supporting the Parliament was timidity. He approved of a middle-way course, not just from good sense, but because it was a way to keep in with both sides. He was also under pressure not to back the King, from his son-in-law. His eldest daughter, Anne, was married to Algernon Percy, Earl of Northumberland, the most powerful magnate in the North of England; and the Percys, like the Herberts and the Cavendishes, were among the noble families prominent under the Tudors who ranged themselves against the Stuarts. The hesitating Salisbury, drawn into their orbit, went along with them; and all the more because his sons Charles, Lord Cranborne, and Robert, both now grown-up and Members of the House of Commons, were violently on the Parliament's side. Finally, Hertfordshire was in favour of Parliament and Salisbury, as its Lord Lieutenant, did not like having Hertfordshire against him.

When the Civil War actually broke out, he still strove to cling to his precarious seat on the fence. Its start found him with Charles I at York, where he signed a declaration of peers supporting him. But two days later he was galloping back

Charles I, by Daniel Mytens, and right *Algernon Percy, 10th Earl of Northumberland, with his wife Anne Cecil and one of their daughters, painted by a pupil of Sir Anthony Van Dyck*

along the Great North Road to London to join the peers who had declared them-selves in favour of the Parliament. However, he contrived to remain on friendly enough terms with the King's party to be chosen by the Parliamentary leaders as a suitable man to form part of a delegation sent to try to make peace with Charles I.

Throughout the war he remained on the Parliamentary side, but hesitant and wavering. Its end, however, meant the end of any role for any peer, however anti-royalist he might have shown himself. For the real victor was not Parliament but Cromwell and his New Model Army, and this was a revolutionary body with hardly more use for peers than it had for kings. In fact, when the motion for trying the King came up, the majority of the House of Lords voted against it, and signed its own death warrant by so doing. Salisbury voted with the majority; there was never any question of his being personally disloyal to the King. On the contrary, when in the summer of 1647 Charles I, now a prisoner in the hands of Parliament, stopped at Hatfield on his way to Windsor, he found himself treated by Lord Salisbury and his servants with what was now to him an unaccustomed respect. Charles I could be depended upon to act tactlessly, and the effect of this polite treatment was that – looking, one imagines, obstinate and nervy as in his portrait at Hatfield – he began to assume so dictatorial a manner that the officer in charge felt bound to remind him of his situation.

The Parliamentary leaders heard of the King's behaviour with displeasure and were still more disturbed when they learned that Lord Salisbury had agreed to the King's attending a service in Hatfield church conducted by his own chaplain 'with divers superstitious gestures' and according to the now forbidden rites of the Anglican Prayer Book. Since, two years before, Lord Salisbury had ordered the stained-glass windows in the Chapel to be taken down for fear the Puritans should break them, his conduct over the church service showed unexpected and creditable spirit on his part. So far as we know, he and the King never met again. But two years later, in the cold grey of a January morning, he was observed in company with Lord Pembroke, standing at a window to watch the King walking across the park to his execution.

This was criticized by loyal Cavaliers as an act in poor taste. I cannot think why; it showed no approval of the execution. On the other hand, Salisbury's conduct in the period following was a trifle ignominious. Just as, during the period of Charles I's personal rule, he capitulated to strength and did all he could to propitiate the new government. A few months after Charles's death we find him attending a public banquet at Grocers Hall in honour of Cromwell, where he sat in a prominent place near Cromwell himself; he also accepted a place in a Council of State largely composed of regicides. When the House of Lords was abolished, he joined the House of Commons as member for King's Lynn. His sons were also members; but, as they had opposed the King all along and even fought in the Parliamentary forces, their position was more consistent.

Salisbury's *volte-face* did not in the end do him any good. During the first two

Sir Thomas Fairfax commanding the New Model Army, and a Dutch caricature of Cromwell trampling on England's peace treaty with the Dutch Republic

Commonwealth parliaments, he was employed on a committee appointed appropriately enough to draw up a scheme for improving the breed of horses. Later Cromwell, moved by suspicion or contempt, excluded him from serving again in a parliament: he spent the last years of the Commonwealth at Hatfield in retirement. His changes of front had at least helped him to preserve a substantial part of his property. Meanwhile, some years earlier, Prince Rupert and his Cavaliers, in revenge for what they considered Salisbury's apostasy, had sacked Cranborne Manor, killing an ox in the Great Hall and leaving the place, said Salisbury's agent, 'as nasty as a butcher's yard'.

The Restoration made little change in his fortunes. Charles II came back, cheerfully and cynically ready to let bygones be bygones. Within a short time active enemies of the past, like Salisbury's son-in-law Northumberland, were readmitted to the Privy Council. But, so far as Salisbury himself was concerned, Charles II's opinion seems for once to have been the same as Cromwell's. Hopefully Salisbury entertained him at Hatfield as, forty years earlier, he had hopefully entertained James I. But the result was the same. The King showed his host no more favour after the visit than before. And, once again, after his Court's departure, some silver plate was discovered to be missing. The Second Earl of Salisbury lived on to die at Hatfield in 1668.

I must confess to a weakness for this horse-faced inglorious ancestor, so peaceable and persuadable and confused and inadequate. But he was not a character to make himself respected. During the 1660s Samuel Pepys visited Hatfield. He much admired the House and the Chapel and above all the gardens, 'such as I never saw in all my life; nor so good flowers, nor so good gooseberries, as big as nutmegs'. The owner of the gooseberries impressed him less. 'Got to Hatfield in church time,' Pepys related. 'And saw my simple Lord Salisbury there in his gallery.'

II

The Second Earl's immediate heir did not succeed him: Charles, Lord Cranborne, blond and bony like his father, had died in 1660. He had been married for twenty years to Diana Maxwell, daughter of Sir James Maxwell, afterwards Lord Dirleton, and heiress to a large fortune. The gossip of the time accused Cranborne of marrying for money. But Miss Maxwell, as depicted by Lely, was remarkably

James Cecil, 4th Earl of Salisbury, with his sister Lady Catherine, painted by Michael Wright

Overleaf *William Cecil, 2nd Earl of Salisbury, and Lady Catherine Howard, Countess of Salisbury, both by George Geldorp*

pretty, with bright eyes, a brilliant complexion and wavy brown hair. There seems no reason to suppose he did not also marry her for love. Certainly he loved her well enough for her to bear him five daughters and seven sons; the eldest of these, the twenty-year-old James, now became the Third Earl Salisbury.

He turned out as undistinguished as his grandfather. But he was clearer about his political convictions and firmer in sticking to them. He seems to have started off with a clean slate in the King's eyes; for he was a royal page at the Coronation and had served at sea on the *Royal Charles* against the Dutch in 1666. Soon, however, the struggle between King and Parliament was resumed, though it was to be conducted on both sides more moderately than in earlier days. James Cecil, following his father, came out strongly in support of the Parliamentary and extreme Protestant side. First as a Member of the House of Commons, and then as a peer, he belonged to what was called the Country Party, which, led by the celebrated and unscrupulous Anthony Ashley Cooper, Earl of Shaftesbury, opposed the Crown.

In 1675 Charles II – rendered for the moment independent financially by money he had secretly obtained from the King of France – took advantage of such power he still possessed to prorogue Parliament; that is to say he temporarily suspended its sitting. After this had gone on for two years Salisbury, together with Shaftesbury and the dazzling George Villiers, Duke of Buckingham, came forward and claimed that such an extended suspension meant that Parliament was dissolved and demanded the election of a new one. Charles II was sufficiently put out by this to send all three to the Tower. Salisbury was not prepared to be what he considered a martyr to political principles; imprisonment made him feel ill, and besides his wife was shortly to be confined. Accordingly, after five months, he made formal submission to the King, who ordered him to be released. A year later he felt friendly enough to make him a Privy Councillor.

This did not lead Salisbury to become a King's man. James, Duke of York, Charles II's brother and heir to the throne, was a Roman Catholic, and the burning political question of the next few years was whether, on this account, he should be excluded from the throne. Salisbury was all for exclusion. He showed his antagonism in a very practical way. In 1679 the feeling against James in London had got so bad that he decided to leave for the north, and he wrote proposing that he and his family and retinue should spend the first night of their journey at Hatfield.

Salisbury felt unable to refuse what amounted to a semi-royal command; but he thought it due to his principles to show himself as unwelcoming as he possibly

James Cecil, 5th Earl of Salisbury: attributed to Charles Jervas

could. He wrote back explaining that he could not be there himself to receive his princely guests, on the unconvincing ground that he was going to be bled by a surgeon five days before and would still be convalescent at Quixwood, a small house of his six miles away. Worse was to follow; the Duke and his party arrived at Hatfield to find the Great House unlit, unheated and uninhabited. Only a small bundle of faggots had been left in the hall by way of fuel, and there was nothing in the cellars but one barrel of small beer, and nothing in the kitchen but the carcasses of two does, thought to have been surreptitiously left there by Salisbury's son and heir, who did not agree with his father about the Exclusion question. To crown everything else, Lord Salisbury had ordered all candles and candlesticks to be taken away, so that the poor York family faced the prospect of groping their way to bed chilled, supperless and in the dark. They sent servants down to seek help in the town of Hatfield, where they found persons more sympathetic to the royal cause or at any rate more generous to benighted travellers; so that their basic wants were supplied. Next day the Duke of York, to arouse a sense of shame in his host, gave orders that eight shillings should be left on the hall table as payment for the faggots and the small beer.

The sad story of the Duke of York's visit to Hatfield became the talk of Court and town. History does not record how Charles II reacted to it. But he had never cared for his brother and is more likely to have been amused than otherwise. Certainly he remained friendly to Salisbury. In 1680 he made him a Knight of the Garter. Salisbury accepted the honour; but against Charles's strong wish he voted in favour of the Bill for excluding James from the throne. It was his last political gesture. He had been married in 1661 to the Earl of Rutland's daughter, Lady Margaret Manners, whom he is said to have passionately loved. They had five sons and five daughters. She died in 1683. Stricken with grief, he died soon after.

His son and heir James succeeded him at the age of eighteen. In two ways he differed conspicuously from his predecessors. For one thing, he was from his early years enormously fat; for another, he was notably imprudent. His father and great-grandfather, though far from brilliant, had yet sense enough to know how to avoid getting irretrievably into trouble. Not so the Fourth Earl; he could never grasp the essential facts of any situation he was involved in, so that he was liable to take the one step fatal to the accomplishment of his intentions. Moreover he lacked the instinct for self-preservation that often saves stupid but more selfish men. When his father died, he was abroad finishing his education by a course of

Far left *James Cecil, 4th Earl of Salisbury, painted by William Wissing over his portrait of James, Duke of Monmouth, and* top to bottom *Charles, Viscount Cranborne; Diana Maxwell, Viscountess Cranborne; James, 3rd Earl of Salisbury; and Frances Bennett, 4th Countess of Salisbury*

foreign travel. He came back, the first Lord Salisbury to be an out-and-out supporter of the Stuart family – this in itself was a sign of his lack of good sense –
and hurried off to Court to beg Charles II's pardon for any annoyance his father's
conduct may have caused him.

The next step he took showed him as imprudent about his private affairs as
he was about politics. A year or two earlier his father, anxious to repair his
family's declining fortunes, had opened up negotiations with a rich city magnate,
Sir Simon Bennett, with the aim of arranging a marriage between Bennett's
daughter and co-heiress Frances and his own eldest son. However, while James
was away, both fathers had died and, when Sir Simon Bennett's will was opened,
it was found to contain a proviso that, if Frances should marry before she was
grown-up, all her fortune except ten thousand pounds should go to her married
sister Grace, and that, if she ever married without her mother's consent, she
should lose that also. At the moment of James's return Frances was still a child of
thirteen. Clearly it would be to the advantage of Grace and her husband that
she should be married before she grew up; and if possible to Lord Salisbury,
whom her mother much opposed. It was therefore not surprising that her sister
Grace should try to persuade Lord Salisbury to marry Frances. What is surprising
is that Lord Salisbury let himself be persuaded. Perhaps he was already in love:
Frances was to grow up into a woman of curiously attractive appearance, pale
and dark-haired, with sad beautiful eyes and a sensitive pouting mouth. But it is
more likely that he had not understood Sir Simon Bennett's will. Certainly he
spent time and money during the ensuing years in vainly trying to recover the
ten thousand pounds.

Meanwhile in 1683, having married Frances, he returned to the Continent for
two more years of instructive travel. Before he left he removed his child bride
from her middle-class home and sent her down to Hatfield under the care of a
governess, to be educated in such a way as to fit her for her future role as a countess.
The idea behind this plan was reasonable; countesses in those days were expected
to conduct themselves very differently from the daughters of city magnates.
But James, Fourth Earl of Salisbury, had not realized that his plan could be
fulfilled only in the right conditions.

These were not forthcoming. Hatfield had by now fallen on evil days. The
family had lost and spent so much during the last fifty years that it could no longer
be properly maintained. Its furnishings were dilapidated and decaying and there
were too few servants to keep the place clean. Sometimes also there was not
enough ready cash to see that the young countess was adequately fed. Nor
adequately educated either; she had some lessons in music and dancing – the bills
for these are still to be seen at Hatfield – but very little else seems to have been
done for her. The next thing that happened was that the governess appointed to

take charge of her was dismissed for some unspecified misdemeanour. After this the child countess had a dismal time, staying on at Hatfield companionless, uncared for and unfed: a forlorn little figure with hardly anything to do by day but to roam the crumbling terraces and unweeded lawns of the spreading gardens, or by night to wander through the echoing apartments of the great, gaunt empty house with their fading tapestries and tarnished silk hangings. Indeed, her situation was such as to shock the neighbourhood. At last the steward, the chief domestic officer left in charge of the place, took matters into his own hands and sent her back to her family in London.

In 1688 Lord Salisbury returned from abroad, forty thousand pounds poorer than when he had left. The story was that he had been taken prisoner by the Turks and forced to pay this vast sum as a ransom. It seems more likely, though less romantic, that he lost it gambling in Paris. Meanwhile, the year before, he had gone to Rome, where he had visited the Pope and was received into the Roman Catholic Church. His subsequent history inclines us to believe that his conversion was sincere; but it was also opportune, or must have seemed so to him. For, two years earlier, Charles II had died, to be succeeded by the Roman Catholic James II. It cannot but have crossed Salisbury's mind that his conversion was likely to improve his earthly as well as his heavenly prospects. Whatever his chief motive may have been, he lost no time in coming home to protest his loyalty to his King.

Once again he had calculated wrongly. It is true that James welcomed the new convert and showed his pleasure by appointing him Gentleman of the Bed Chamber and colonel of a regiment of horse. But, as it turned out, Salisbury had little time to enjoy these honours. The year of his return was also the year of the Glorious Revolution of 1688, when James was driven from his throne and his Protestant daughter and son-in-law were summoned from Holland to rule in his place. Their succession was the occasion for a violent outburst against Roman Catholics, especially newly converted ones. First a mob tried to burn down Salisbury House and had to be dispersed by the Earl's armed retainers. Then the Grand Jury of Middlesex issued a warrant to arrest eminent converts, notably young Lord Salisbury and old Lord Peterborough, for changing their religion. They were taken, but managed to jump out of the coach in which they were being driven to prison. Since Lord Peterborough was nearly senile and Lord Salisbury so fat that he could hardly move, there was little difficulty in recapturing them. At his trial Salisbury was sentenced to imprisonment in the Tower; four years later he was released on payment of five thousand pounds. He had no more power of getting himself respected than had his father. Already, a year earlier, a paper had been found pinned on the front door of Salisbury House declaring:

> If Cecil the wise
> From his grave should arise
> And see this fat brute in his place,
> He would take him from Mass
> And turn him to grass
> And swear he was not of his race.

After the revolution the story went round that, when Salisbury heard of William III's victory, he swore and lamented and cried out, 'Oh God, I turned too soon, I turned too soon!' It is an entertaining anecdote, but improbable. For, if he had become a Roman Catholic only for worldly reasons, he could easily after a decent interval have turned Anglican again; many people did. In fact, he stuck to his new faith and continued to stand up for his former King. Sitting in a London coffee-house one day after he had left the Tower, he heard a man stating that James II was a coward. Salisbury drew his sword in indignation and nearly got himself sent back to prison for brawling. This incident indicates something likeable about the fat Fourth Earl. Surprisingly enough, his wife seems to have liked him. Countess Frances, now arrived at the mature age of eighteen, had rejoined her husband when he got back to England; and, in spite of her memories of dismal days as a girl at Hatfield, she took to him so much that she shared his imprisonment in the Tower and enjoyed doing so. 'They lovingly cohabitated in the Tower' – so a contemporary writer curiously phrased it.

Out of the Tower, Salisbury was soon in trouble again. He had three brothers: Robert, William and Charles. By the time he got back from abroad, Robert was grown up but William and Charles were still schoolboys at Eton under the legal guardianship of a cousin, the Countess of Burlington. During their summer holidays Salisbury entertained them on a visit to Hatfield. They complained to him that they did not like Eton, and it struck Salisbury, still burning with Roman Catholic zeal, that he might use their dislike as a means to lure them into the true Church. If they would become Roman Catholics, he told them, he would arrange for them to go and live in Paris no longer as schoolboys but as independent young gentlemen.

Charles and William found the idea of the true Church, as seen in this context, extremely attractive; they agreed. During the following term Salisbury drove down to Eton in his coach, picked them up and smuggled them over to France. This was before the Revolution. Afterwards, when Salisbury was in the Tower, the Countess of Burlington demanded that Salisbury should arrange for his brothers to be brought back to England. This he refused to do; he would not even reveal their Paris address. Up to date this story has its comic side; now it becomes tragic. Charles and William were a pair of budding rakes quite unfitted to be left in Paris, except under supervision. As was common at that period, they

The Hon. William Cecil, by William Wissing and right *the Hon. Robert Cecil, by Charles Beale*

shared the same bed. One night in 1691, they quarrelled and one pushed the other out of it. Within a minute each had grabbed his sword; and there and then they fought a duel in their nightshirts and by the dim light of bedroom candles. It was a duel to the death, and William, the older, was killed. Charles was wounded in the struggle, but he managed to escape to Italy.

It is a lurid tale. For this reason it caught my imagination as a boy, and I used to gaze with curiosity at the portrait of the victim William, a pallid heavy-cheeked youth in a lace jabot, disappointingly unlike the daredevil suggested by the story of the duel. Indeed, he looks not so very different from the second son of the family, his brother Robert, who was a pillar of the Protestant Establishment, ruthlessly respectable and much interested in acquiring money. He had made trouble for the recently released Lord Salisbury by also clamouring for the return of his two brothers from France. He further tried to restrain his elder brother, Lord Salisbury, from selling land to pay his debts, which by now were enormous; for, so long as Lord Salisbury was childless, Robert was his heir-presumptive and therefore concerned that the family patrimony should not be diminished. The land in question was entailed, and the Fourth Earl had to get a private Bill introduced in Parliament enabling him to sell it. Robert took measures to get the Bill opposed; and a violent controversy followed. Luckily it was soon stopped when the Countess Frances gave birth in 1691 to a son and heir. After this the respectable Robert disappears from the family history. All we know of his later life is that he married a widow and had a son who later became Bishop of Bangor, and a daughter who married a celebrated miser called Sir Robert Brown. It was said of him that, when one of his daughters had just died of consumption and another seemed about to do so, he hastily contracted with an undertaker for a double funeral because he had heard that this would cost less than two single funerals.

That was many years later. To return to the Fourth Earl, his religion could still get him into political trouble. In 1692 a dubious character called John Young came forward with allegations of a conspiracy to restore James II to the throne. This, he said, had been organized by several leading men of position, including Lord Salisbury; and he produced as evidence a document signed with their names. There seemed a good chance that the poor Earl would be back in the Tower once more. Fortunately another of the alleged conspirators was John Churchill, afterwards the great Marlborough. He was soon able to show that the report of the conspiracy was false and the signed document a forgery. Lord Salisbury did not long survive this last embarrassment in which his conversion had involved him. He retired to Hatfield, where he is said to have entertained Dryden, the greatest poet of the age. It is likely that he did so less for love of poetry than because Dryden was also a Roman Catholic convert. Still, it is pleasing to think of any gleam of culture that illuminated, for whatever reason, the dull life at the now dilapidated Hatfield. Otherwise the Fourth Earl's life was mainly occupied in struggling with his debts; he was forced to sell Salisbury House in London to repay them. In 1694 he died, aged thirty-five.

What became of the woman, once his child-bride and now his girl-widow, who had so unexpectedly loved him? The little we know is curious enough to make us wish we knew more. She spent much of her time abroad, where it is interesting to discover that she became a close friend of her brother-in-law Charles, who had killed his brother William in Paris. We hear of them travelling together in Rome in 1701. A year later Charles was stricken with fever there and died, his imagination haunted to the last by the spectre of William dead by his hand eleven years before. The curse of Cain had fallen on the man who had slain his brother. Frances may well have thought that there was a curse on her too, or at least on her relations with any member of the household of Cecil. She lived on to die in London in 1713.

The story of this last generation – with its episodes of the forlorn child-bride, the fraternal duel fought at midnight in Paris and Charles's guilt-haunted death-bed far away in Papal Rome – strikes the single note of exotic melodrama in all the long chronicle of the Cecils of Hatfield. In the next generation this reverts to describe lives wholly English, and so uneventful as to leave the historian nearly speechless. The early eighteenth century in England is a peculiarly prosaic period. Of this period the Salisbury family was peculiarly and prosaically characteristic.

James, the Fifth Earl, who succeeded to the title at the age of three, is chiefly memorable for the fact that in his youth his family were always having his portrait painted. This is understandable. At ten years old he appears as a very pretty child, blond, bright-eyed and dressed in a classical tunic. At fifteen his nose has become bigger and his eyes smaller, but he is still pretty, with fair curls and a milk-and-roses complexion tastefully set forth by a green velvet coat and a white muslin neck-ruffle. By the time he is an Oxford undergraduate the man, though still pleasant-looking, has come to matter less than his clothes. This portrait is mainly interesting to posterity because it depicts him in the academic dress that in those undemocratic days was reserved for men of high birth: a nobleman's gold-embroidered gown and a mortar-board with a gold tassel. The last picture of him, done in his mid-thirties, shows him matured into a heavy, stodgy-looking Georgian gentleman with prominent features, double chin and huge feet. He looks undistinguished; and was so. There are hints that he did at moments aspire to wider and more cultural interests. He kept up the Dryden connection by making friends with the poet's son, added substantially to the library and took sufficient interest in foreign affairs and foreign personalities to buy two very poor portraits of the Tsar of Russia and the King of Sweden to hang on the walls of Hatfield.

Otherwise, if the Fifth Earl is mentioned at all by his contemporaries, it is disrespectfully as a man with a taste for low company and henpecked by his wife. For the dominating figure at Hatfield House during this phase of its story was the Countess of Salisbury, born Lady Anne Tufton and daughter of the Earl of Thanet. She looks dominating in her picture, black-eyed, sharp-featured and a touch shrewish, dressed in the red velvet and ermine robes she wore at George I's Coronation. There seems never to have been any question of her husband's being a Jacobite or a Roman Catholic like his father. At this same Coronation the Earl of Salisbury was recognized as a firm enough supporter of the House of Hanover to be given the honour of carrying the staff of St George in the royal procession. This was the nearest he ever got to taking part in Court and political life. He was the type of English peer who feels happiest residing in his country home and surrounded by his own estates. His Countess was the same. It was domestically and in the locality that she exercised dominion.

Here she was very active. Countess Anne, as she was popularly called, had Hatfield House cleaned and tidied. She also did a great deal to improve the garden, sadly fallen away from the *Faerie Queen* splendour of the First Earl's plans. There was no question indeed of her trying to revive its fountains and its vineyard; such things were no longer to the taste of the time. But it was Countess Anne who planted the great copper beeches that shadow the West Garden on its south side. She took an interest in the people of the place, too, and founded a charity school, where forty Hatfield girls between the ages of nine and fifteen, dressed in a uniform of hooped skirt, starched collar and close-fitted cap, were

Hatfield House about 1740, and opposite *Lady Anne Tufton, 5th Countess of Salisbury*

taught knitting, sewing and the Church Catechism to fit them for decent domestic service. Countess Anne drew up the regulations for the school herself. They were fairly stringent. The children were kept at it for seven hours a day; and one regulation gives warning that the Countess was not the type of person to stand any nonsense and that she expected from her inferiors the obedience due to her exalted rank:

> *Number Nine.* That whoever take their child or children out of the school without consent and approbation of the said Countess of Salisbury, neither themselves nor their children shall for the future partake of her Ladyship's bounty in any kind whatsoever.

It must be noted to the Countess's credit, however, that her sense of her rank did not lead her to treat her inferiors with a special harshness. On the contrary, there is nothing in the school regulations about corporal punishment. But it was the talk of the county that she had her eldest son beaten for his own good, even after he had reached the age of seventeen. She was also accused, when in a better temper, of spoiling him recklessly.

Whichever the cause – the County thought it was the beating rather than the spoiling – he turned out badly; so much so that, as a child five generations later, I always heard him spoken of as the 'Wicked Earl'. This is a misleading name, in that it suggests something sinister and criminal, whereas James, Sixth Earl of Salisbury, was nothing of the kind, but merely a dissipated, irresponsible figure, deplorably unequal to his position. There is a satirical reference to him in Hogarth's cartoon *Night*, and in fact he was a thoroughly Hogarthian personality. One imagines him as the hero of a series of moral prints depicting the phases in the career of a dissipated heir to a rich peerage, wasting his substance and sinking in the social scale, surrounded by a crowd of low-born hangers-on: card-sharpers, tavern-keepers, jockeys, flaunting trollops. He early became his own master; the Fifth Earl, like his father, died young – in 1728, when he was only thirty-seven. His heir grew up, made the grand tour of Europe – he had his portrait done at

Venice by Rosalba Carriera – and came home to start immediately on his downward progress. Neither then nor afterwards does he seem to have associated with his social equals; even his more respectable companions were of humbler origin than himself.

As a matter of fact this was to lead him to perform the one action of his life that benefited the Cecil family. In 1744 he married Elizabeth Keet, sister of the Rector of Hatfield. In those days the Anglican clergy tended to be divided on the one hand into men of rank – it was only these who were likely to be made bishops or deans – and parish parsons, who came mostly from the same class as upper servants and enjoyed themselves drinking beer with their patrons' butlers. Miss Keet's brother did not belong to this humblest type of country parson, but equally he was not a man of rank as the eighteenth century understood the phrase. In marrying the Reverend Mr Keet's sister, the Earl of Salisbury was judged by the world to have married noticeably beneath him.

However, it was soon apparent that it was Miss Keet who, in any true sense of the word, had made a misalliance. All that we know of her, including the intelligent, decided countenance shown in her portrait, indicates that she was a superior woman with a just sense both of the dignity and difficulties of her position. Too much sense of them, indeed, to endure indefinitely the riotings and infidelities of her blue-blooded husband and his coarse boon companions. After eleven years of marriage, she took herself off to London with her son and daughters. For the rest of their lives Lord and Lady Salisbury lived separately. Oppressed it may be by the grandeur of Hatfield, which anyhow he found too expensive to live in, the 'Wicked Earl' soon retired to Quixwood, the same small country house six miles away to which his great-grandfather had retreated in 1679 to avoid having to welcome the future James II. There he spent his later days quietly, if not virtuously, a semi-recluse but for the company of his mistress Mrs Graves and the family of children that she had borne him. He gave up all pretence of behaving in a manner appropriate to his station; he had already created scandal and amusement on several occasions by appearing in the role of a public coachman, driving the stage coach to and from London. The 'Coachman Earl' became a byword. It is this activity of his that Hogarth made fun of in his cartoon, and Pope alludes to it in the fourth book of the *Dunciad*:

> From stage to stage the licensed Earl may run
> Paired with his fellow charioteer – the sun.

In spite of his reduced scale of living, the Sixth Earl still contrived to overspend, with the result that the deserted Hatfield House fell into worse disrepair than ever. More and more of its treasures had to be sold. All the good silver went, except for a set of Charles II silver candle-sconces moulded with figures of Cupid and

Psyche. The tradition is that old Countess Anne – she lived till 1751 to witness the disastrous effects of her educational methods – got hold of them and had them painted brown to make them look as if made of wood and so not valuable enough to be worth selling.

Elizabeth Keet, 6th Countess of Salisbury,
by Benjamin van der Gucht

Meanwhile, up in London, Lady Salisbury lived very quietly, devoting herself to bringing up her children. She brought them up well, to judge by results, and in general got herself respected. This was a credit to her considering alike her origin and her situation as a separated wife; for the eighteenth-century English, though less prudish than their Victorian descendants, believed equally strongly in indissoluble marriage and much more strongly in distinctions of rank. Lady Salisbury had the luck to be much helped by her husband's cousin Lady Brown, the wife of the celebrated miser. People said that Lady Brown was a miser too; but it is hard to believe this in view of the generous kindness she showed in her relations with her Cecil cousins. She got on well with the former Miss Keet, and was able to give her valuable advice on how best to educate her children so as to suit them for their future place in society. She was also one of his few respectable relations who were on friendly terms with Lord Salisbury. She had been left his guardian when he was a minor; and during that time had managed to make him fond of her. The result of this was that for the rest of her life she was able to keep an eye on the whole family and do something to prevent it from disintegrating. She acted as a mediator between husband and wife and a link between father and children. In consequence they did not grow up wholly alienated from him. When he came to die, his son and heir was with him at Quixwood.

2
RECOVERY

THE REPUTATION of the Cecils at Hatfield, on the wane for five generations, reached its lowest point with the Wicked Earl. After him it began to rise again. This rise was due less to the Cecils than to their wives. The Cecil stock, apparently exhausted by the efforts of its sixteenth-century representatives, was revitalized by union with a succession of women of character or intelligence or both. The middle-class Miss Keet was the first, and her effect was most likely due to her being middle-class. It is one of the ironies of history that the English aristocracy maintained its power and position longer than foreign aristocracies mainly because, unlike them, it did not believe in noble birth as such. Whereas foreign aristocrats were only permitted to marry other aristocrats, the English could marry whom they chose, so that their blue blood was always being refreshed and invigorated by the infusion of red blood drawn from the veins of other ranks of society.

It is true that, to be readily accepted, these unaristocratic brides had to be rich and so able to help in keeping up the position of the family they married into. Miss Keet was not rich, and therefore not so immediately acceptable. But accepted she was; and the Keet strain, steady and worthy, and the Keet method of education, different from that employed by the high-born Countess Anne, arrested the downward trend of the Cecil family. Not that they produced anything spectacular: none of Miss Keet's children were brilliant. But they were all three respectable, and the son and heir James, Lord Cranborne, though like many men of his period addicted to strong language – he was nicknamed 'Blastus' – was in taste and manners notably gentlemanly. If his father was a fit subject for Hogarth, he was a fit subject for Reynolds and Romney. In fact Romney did paint him, in a peer's crimson robes standing under a classic colonnade and looking mild and bland and handsome.

From the first he seems to have sought to live in a manner appropriate to his

James Cecil, 7th Earl and 1st Marquess of Salisbury, by George Romney

position. He reverted to the political tradition of his family, entered the House of Commons at the age of twenty-six and stayed there till 1780, when his father died. Afterwards he was a reasonably active member of the House of Lords. The political situation had changed since the days when last a Lord Salisbury had occupied himself with it. The battle between King and Parliament had ended in the victory of Parliament; in the late eighteenth century the struggle was between the Whig and the Tory parties. The King, in the person of George III, was now attempting to revive some of his lost power by organizing a group to further his views among members of Parliament. James Cecil was one of them, first as Lord Cranborne, then as Lord Salisbury. He was a High Tory, as the term had come to be understood, and he strongly supported the King; in particular he backed his opposition to the rebellious American colonies. George III showed his gratitude to this reliable and gentlemanly supporter. Once more, after a lapse of one hundred and fifty years, the Salisbury family began to rise in the world. In 1783 the Earl became Lord Chamberlain, in 1789 a Marquess and 1793 a Knight of the Garter. By the closing years of the century the Cecils of Hatfield were again a leading political family, but now definitely committed to the Tory side.

It is hard to believe, however, that the family rise was due to the first Marquess's unaided talents. We know little about him; what we do know is unimpressive. Horace Walpole mentions him once or twice rather disparagingly; the rumour that Lord Salisbury has written a poem strikes him with 'astonished amusement'. Clearly, and in spite of his oaths and gentlemanly manners, he did not make much mark on his contemporaries. Lady Salisbury on the other hand did. For the second generation, and more dramatically, it is the mistress of the House who is the memorable figure in the history of Hatfield. The family rise seems to have been largely her doing. It is significant that she had her own picture painted wearing her husband's Star of the Order of the Garter, though there was no question of her having any legal right to do so. It is also significant that it was she who performed the only political act recorded either of her or him.

During the Westminster election of 1784 the beautiful Duchess of Devonshire, leader of Whig fashionable society, took the unusual step of going down herself to canvas the free and independent electors of the borough on behalf of the Whig candidate, Charles James Fox, and, it is said, kissed a local butcher to obtain his vote. Next day Lady Salisbury followed her to Westminster to restore the balance. Alas! her blandishments were less successful. Partly because her manners were not as friendly – she does not appear to have kissed any butchers – and still more because she was thirty-four and by the standards of the time well past her prime as a beauty. Fox won the seat. The story is evidence however that, unsuccessful or not on this occasion, by 1784 Lady Salisbury was looked on as the Duchess of

Devonshire's Tory counterpart and the leading Tory lady of fashion.

This does not mean she was as attractive as the Duchess, who was the exquisite fine flower of Whig Society when this was the most agreeable in the whole history of English aristocratic life. Compared with it, the Tory aristocracy of the time was a crude affair, not so very different from the hard-drinking, hard-riding country squires who were its chief supporters. Still, Tory aristocrats were not without their attractions. They had the vigour of the period and the confidence of their rank; there was nothing timid or conventional about them. Racy and full-blooded, they were not afraid to give full rein to individual idiosyncrasy and even individual eccentricity. Moreover, though less intellectual than the Whigs, they shared their elegance. If the talk at the great Tory houses was less brilliant, the houses themselves were decorated with equal taste and magnificence.

The first Marchioness of Salisbury was the epitome of this Tory society. She had been born in 1750, as Lady Emily Mary Hill, daughter of the Irish Earl of Downshire, and she was a very Anglo-Irish type, forceful and flamboyant. As depicted by Sir Joshua Reynolds, she was also beautiful, with a proud small head,

Georgiana, Duchess of Devonshire, and her daughter, painted by Sir Joshua Reynolds, and a caricature of Charles James Fox, supported at the Westminster election of 1784 by the Duchess but opposed by Lady Salisbury

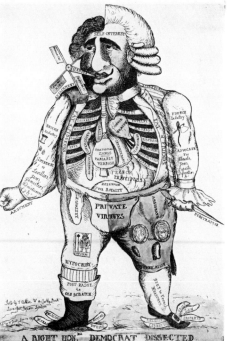

Hatfield House: the South Front in 1785

an erect graceful figure, and an air about her at once dashing and imperious. Her manners were imperious, showing, it was observed, a consciousness of her rank and a determination that others should be conscious of it. Perhaps this is why she failed to please the Westminster butchers. Her sense of her position also appeared in the way she liked to live. She enjoyed showing off, dressed with conspicuous splendour in rich stuffs, vivid colours and sparkling jewels, and compelled attention by the equipages in which she appeared in public; sometimes she was carried by gorgeously attired footmen in an ornamental sedan chair, sometimes she drove in a carriage drawn by four horses in harness of the family colours of blue and silver and attended by a retinue of postilions in blue and silver livery. When she was driving round the estate, one of these postilions was commanded to carry a bag of golden guineas; now and again she ordered the coachman to stop and asked for the bag, from which she drew some guineas to toss to the grateful tenantry.

She also entertained on a huge scale and in semi-royal state both in London and at Hatfield, which she had largely redecorated and refurnished in the taste of the period, with tall mirrors, Chinese silk curtains and chairs of gilded Chippendale. At Hatfield in particular she kept open house to throngs of guests. On Sundays in summer the Park was thrown wide open to admit the people of the place so that they might listen to Lady Salisbury's band playing on the terrace; or, to vary the entertainment, the band would play on the banks of the River Lea at the north end of the Park, where she herself listened to it from a state barge rowed up and down the river by twelve men in full livery. The most famous of her entertainments took place in 1800 when George III and his Queen came on a visit to review the local militia in the Park. It was to commemorate this occasion that George III presented his host with the red-faced, red-coated portrait of himself standing in Hatfield Park.

Though grand, the first Marchioness was not stiff. Indeed, her love of show went with a love of pleasure which made her much the reverse. Indoors she liked to dance and gamble till dawn; outdoors she was an enthusiastic sportswoman who delighted in archery, in riding, above all in hunting. She took on the mastership of the local hunt when her husband got bored with it and directed the chase with zest, dressed in a specially designed costume which included a blue and silver riding coat and a black velvet jockey cap. Her days and nights passed in a whirl of enjoyment, outdoors and in, that staggered and dazzled observers. 'I never heard anything like the manner of living at Hatfield,' writes one of them; 'five hundred fed every Tuesday and Friday for six weeks at Christmas, the house full of company eating and drinking all day long . . . Lady Salisbury goes a-fox-hunting in the morning or in her open carriage and to all balls in the county at night. In short she does anything and everything all day long.'

There is a note of disapproval in this. People did disapprove of Lady Salisbury. There was no scandal about her love life, as there was about that of the Duchess of Devonshire; perhaps her Irish flamboyance went along with an Irish coolness of sexual temperament. But otherwise her way of living was such as to scandalize the staid and the strict. They were shocked by her hunting – not a decorous activity for a lady, they thought; they were shocked by her talk which, uttered in harsh masculine tones, was startlingly free-spoken; they were shocked by her extravagance and her gambling. The floor of the gallery at Hatfield late on Sunday night was sometimes ankle deep in cards from the packs discarded and thrown on the floor, for – and this shocked people all the more – Lady Salisbury held card parties on Sunday. Indeed, she did not revive the family religious tradition. Her Sunday concerts often took place at the same time as a church service, to which they provided such a powerful counter-attraction as to corrupt the Rector of Hatfield himself. Before the service began he would look up and down the street to see if anyone was coming. If no one was, he would lock the church door and go off to join the concert audience.

Lady Salisbury herself seldom went to church; when she did, it was in a secular spirit. Once she arrived with her daughters late at a service held at the Chapel Royal in London and found the place full. 'Where shall we go, Mamma?' asked one of the daughters. 'Home again, to be sure,' replied Lady Salisbury; 'if we cannot get in, it is no fault of ours – we have done the civil thing.' On another occasion – this was at Hatfield – she sat listening to what was to her the hitherto unknown story of Adam and Eve, which told how Adam, rebuked by

God for eating the fruit of the Tree of Knowledge, put the blame on Eve. 'The woman tempted me and I did eat,' he said. Lady Salisbury was outraged. 'Shabby fellow indeed!' she exclaimed in angry and audible tones. She was no respecter of persons dead or alive. For all her Toryism, she did not mind inconveniencing the King himself to get what she wanted. Once George III and the royal family were attending the Handel Festival in Westminster Abbey. Lady Salisbury arrived after it had started – she seems to have been very unpunctual – and entered the box put up for the Lord Chamberlain's party. Soon a loud sound of hammering was heard disturbing the celestial harmony of the music. The King asked the cause; he was told that Lady Salisbury, finding the box divided in two by what she thought was an unnecessary partition, insisted that carpenters should be sent for to take it down at once.

The 1st Marchioness of Salisbury,
by George Engleheart

The Marchioness of Salisbury, entertaining personality though she was, could be a great nuisance. Her husband died in 1823 and was succeeded by his married son and heir. But, though over seventy, his widow showed no intention of taking on the depressing role of retired Dowager. She lived for ten years more, during which time she continued to cut an arresting figure in the social life of the day. The gossip writers of the time are full of anecdotes about 'Dow. Sal' or 'Old Sarum', as she was nicknamed. They are not dignified nicknames; in spite of her sense of rank, she was not a dignified figure, especially at this stage of her career. Rejecting old age, she insisted on surrounding herself with young people and behaved like a young person herself. Wilful and tireless, her withered body decked out in girlish gauze and coloured ribbons, she continued to dance and gamble and drive a four-in-hand and even to hunt. At eighty she was too weak

A commemorative festival to Handel in Westminster Abbey, 1784

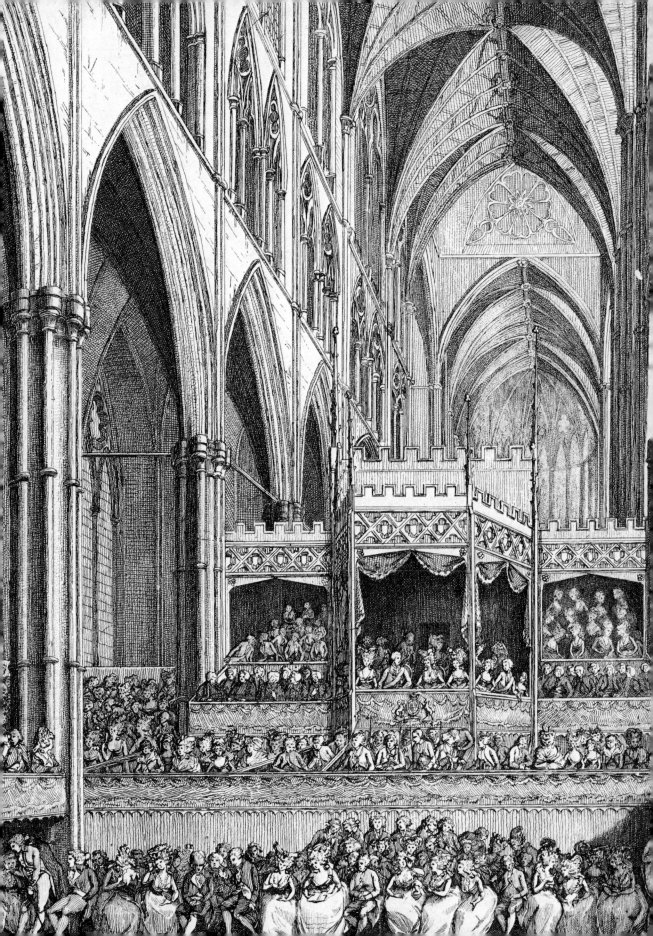

to sit on her horse without being strapped to it, and too blind to guide it, so it was attached by a leading rein to a groom. When they came to a hedge, 'Damn you, my Lady, jump!' cried the groom, and the odd couple scrambled together over the hedge.

During the London season Lady Salisbury's house was crowded with famous people; out of season she imposed herself as a visitor on any country-house where she fancied she might be amused. Creevey's diary gives us lively glimpses of her on these visits.

> Old Salisbury arrived yesterday . . . in her accustomed manner, in a phaeton drawn by four long-tail black Flanders mares – she driving the wheel horses, and a postilion on the leaders, with two out-riders on corresponding long-tail blacks. Her man and maid were in her chaise behind; her groom and saddle horses arrived some time after her. It is impossible to do justice to the antiquity of her face. If, as alleged, she is only 74 years old, it is the most cracked, or rather furrowed piece of mosaic you have ever saw; but her dress, in the colours of it at least, is absolutely infantine. I wish you just saw her as I do now. She thinks she is alone, and I am writing at the end of the adjoining room, the folding doors being open. She is reclining on a sofa, reading the Edinbro' Review, without spectacles or glass of any kind. Her dress is white muslin, properly loaded with garniture, and she has just put off a very large bonnet, profusely gifted with bright lilac ribbons, leaving on her head a very nice lace cap, not less adorned with brightest yellow ribbon . . .

And again:

> We have just lost our Sally, and I only wish you could have seen her four long tails with white reins, and huge tassells on each horse, and herself driving her dogs 20 miles to London.
>
> Saturday and Sunday were so hot that none of us were able to ride, but yesterday my Lady with her four Daughters, and two Sons, and old Sally and I took the field to Bulstrode, and its environs – Sall being the only one who mounted her horse like an arrow from the hand of her groom, the horse too being an uncommonly high one . . . I had a good deal of jaw with her yesterday in our ride, her opinions upon different matters were very amusing. By the way of an outing for her, we have driven out the last two nights after coffee, about ten o'clock in two open carriages, taking the road to Salt Hill, and so seeing the London Mails to the West of England arrive and change horses etc.; and, poor as such amusement may appear to be for persons of our rank and age, I assure you it gave very great and general satisfaction, and so after a cool drive of ten miles about, we returned to our tea; and, as near 12 as might be each night, we have made up a rubber for Sally at crown points; and about $\frac{1}{2}$ past one and after finishing 3 or 4 rubbers she has retired to her couche . . .

These accounts suggest that 'Old Sal' was an exacting guest and, if crossed, a tiresome one. Once, when she was staying with her son at Hatfield, one of her dogs went mad and bit a footman who, poor fellow, had to have the wounded piece of flesh cut out for fear of hydrophobia. 'Lady Salisbury', reported her daughter-in-law indignantly, 'remained perfectly unmoved and refused for a long time to part with this or another dog which had been bitten, and seemed to have no thought in the whole transaction but her own privation in losing her dogs.' Lady Salisbury's conduct on this occasion was far from being the only thing that her son and daughter-in-law had to complain of in her. Clinging to the habits of her youth, the Dowager clung also to its privileges. She refused to give up the family jewels, including the diamond Star of the Order of the Garter in which she had been painted but which in fact belonged to her husband; and she spent as much money on gambling and entertaining and dress as when she was Marchioness of Salisbury. In consequence, though she had been generously provided for, she managed to overspend on a large scale. Gradually her capital diminished and her debts mounted, till in the autumn of 1835 she faced a financial crisis. 'Some measures must be taken about it. Her income is so much reduced that it is impossible for her to go on,' commented the young Lady Salisbury in disapproving tones.

In the event the crisis was averted by death. The end of 'Old Sarum' was characteristically spectacular; and all the more because it nearly involved the end of Hatfield House as well. On the evening of the 22nd of November 1835 Lord and Lady Salisbury were sitting quietly reading when a maid rushed in breathlessly to tell them that clouds of smoke were issuing from the Dowager Lady Salisbury's bedroom in the West Wing. They hurried out to find the house

After the fire in 1835: the West Wing of Hatfield House

on fire and a high wind blowing; soon the whole West Wing was in flames. Lord Salisbury tried again and again to fight his way through to his mother's room, only to be beaten back. Throughout the night the blaze roared higher; all the fire-engines of the district arrived but could do nothing. It looked as if the first Earl's image of the Earthly Paradise would soon be a heap of ashes. Then, shortly before dawn, the wind changed and the fire was got under control. But the West Wing was now only a shell, in which were found a few charred bones, all that remained of the Dowager. It was thought that she had been writing and that the feathers in her high-piled hair – she still wore it in the fashion of her youth – had caught in the candle and so started the fire. Besides her bones, a few scraps of metal were discovered, thought to be what was left of the family jewels that she should long ago have handed on to her daughter-in-law. Further investigations, however, suggests that most of these had been already sold to pay gambling debts. The starry parures that had glittered on her ancient person during recent London seasons were fakes.

II

The first Marchioness was a picturesque rather than an edifying figure. But, to make use of a metaphor that would have appealed to the horsewoman in her, she improved the breed. To the solid middle-class qualities of character brought into the family by Miss Keet, Lady Emily Mary Hill added the toughness, the fighting spirit, and the contempt for convention of her Irish ancestry. All these qualities appear in her son and heir, James, Second Marquess of Salisbury.

Without his mother's beauty – he was short and stocky, with a plain, strong-featured aggressive countenance – he was yet very much her son in his oddity and self-confidence. He too had got himself known by a nickname, the Matador, which suggests a man who enters life as a bullfighter enters the arena alone and sword in hand. He would have liked to be a professional soldier, but, since he was the only male of his generation and the heir to a great position, his parents forbad this. Instead, according to the common practice of the more energetic sons of the English governing class, he went into public life, first in the House of Commons and then, when he succeeded to the peerage in 1823, as a Member of the House of Lords. Vigour and industry united with the advantages bestowed on him by birth to push him some way up the political ladder: he was made a Privy Councillor before he was thirty-five and in later life was twice for a short time in office, as Lord Privy Seal in 1854 and Lord President of the Council in 1859. But he never made much of a mark in national politics. It was as a local magnate – autocrat of his estates, Colonel of the local Militia Regiment and general self-appointed dictator of the Hatfield district – that his energies found fulfilment.

It was an active fulfilment. His career coincided with a dramatic period of change, in which the liberal ideas of the French Revolution and the practical facts of the Industrial Revolution were combining to alter English life and institutions as they had not been altered for centuries. Politically the Second Marquess was an extreme High Tory, believing whole-heartedly in rank and privilege and violently opposed to the whole 'progressive' movement. His style of living was in harmony with this *ancien régime* outlook: a regal, feudal open-house affair whose festive occasions were marked by huge gatherings where retainers and tenants were lavishly entertained with gallons of beer and specially slaughtered oxen, and the nobility and gentry with balls and banquets and garden parties. 'There is a grand baronial style of living kept up at Hatfield,' writes a visitor. 'Prayers are said in the chapel every morning by the Chaplain. Dinner takes place in the old Elizabethan hall. The band of the militia, of which the Marquess is Colonel, plays during the meal in an outer apartment. Each lady as she passes into the Dining Hall is presented with a handsome bouquet.'

All this took place against an appropriate background. The Second Marquess did a great deal to the house. He had to rebuild the West Wing after the fire. But he found much of the rest of the building in bad repair and set to work to put it right. He did so in what was thought to be the original style of the house. The elegant eighteenth-century furnishings and decoration put up by his parents were removed and in their place the walls were hung with tapestry and lined with panelling and carving, sometimes new, sometimes made up from fragments of ancient work. The effect could be odd: a huge bed was composed from woodwork taken from a foreign church, with an altar-rail forming the end of the bed and the Holy Ghost in the form of a dove hovering over the sleeper on the underside of the bed's canopy. The historical imagination was further stimulated by wooden figures dressed in ancient suits of armour disposed about the entrance hall and landings.

Politically and artistically, then, the second Marquess looked back. But in practice he often behaved like a go-ahead man of the present. He encouraged the education of the working class by starting night schools for boys on his estates; he insisted that the local Board of Guardians should pay a higher rate of relief wages than they wanted to and also pay bachelors at the same rate as married men.

As for new inventions associated with the Industrial Revolution, he went in for these enthusiastically: he modernized agricultural methods and machinery, built cottages with new systems of drainage and, when many landowners were resisting the railway as a hideous modern intrusion to be kept as far away as possible, Lord Salisbury welcomed it on to his property, if its promoters would agree to place a station near enough to Hatfield House to be of use to himself. 'People who talk much of bridges and railways are generally Liberals,' said Lord Melbourne to the young Queen Victoria. The Second Marquess of Salisbury was an exception to this ironic generalization. His views on railways and wages were of the future, but he sought to impose them with the authority of one who maintained his right to act as their hereditary overlord. Once there was an outbreak of cattle disease near Hatfield. Lord Salisbury was up to date enough to recognize the importance of segregating cattle coming from the district where the disease had appeared. But he did not wait to get this done through the local authority legally responsible for such matters. Instead he went down himself, stood in the middle of the highway and turned back any cattle coming from the infected area.

What the farmer who owned the cattle thought of this arbitrary interference is not recorded. But it is possible that he accepted it submissively enough. The rural population around Hatfield did not dislike the Second Marquess: they were rather proud of him. If he bullied them, so did most of their social superiors; and they realized that, unlike many of these, he had their interests at heart. Moreover, like his mother, he was a 'character' and they enjoyed hearing and telling anecdotes about him. He was less popular with his equals, especially if they were neighbours. The Matador had the defects of his fighting spirit and his independence. He was irascible, high-handed and egotistic; and these weaknesses were increased by the fact that fate had placed him in a position of power and privilege, surrounded by persons who dared not stand up to him. The result was that on his own ground he was domineering and quarrelsome. He had little respect for the opinion of others and a high respect for his own. He liked to record his achievements as landlord or builder or agriculturalist. At the end of each record he noted with satisfaction 'All done by me!'

III

He married twice. The first wife inaugurates a new phase in this history. She kept a diary; and, though it is a discreet ladylike affair, innocent of confessions and revelations, yet it does enable us to know her more intimately than any previous member of the family. She is worth knowing, too. For the third successive generation in the Salisbury family, the wife was superior to the husband: more intelligent and more civilized. Frances Mary Gascoyne came, indeed, from a more civilized milieu. She was the only child and heiress of Bamber Gascoyne the second, grandson of a Lord Mayor of London, Sir Crisp Gascoyne. He himself was during a short period a Member of Parliament; but he spent most of his life as a man of leisure, cultivated and intelligent, who – for he had inherited several fortunes – was able to pass the time in a manner appropriate to what his contemporaries called a 'man of taste and sense', collecting rare books and pictures, and with enough imagination to respond to the growing taste for romantic scenery.

Frances Mary, 2nd Marchioness of Salisbury, by Sir Thomas Lawrence, and James Gascoyne-Cecil, the 2nd Marquess, by John Lucas

His wife, Sarah Bridget Price, came from a similar background; she was the daughter of the prosperous Mr Chase Price, a genial vigorous personality, noted as an amusing talker, who was intelligently enterprising enough to have made friends with Rousseau during his sojourn in England. Through his half-sister-in-law, Mrs Boscawen, Chase Price was connected with a circle that included Dr Johnson, Dr Burney and Sir Joshua Reynolds. How far his wife shared his cultured interests we do not know; but her entertaining gossipy letters recall, if not Jane Austen's own, at least letters that one can imagine written by her livelier characters – Mary Crawford, perhaps, or Emma Woodhouse. The name of Jane Austen strikes a keynote. For though, because they were richer, the Gascoynes moved in grander society than she did, the tone audible in their letters and diaries is that of her world and characteristic of the late eighteenth-century English

A rainy country morning, drawn by Olivia de Roos and preserved by the 2nd Marchioness of Salisbury in one of her albums

gentry – the gentry rather than the nobility – at its best: respectable and sharp-witted and cultivated.

Frances Mary, born in 1802, showed herself from the first such a daughter as her world would approve of. As the only child of doting parents and the heiress to a large fortune, she was brought up with love and anxiety. But in fact she never seems to have given the slightest cause for worry. She was a pretty little girl good at her books and, says her mother, 'very desirous of doing Right and being a Young Lady as she calls it'.

*Reading the immortal Byron: another drawing by Olivia
de Roos from an album of the 2nd Marchioness*

This desire was satisfied. The Gascoyne heiress at seventeen years old was a model of what, by the standards of her age and rank, a young lady should be. Tall and graceful, with fine eyes, wavy dark hair and a sweet smile, she was above the average in looks; and her beauty was matched by her accomplishments. This appears in the albums and commonplace-books still to be seen at Hatfield. The albums were made up of contributions by herself and her friends: watercolour sketches of lakes and rivers, skits and caricatures of fashionable life and lyrics on lace-edged paper in the manner of Tom Moore. The commonplace-books reveal her serious side and contain passages from an impressive list of authors English and foreign, ancient and modern: Rousseau and Montesquieu, Bossuet and Johnson, Cowper, Clare and Coleridge. It is likely that the standard of culture in England was higher in the early nineteenth century than today. But Frances Mary Gascoyne was unusually cultivated even for her period. Her culture was expressive of solid qualities. She was sensitive and conscientious and modest and pious. She also had the brain to take an interest in public affairs and the touch of imagination which, nourished by the novels of Scott and the poems of Byron, led her to respond to the romance of history and of foreign lands. She added to all this an unusual capacity for hero-worship.

Hero-worship is not a humorous activity. Frances Mary, in spite of the skits and caricatures, did lack humour. The model young lady, as disclosed in her diary, had her limitations: her well-informed mind was not original and her excellent moral principles tended to make her narrow. Once more the reader is reminded of the novels of Jane Austen. Frances Mary recalls their more solemn heroines: Elinor Dashwood, without her saving touch of irony; Fanny Price, if she had not been shy in company. She also had Fanny's anxious care for propriety and her taste for the romantic and picturesque. In all this she was of a new generation. The Victorian Age had not yet arrived, but it had begun to cast its shadow before it, especially in its ideal of what a young girl should be. There was something Victorian about Frances Mary Gascoyne.

Meanwhile her future looked like being rosy. Marriage was then the object of a girl's life, and she had every chance of marrying well. In the higher ranks of society marriage was not a wholly private affair entered into for personal reasons but rather a social arrangement for maintaining the institution of the family. A young man grew up accepting the view that he should choose a wife likely to help him to support his fortunes and carry out his duty in the state of life to which it had pleased God and the social order to call him. Further, since marriage was a social arrangement, he ought at least to consider the opinion of his parents in selecting his bride. For her the approval of parents was a necessity. Good parents would have thought it wrong to impose a husband on a girl against her will; but there was no question of her marrying someone they disliked. Finally, it was usual, though not universal, that a young man should ask permission of parents before paying addresses to a daughter.

This was soon to happen to Frances Mary Gascoyne. Within two years she was to have four suitors, all peers or heirs to a peerage. There was Lord Garvagh, Lord Burford, Lord Erroll, and Lord Cranborne. Lord Garvagh, forty-one years old and a widower, was first in the field. He proposed directly in a letter; but, to comply with convention, enclosed it in one to Mr Gascoyne to be forwarded only if it was thought likely to be well received. It looks as if Mr Gascoyne did not think so; no more is heard of Lord Garvagh. Lord Burford might be thought to have a better chance, for he was heir to the Dukedom of St Albans. Moreover his mother was anxious for the match. The trouble was with Lord Burford himself, described by the lively Lady Cooper as 'neither bad or actually an idiot but yet a very raw uncultivated strange cub'; and even his mother could find no more to say in his favour than that the Headmaster of Eton had once praised him for backing the authorities during a school rebellion. This was hardly enough recommendation to melt the heart of a pretty and accomplished heiress.

In June 1820 she went to stay with Lord and Lady Verulam at Gorhambury and found herself the first morning at breakfast seated next to young Lord Cranborne; the same night the party drove over to Hatfield for a ball. By the time the visit was ended both had become interested in each other. The interest was both worldly and sentimental. Lord Cranborne felt drawn to Miss Gascoyne's personality and also to her fortune. Miss Gascoyne's heart and imagination was stirred alike by the Matador's personality and by the historic associations of his home and name. Lady Salisbury heard of the budding romance and approved. She wanted her son and heir to marry someone with the money to repair the ravages in the family fortunes made by her parties and card debts. Accordingly she opened negotiations by arranging a meeting with the Gascoyne family where, after pointing out her son's advantages of birth, she proposed that the young people should be encouraged to see much of each other with a view to marriage. Mr Gascoyne received this overture with polite caution. Though he realized, he said, that it would be an honour to be connected with the Cecil family, he did not want it to get about that the young people were already, as it were, earmarked for each other, so that Frances would lose all chance of ever getting to know other young men. Lady Salisbury tactfully agreed that it might be wiser that things should be left as they were.

Even so, the romance became sufficiently talked about to disturb the Duchess of St Albans, who saw Lord Burford's chances of getting his heiress receding. She therefore wrote a letter to Mrs Gascoyne alluding lightly to the fact that she understood that Lord Cranborne kept 'a little French establishment' in London; also that he was on very friendly terms – she *hoped* that these were Platonic – with Lady Mary Dewhurst. Mrs Gascoyne hurried round to Lord Verulam to inquire agitatedly about Lord Cranborne's morals. Lord Verulam soothed her fears. It was now that Lord Erroll, rather late, entered the scene with a letter of proposal, cool and formal in tone and explaining that he would have come in person had he not been suffering from a cold in the head. The only effect of this unromantic communication was that within a few weeks Frances Mary became engaged to Lord Cranborne. Lord Erroll quickly cut his losses, and six months later he married Elizabeth Fitzclarence, the illegitimate daughter of a royal duke. Meanwhile Lord Burford had made a final offer, only to be refused. Five years afterwards he wedded Mrs Coutts, the rich widow of a banker but twenty-six years older than himself.

The Cranborne wedding was delayed by complex legal negotiations about the marriage settlements. The bridegroom's mother was characteristically impatient. 'Those infernal lawyers cannot be ready; so the infernal ceremony cannot be till Tuesday,' she protested. At last on the 22nd of February 1821 the marriage took place at eight in the evening in the saloon of Mr Gascoyne's house in London.

The Cecils of Hatfield House

Though small and private, as weddings were at that period, it was a sufficiently grand affair; for the Duke of Wellington, the greatest man in England, gave away the bride. Later there were lavish feudal celebrations at Hatfield, with a ball for the County and unlimited ale for the tenants.

The marriage was a success. It is true that Lord Cranborne was said to be a hot-tempered husband; there is even a story of poor Frances Mary bursting into tears because he scolded her in front of the gardener. Yet in 1835 we find her writing, 'Few persons can boast as I can thirteen years have only added to my attachment and sense of my husband's worth'; and he wrote after her death that, during the nineteen years they had lived together, they had not known what it was to have a difference. He seems to have forgotten the scene in the presence of the gardener.

Happy or not, the Second Marchioness's life was fully occupied. Before 1834 she had given birth to seven children, five of which lived to grow up. In 1823 her husband succeeded to the title and a larger life now opened before her, politically and socially. Frances Mary, following her husband, became a militant High Tory, violently opposed to the Liberal Movement. The campaign for the Reform Bill of 1832 found Lord Salisbury in the thick of the fight. Stones were thrown at his carriage as he drove through the neighbouring town of Hertford; and when he got up to speak at a public meeting he was hardly allowed to utter a word. 'Poor, dear little Lord Salisbury', said an observer, 'in a large drab grey coat looked very miserable.' Such happenings made his wife's blood boil; so did the sight of Lord Grey, the promoter of the dreadful Bill. 'The Wilful Destroyer of his Country,' she called him; and when she heard that her friend Miss Grimstone was engaged to a member of the Whig Party – 'I regard her as lost to me!' wrote Lady Salisbury.

Meanwhile she must play her part in a crowded social life in London and at Hatfield; presiding at dinner parties, and garden parties, and house parties and private theatricals – Lady Salisbury's performances in these were a little too much like those of a professional actress, commented aristocratic and sharp-tongued Miss Eden – and at a magnificent series of tableaux in which the rank and fashion of England appeared as characters in the Waverley novels. Lady Salisbury was an admired social figure. But I doubt if she enjoyed herself very much. She did get pleasure out of talking to interesting men; it is a proof of her genuine intelligence that she forgot her prejudices when conversing with witty, wicked Talleyrand, or Brougham, that sinister architect of the accursed Reform Bill: 'I thought him one of the most agreeable men I ever saw,' she said; and, though

Lady Emily Mary Hill, 1st Marchioness of Salisbury, by Sir Joshua Reynolds

Overleaf The Grand Review of Troops at Hatfield by George III on the 13th of June 1800

she described the young Disraeli as 'superlatively vulgar', she liked him. But, except for these pleasant interchanges with clever men, she seldom speaks with zest of her social experiences.

Indeed, the effect of her diaries in general is low-spirited and anxious. One wonders why. She did, it is true, have one considerable cause for anxiety. Her eldest son, Lord Cranborne, born sickly and undersized, was gradually showing signs of also growing blind and deaf. Yet this does not completely account for her depression. She seems to have been a conscientious rather than a devoted mother – there is little about her children in the diary – and moreover her sadness seems the expression of a general mood rather than of a particular trouble. Was it caused by some emotional frustration, a sense of something lacking in her marriage? Or was it the result of a feeling of insecurity arising from a perception that the world was changing and, from the point of view of one who believed in ancient traditions, changing for the worse?

No doubt, too, she was made graver by her responsibilities. Frances Mary's position matured her and brought out her fundamental seriousness. By the time her diary starts in 1837, she has lost all outward trace of girlishness and is now a pattern Tory great lady deeply conscious of her duties and growingly concerned in those political issues which have always been the chief serious interest of the English aristocracy. In her case there was a personal reason for this, her friendship with the great Duke of Wellington. We do not know when she first met him. He was already a friend of the Salisbury family when she married, for, as we have seen, he was asked to give her away as a bride. Starting, however, as a friend of both husband and wife, he gradually became the special friend of the wife. By 1832 this friendship was the chief interest of her existence.

It was a friendship, not a love affair. Apart from anything else, there were thirty years between them; and the passions of the Duke, now in his late sixties, may be presumed to have cooled enough to prevent him from entering into a love affair with the wife of an old friend. But he was the type of very masculine man who is dependent on women's society. He needed a sympathetic female friend, and it did not matter if she was young. On the contrary, the Duke liked to take a paternal role instructing delightfully a youthful admirer. Further, though he appeared indifferent to flattery, in fact he enjoyed admiration more than most people; and he got it from Frances Mary. The Duke was exactly the hero to call out all her natural capacity for hero-worship: the greatest man in England, victor of Napoleon, champion of the old traditions against the new Liberalism, and all this besides being, in his own curt, caustic style, a man of considerable charm. As

Hatfield House: Queen Victoria's Bedroom

for his age, it made him appear wiser, and perhaps safer. The fact that she became so deeply absorbed in him suggests that, consciously or not, she felt the want in her life of a man to look up to; but prudence and principle alike led her to shrink from a man who might approach her in the role of a possible lover. There was no such reason to shrink from one who assumed that of a father. From this time on, the Duke is the main subject of the diary. They met regularly in London or at Hatfield, and she stayed with him at his home at Strathfieldsaye, or accompanied him on other country-house visits. They walked together, rode together, conversed together of an evening.

The talk was often about current politics. The Duke confided to Frances Mary his political plans and anxieties and asked her advice, all in a delightfully easy and relaxed fashion. 'With you I think aloud,' he told her. In return she would sympathize and make suggestions: perhaps it would be wise for him to see more of Sir Robert Peel, or was the Duke sure he was right to threaten resignation over the Irish Tithe Appeal? In the small, homogeneous social and political world of those days, personal relations counted for a great deal, and women as rulers of the social world often played an important part in easing these relations. Frances Mary was also the Duke's confidante in more private matters. He talked to her about his late wife – 'one of the most foolish women that ever existed', he said; and he complained that she had spoiled her sons by giving them too high an idea of themselves. The Duke thought poorly of his sons, especially of his heir, Lord Douro. On one occasion Frances Mary thought to improve relations between the two by carrying a friendly message from Douro to the Duke. For once the Duke was not pleased with her. Kindly but firmly he warned her not to intervene between father and son in this way.

His own problems formed only a part of the subject-matter of the Duke's conversation. The diary records him as giving voice to his forcible and individual opinions on every sort of subject: on English public schools, which he praised unexpectedly as encouraging independence and originality of character; on the fact that, in his experience, women were generally better read and better educated than men; on alcohol, which he thought should not be drunk except for medical purposes; and on poets – 'I hate the whole race of them,' said the Duke; 'there never existed a more worthless set than Byron and his friends'; on the royal family – he called George IV the 'greatest vagabond that ever lived' and Caroline, his Queen, the 'most impudent devil and never handsome'. These pungent pronouncements often raise a smile and, from what we know of the Duke, it is likely that he meant them to do so: a tough irony was one of his characteristics. Frances Mary, however, was innocent of irony, and reports his sayings with a reverent gravity which adds to their comic effect.

Much of the Duke's talk was taken up with reminiscences of his campaigns,

Sir Crisp Gascoyne, ancestor of the 2nd Marchioness of Salisbury, by William Keable, and right Arthur Wellesley, 1st Duke of Wellington, by Sir David Wilkie

in particular about the Waterloo campaign, both during the battle and afterwards while he was riding through the streets of Brussels. 'While you were riding then,' she interrupted excitedly, 'did it never occur to you that you had placed yourself on such a pinnacle of glory?' 'No,' he replied, 'I was entirely occupied with what was necessary to be done.' In 1831 the Salisburys and Wellington went to Belgium together, and Frances Mary had the thrilling experience of being taken round the field of Waterloo by its hero. Equally thrilling was a week's visit to Oxford in 1834 to watch the Duke presiding as Chancellor of the University at the annual June celebrations. Frances Mary's imaginative sense of the romantic past was deeply stirred by Oxford's medieval buildings. 'When one looks at these beautiful and peaceful cloisters,' she writes, 'one may for a moment understand the fascination that would induce the choice of a monastic life.' Even more stirring was the reception given there to the Duke by the students. 'They roared,' she related, 'they screamed, they waved hats and handkerchiefs, they actually jumped and danced with delight. It was quite overcoming: such a moment, the witnessing of such homage to the greatest man existing was worth any trouble and any sacrifice!' She fully shared the students' feelings and, if it had been decorous, no doubt she would have roared and jumped and danced with delight herself.

The Cecils of Hatfield House

By this time hero-worship had warmed to a steady, unchanging white heat. Almost every reference to him in the diary is followed by a word of praise for some fresh quality she has noticed in him: his kindness to children, his beautiful seat on a horse, the graceful dignity of his appearance in an academic gown. As for those who dared to criticize him, she cannot mention them with patience; she even speaks severely of Lady Frances Egerton for spreading the rumour that the Duke is 'low in spirits'. Once or twice in the diary she recognizes that her hero had his weaknesses. For instance, she notes that he has come to expect praise and is liable to be offended if he does not get it. Such a criticism, however, is very rare; indeed, it comes oddly from one who herself has overwhelmed him so often with unmeasured praise. 'There must be a satisfaction', she told him, 'and a lasting one in that feeling of superiority you always enjoy . . . you are equally great in the Cabinet and in the field.' Her own highest point of happiness was when the Duke called her his friend. She writes with rapture, 'He called me his friend twice over with emphasis as if he would have said "my first and best friend" . . . I sometimes think how can I be worthy of the friendship of such a man; what have I done to deserve the highest honour a woman can attain to be his friend?'

In these passages she shows that beneath her mature and dignified demeanour Frances Mary preserved all her innocent girlish faculty for hero-worship. Alas! fashionable society was still too near the days of the rakish Regency to believe in innocent hero-worship. The friendship began to give rise to talk. One day Lord Salisbury got an anonymous letter coarsely accusing Lady Salisbury of being Wellington's mistress. It was the good side of the Matador's contempt for public opinion that he seems to have taken no notice of this. The Duke, however, was more concerned: the fact that he was fond of Frances Mary made him feel especially responsible for her reputation. In 1837 she proposed visiting him at Walmer. He replied that he would be delighted to receive her, but that for the sake of her reputation she simply must bring her husband with her.

The Duke's figure dominates the diary, but Frances Mary also talks about her relations-in-law. These were a source of more anxiety than pleasure. Lord Salisbury had two sisters, Lady Westmeath and Lady Cowley. Lady Westmeath would have been a trial to any respectable family. First she got heavily into debt, and her brother had several times to pay up for her. Then Lord Westmeath divorced her, a rare occurrence in those days and one that was looked on as a shocking disgrace to her relations. It led to a violent quarrel with her mother, the Dowager Sally, who rebuked her erring daughter with eighteenth-century outspokenness. Lady Cowley was an improvement on her sister in that she never ran up debts or got divorced, but Frances Mary did not care for her either. She found her unreliable and ill-tempered. Worse, she actually refused on one occasion to accompany her as chaperone on a visit to the Duke.

As for the old Dowager, she was the most troublesome of them all. Frances Mary admitted that she was friendly enough to herself, but she could not but resent the endless anxiety she caused her son Lord Salisbury by her extravagance and her caprices. Besides, she was a character of a kind Frances Mary especially disliked – coarse, showy and selfish. After the Dowager's death, her daughter-in-law wrote in her diary, 'If it had happened in the common course of nature I could not pretend to grieve; her conduct has not been such as to inspire me with respect or affection; though personally to me she had always been kind and obliging . . . for the rest God is her judge. She had far more excuses and more temptations probably in the course of her long life than many of us have and I trust stands acquitted in His sight.'

IV

The Second Marchioness of Salisbury did not long survive her mother-in-law. In the autumn of 1838 she was seized with a mysterious illness; she got steadily worse during the next year. On the 19th of October 1839 she died. Lord Salisbury was grief-stricken. It is evidence of his affection and also of the value he put on her judgment that he set to work to continue his children's education on lines she had started and to supervise it himself. He corrected their essays and had the children into his dressing-room to give them lessons in history. Unlike many of his contemporaries, he thought that it was as important to educate girls as boys, and on the same lines. Indeed, he made little allowance for feminine weakness. It was not uncommon for him, after coming back from the House of Lords at eleven at night, to be seized with a sudden wish to be at Hatfield; and then, 'Get up and dress, girls!' he would shout, and he would be much annoyed if they were not ready to start within a few minutes.

His character was such as not to make him an easy father; and he grew less of one. Bereft of Frances Mary's influence, he grew more unreasonable and more domineering. As the years passed, ill humour went along with a growing pessimism about the state of the world. We who are living in the precarious twentieth century are disposed to look back to the Victorian age as a peaceful period with England growing every year stronger and more prosperous. It did not look like this to the Second Marquess of Salisbury. On the contrary, all the fears he had entertained in 1832 seemed in the process of being confirmed. Even those persons who set up to defend ancient traditions roused his disapproval – what did the Tory Party mean by choosing a vulgar Jew like Disraeli to be their leader? – and he suspected that the High Church movement, conservative though it claimed to be, was really a plot to sell England into the power of the Pope. Finally, like ageing persons in every period, he complained that the younger generation showed no respect

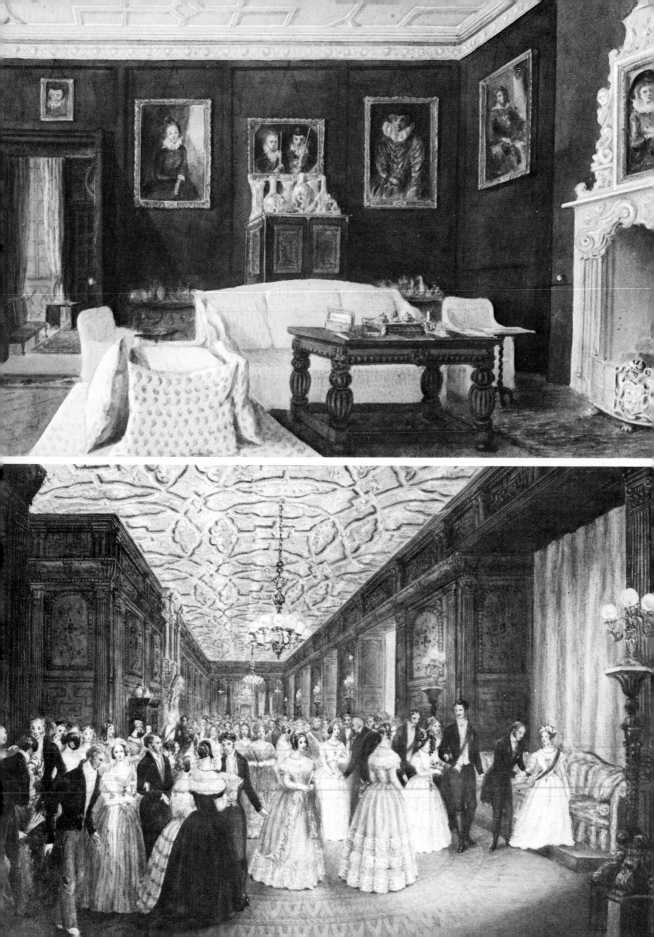

for law and order. Altogether the future looked dark. Every morning he opened the newspaper; and then, 'It is all very bad. Depend upon it, the end of the world is coming,' said Lord Salisbury.

This gloomy prospect, however, did not affect his mode of living. Existence at Hatfield continued on its splendid and spacious way. In 1846 Queen Victoria and the Prince Consort came to stay. The state bedrooms were redecorated in red and gold for them and a ball was held in their honour. Neither guest made a good impression on the company. The Prince Consort smiled at nobody; instead, he stared restlessly about, now and again fixing his eyes on someone and then whispering about that person to the Queen. She was more affable; but she joined in the whispering and looked unbecomingly fat.

In 1847, at the age of fifty-six, Lord Salisbury married again; his bride was twenty-three, Lady Mary Sackville-West, daughter of the Fifth Earl de la Warr. She was a very different character from Frances Mary: a sharp-witted, ambitious young woman out to cut a figure in the world and not very scrupulous about how she did it. It seems unlikely that she married the elderly Matador for any but worldly reasons, and she was later to acquire a reputation for intrigue and mischief-making. However, she filled her position effectively enough; Hatfield was more than ever a centre of social and political life, and she herself became an influential figure in the great world and the friend of some of the most important men of the day.

In the intervals of her social activities she helped Lord Salisbury with the work of embellishing his houses. During these later years he restored Cranborne, fallen into disrepair, into something of its original beauty; at Hatfield he gilded the Gallery ceiling, refashioned the Library and pretty well re-created the gardens. One evening in 1868 he went round house and grounds on a tour of inspection. 'There is not a more perfect place in all England,' he remarked with satisfaction. A few months later he was dead.

The Yew Room, Hatfield House, in 1843, and Queen Victoria at the ball given for her in the Long Gallery on the 23rd of October 1846

Part III
I
ROBERT CECIL
Third Marquess of Salisbury

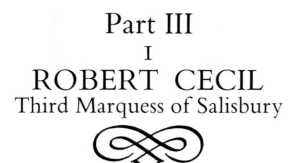

LORD CRANBORNE, the blind invalid, died in 1865, so that the Second Marquess was succeeded by his second surviving son, Robert. With him a new epoch opens in the family history. The next batch of Hatfield ghosts is very different from its forerunner, and is more interesting. For the first time in two hundred and fifty years the Cecils of Hatfield were important by virtue of their own talents and not just because they happened to be born rich and blue-blooded. They remained so for more than one generation. The members of these generations, along with strong individual characteristics, do bear a common and family stamp, put on them by their originator, Robert, the Third Marquess.

He was my grandfather; and, though I cannot remember him – he died when I was a year old – his spirit persisted as a living influence over my childhood and I knew his children very well indeed. This means that it is impossible for me to write of him or them in the tone of objective detachment with which I have sought to write about their ancestors: I am too close to them to be able to see them in any kind of general perspective. Further, though I have grown up to diverge from them in many ways, yet I so much admired and delighted in those I knew, that it would be disingenuous for me to write of them except from a point of view confessedly personal and affectionate.

The fact that my relationship with them was personal, not to say private, also means that my portrait will concentrate on their private and personal aspects: I shall not do more than touch on their professional lives. Since, like their Elizabethan ancestors, they were servants of Church and State and equally dedicated to their work, it might seem that so private a portrait would be hopelessly inadequate as a likeness. But – and here they differed from the Elizabethans – they wore no masks. To know them privately was to know them publicly.

As I have said, it was my grandfather who set the tone for them. He was the most original personality the Cecils ever produced, and a man of remarkable

Robert Cecil, 3rd Marquess of Salisbury, by George Richmond, 1861

217

character and intelligence. Why they should have started producing remarkable people at this moment in their history is as unaccountable as why they should have stopped doing so at the beginning of the seventeenth century. It seems unlikely that the gifts of the Elizabethan Cecils should have suddenly and inexplicably reappeared after lying latent for two hundred and fifty years. On the other hand neither the Keets, nor the Hills, nor the Gascoynes, separately or in combination, were of a mental calibre to account for my grandfather.

His was a success story, a success that would have come as a surprise to those who had only known him in his youth. I know of him mainly from my mother, and as he appeared in his old age: an archetypal father-figure, bearded, venerable, benignant, surveying the world with a contemplative gaze and uttering from time to time sentences, brief and ironic, which yet seemed the expression of a profound wisdom. My mother, when she was young and eager and idealistic, once spoke to him agitatedly about the failure of some philanthropic scheme which she believed in. He answered her soothingly. 'But, Lord Salisbury,' she urged, 'surely this failure matters very much.' My grandfather smiled gently. 'My dear,' he said, 'nothing matters *very* much.' Taken in isolation this statement did not represent his point of view. He had religious and moral convictions that mattered supremely to him and also a fighting spirit which even in old age could break out and ruffle his detachment. But it is true that he had grown to look at things in the context of God's eternity and in relation to the whole long perspective of human history; with the result that he had learned to feel, genuinely and not just in theory, that nothing that occurred during his transient lifetime did matter very much.

This was my grandfather in old age. In youth he appeared very different: a lean, awkward, angular young man at once intolerant and lacking in self-confidence, quivering with nerves and strong convictions and subject to acute fits of melancholy. His early experience had not been such as to make him cheerful. By nature he was the kind of boy that finds it hard to adapt himself to life; on the one hand hypersensitive and precociously intellectual, on the other clumsy, sickly and unsociable. Nor did his parents help him to be adaptable. His father was remote and unsympathetic, and his mother died when he was nine. In any case he had already for three years been out of her hands. He had been sent when only six years old to a boarding school near Hatfield kept by a Mr Faithful. There he was so horribly tormented that, up to the very end of his life, he could hardly bear to speak of it. 'My existence there was an existence amongst devils,' he said.

At the age of ten he went to Eton. This proved as bad as Mr Faithful's. His housemaster, indeed, was impressed by the intelligence of the 'frail little boy who wrote such clever essays', though he complained that he was inexcusably grubby and untidy. The boys persecuted him. What made their persecution especially

Eton College in 1890

unpleasant was that, since he was advanced for his age, those he had to associate with were older than himself and therefore bigger and stronger. Moreover, they decided that, since he was so unnaturally and unpleasantly intelligent, he might make himself useful by doing their homework for them. Here they came up against an unexpected and steely strain in him. The 'frail little boy' did not see why he should do all this extra work; and he refused. This showed more courage than good sense on his part, and he suffered for it. Night after night he crept to bed black and blue from bruises. But he would not give in; instead he tried to get a little comfort from stuffing himself with cakes at the pastrycook's – this gave him indigestion – and relieving his feelings by pouring out his misery in letters to his father, from whom, however, he feared he might get little sympathy.

I know you do not like complaints, and I have tried to suppress them and conceal all this, but you are the only person to whom I can safely confide these things. Really now Eton has become unsupportable. I am bullied from morning to night without ceasing. I am obliged to hide myself all the evening in some corner to prevent being bullied, and if I dare venture from my room I get it directly . . . When I come in to dinner they kick and shin me and I am obliged to go out of dinner without eating anything and to avoid it because of that. I hardly have any time to do lessons because I pass so much time in being bullied. I get a punishment regularly every morning because I have no time to learn my lessons . . .

And later:

I have been kicked most unmercifully since I wrote to you last for refusing to do a fellow's theme and get the sense for it . . . He kicked me and pulled my hair and pinched me, and hit me as hard as ever for twenty minutes, and now I am aching in every joint and hardly able to write this . . . I seldom go to bed till much past eleven, as I cannot get to my room till they are all gone to bed. You see my age is so much against me, for the boys in my part of the school are three years, if not more, older than myself. Then besides, I am not strong nor healthy, both of which things are to be in a great degree attributable to Eton. For though I have tried every method, I have never been able to refrain from those sock-shops, and in consequence I am often ill and so lose a great deal of strength.

Boys at Eton, and Lady Mildred with Lady Blanche Cecil, sisters of the 3rd Marquess of Salisbury, about 1825

After a succession of such communications his father was at last moved to complain to his son's housemaster. But it did no good, and my grandfather's life of torment continued. He grew to hate Eton so much that when in London during the holidays he would never venture into a main street for fear of meeting a schoolfellow there. Gradually his work and his health began to deteriorate; so much so that after two years his father did take him away. But his ordeal had left a permanent mark on him. On the one hand, brought face to face as he had been at an early age with the cruelty and injustice inherent in primitive human nature, he grew up hoping little of man in the mass; on the other, there was burned into him a passionate belief in a man's right to do and think as he wishes, however much the majority of his fellows disagreed with him, and a contempt for those who surrender that right to placate the majority.

The next two years, spent at Hatfield with a tutor, were happier. Insofar as he had company, it was congenial. He was not the only intelligent member of this generation of Cecils. His blind elder brother studied the French Revolution and wrote historical essays; his elder sister Blanche was interested in politics and liked talking to her younger brother about them. But his relations were often away, and he passed much of his time alone in the tranquillity of the Library, reading books in English, French, Latin, Greek and exploring the subjects that specially appealed to him.

These were limited. My grandfather was curiously unaesthetic. He took pleasure in style of the polished eighteenth-century kind and enjoyed an intelligent, entertaining novel – Pope and Jane Austen were to be favourite authors of his – but he had no feeling for painting or music or architecture and was inclined to be impatient with those who set a serious value on such feelings. Nor did he care for metaphysics: he saw no value in philosophic speculation that could not be practically applied. But he was deeply interested in history, biography, mathematics and especially the sciences; in physics, chemistry, biology and botany. Botany was the one thing that took him out of doors. He disliked all forms of sport; but he would pass whole days roaming the countryside in search of plants – looking, incidentally, such a ragamuffin that he was once arrested by a farmer who thought he was a poacher's boy. Throughout his life my grandfather was eccentrically indifferent to his own appearance. In later years, and when Prime Minister of England, he was refused admittance to the Casino in Monte Carlo because his clothes were so disreputable that he was taken to be a tramp.

Meanwhile his most serious attention was already given to the two subjects which were to be the chief interests of his maturity. The first was politics. So long as the English aristocracy was a governing class, almost all its intelligent sons went into politics; and for once my grandfather was no exception to the rule. Already at Eton he was writing to his sister about the Corn Laws and the Irish Question.

The Cecils of Hatfield House

Now at Hatfield he began to study the subject of government more thoroughly and to develop his own views on it. The other topic to engage his most serious attention was theology. Here he does seem a throwback to Lord Burghley: like him he was born with a strongly religious temperament, and this found fulfilment early. Some time before he was out of his teens he underwent a momentous spiritual experience. What form it took no one knows, for he never said. But his daughter Gwendolen, who knew him better than anyone else, thought that it involved an intimate sense of what he believed to be the living and personal presence of Christ. This experience was so overwhelming that it became the foundation of a faith that was to endure unshaken till death; and it conditioned his permanent and basic attitude to life. Naturally enough he grew deeply interested in the theology that interpreted spiritual experiences like his.

My grandfather's nature was an odd paradoxical mixture. His general intellectual approach was practical and realistic; he was interested in science because it dealt with facts that could be proved or disproved by experiment, and in history because it shed useful light on the forces that shaped the fate of man. But he combined this with a mystical, intuitive awareness of spiritual forces that are not to be apprehended through the senses, and which he felt were even more profoundly influential on human destiny. His temperament and his mind were also at odds. His mental attitude was detached, questioning, sceptical of the value of human effort. But his temperament was that of a man of action, ready for a fight and, once committed to it, fiercely combative. All his life these various and incongruous strains were to coexist within him, never to be wholly reconciled. The mixture gave its individual flavour to his personality. But it troubled him and bewildered others.

II

At seventeen he proceeded to Christ Church, Oxford. Here he blossomed; though blossoming, suggesting as it does something festive and flowery, seems hardly the word to describe his strenuous years at the University. But his spirit expanded at Oxford. He plunged into undergraduate politics, joined societies, made speeches, read papers. These were often so disrespectful of authority that some of his hearers thought him a Radical. In fact, he was an aggressive High Tory. Oxford helped him to clarify and strengthen these High Tory opinions. There too his religious views took a more definite shape. The High Church Movement was still active, and my grandfather also came across it at the house of his sister Mildred, who had married a pious newspaper-owner called Beresford-Hope. My grandfather was attracted to the High Church Movement: he liked its definite intellectual position and especially its sacramental doctrine, its

The pond in the Tom Quad, Christ Church, Oxford

teaching that, when partaking of the consecrated bread and wine, the communicant was in direct contact with the living spirit of Christ. The sacrament became the centre of my grandfather's religion. During the rest of his long life he hardly ever failed to partake of it on a Sunday.

For the rest, he spent his time at Oxford working and holding discussions with young men who had the same interests as himself. The drinking and hunting set of the college was displeased by the spectacle of these earnest youths and one day plotted to seize upon one of them, who particularly irritated them, and throw him into a pond in the middle of the college quad. The earnest youths heard of this plot and hesitated what to do. Not so my grandfather: realizing that offence is also the best defence, and also perhaps because he liked the idea of getting his own back on the kind of young male who had made his life at Eton miserable, he organized a plan of resistance. He and his friends waited till the invaders were halfway up the stairs to their victim's room and then swept down and routed them so completely that from that day on the serious were left to be serious in peace. The incident has always interested me, partly because it reveals the fighting spirit that was to mark my grandfather's political career, but still more because it is the only one recorded of his youth where he shows a sense of fun. This is very surprising, because in his later years humour was one of his outstanding characteristics: a robust, mischievous, ironic humour which pervaded his talk and was always glinting out unexpectedly to brighten a speech or a dispatch. Such humour is bred in the bone, and he must have had it in his youth.

My guess, however, is that it was bitterer and harsher than it became later. Good humour is the expression of happiness; my grandfather at this stage of his career was not happy. He had not come to terms with the world; his early experience of it had been too painful, and so he was ill at ease with his fellow beings. Finally, he was also unhappy because he was ill, subject to attacks, partly emotional, partly physical, in which he was at the same time sunk in black depression and physically so sensitive that he could hardly bear the lightest touch or the softest noise. These grew so bad that at last his doctor recommended him to leave Oxford before taking a degree and try if foreign travel might do him good. He passed the next two years in South Africa and Australia and New Zealand.

The records of his travels present us with a curious picture. A pale, round-shouldered youth, very thin and very tall, he seems to have spent his time mainly with clergymen and missionaries, discussing questions of theology. But now and again he caught a glimpse of life in the raw, especially in Australia. Here a gold rush was in progress, so that the place was thronged with shady adventurers and rough ex-convicts, all out for what they could get and all more or less lawless, drunken and immoral. With mingled interest and distaste, my grandfather watched the unedifying spectacle and drew his conclusions. He was confirmed in the view he had acquired at Eton that the natural man was a deplorable object. Moreover, he noted that the better-off were often the worst. The unfortunate ex-convicts could be partly excused because they had been brutalized by what my grandfather recognized as the inhuman system of transportation; but there was no such excuse for the middle-class speculators who, he also noticed, were often irreligious. My grandfather boldly generalized. 'I am convinced', he said, 'that the turbulence as well as every other evil temper in this evil age belongs not to the lower but to the middle class.'

He returned to England improved in health and with a beard. But he was no more reconciled to the world than when he started his journey. All the same he had to live in it, and that meant joining a profession. But what profession? Unhopefully he poured out his thoughts on the subject in a letter to his father. It was only a question of duty, he said, for all modes of life were equally uninviting to him. He would have chosen politics, but he saw no chance of getting a seat in Parliament; or the Church, but he thought he was too bad at getting on with people to be any good as a pastor. His father suggested the law. My grandfather said that he was disgusted by the English law, a monstrous out-of-date machine, whose only practical effect, so far as he could see, was to obstruct the course of justice. Altogether he felt himself at an impasse. However, a parliamentary seat suddenly fell vacant at Stamford, and his cousin Lord Exeter, a man of influence in the district, suggested that he should put up for it. He did, and was elected unopposed. He followed it up by competing for an All Souls Fellowship at Oxford, always regarded as a mark of high intellectual distinction. He won it.

These two events signified the start of my grandfather's career. After this for several years it marked time. He did not make much impression in Parliament: he was too shy to be a natural orator and, extreme High Tory as he was, he agreed with hardly anyone, even on his own side. Further, he found himself very critical of his fellow members, especially the party leaders. They seemed to him men of no principle, mainly concerned with manoeuvring for position and dishing their opponents. Meanwhile he became involved in two disputes with his father.

The first occurred in the spring of 1855 when the Matador proposed to appoint his son Colonel of the Middlesex Milita. Since he himself had loved soldiering, he thought no doubt that this was a piece of luck for his son. His son took a different view. 'Your proposition gave me a stomach-ache all this morning,' he wrote to him. 'I do not know whether I have sufficiently recovered my equanimity to write intelligibly, but I will try. First then as to my inclinations. I detest soldiering beyond measure. As far as taste goes I would sooner be at the treadmill.' He went on to say that he would not be able to combine his duties as a soldier with those at the House of Commons as his health would not stand it, and he ended: 'I have said nothing about my unfitness for the post – for that is your responsibility – not mine; and it is so ludicrously glaring that you cannot have overlooked it. The only point that affects me, the exposure to extreme contempt that I must face, will be rather a benefit to me than otherwise; for spite of many strenuous efforts at self-steeling, I care much too much for other people's contempt; and therefore the more I meet with it, the better for me.'

His father accepted his refusal; but it cannot have improved relations between the two. They were to become much worse a year later. My grandfather, though now twenty-five years old, had, so far as we know, never been in love. The only girls he had met were those he had come across on his rare excursions into London fashionable society, and with these he had nothing in common. Indeed, he had acquired, and was to retain, a distaste for such society. He thought the men in it, natives of what he called Clubland, were a self-satisfied, useless lot; and that the women were no better. As a young man he saw the world of fashion through Thackerayan eyes, as a marriage market where worldly mothers competed ruthlessly to find eligible husbands for their empty-headed daughters. But he was a man of normal sexual instincts; and his melancholy and loneliness of spirit made him particularly susceptible to feminine sympathy and understanding if he could find a woman qualified to give them to him.

In 1855 he found her. But not in fashionable society: Georgina Alderson, my grandmother to be, was the eldest daughter of Sir Edward Hall Alderson, son of a

Recorder of Norwich. After an academic career of extreme brilliance at Cambridge, Sir Edward had risen to be a Judge and a Baron of the Exchequer, the father of ten children, a leading figure in Church affairs and a distinguished ornament of that professional class from which so many of the great Victorians sprang. The Aldersons belonged to what would now be called the right wing of that class: Conservative and High Church, they associated mainly with dons, divines and fellow lawyers with opinions similar to their own. They themselves were cultured and educated, full of purpose and energy and strong convictions and high spirits. In London the men worked hard at their various professions, and the women threw themselves into Church and philanthropic activities. Yet the family also enjoyed itself, dining out, going to theatres and, at their country cottage near Lowestoft, pursuing an intense family life, boating, riding, reading and incessantly talking. Talking often involved arguing heatedly. The word 'Aldersonian' was used by my parents to denote a temperament highly strung, explosive and contradictious.

My grandmother was the most magnetic personality in her family. Though not pretty – she was short and square, with strong, aquiline features – she was yet made attractive by her fresh skin, shapely hands and piercing blue eyes; and still more by the vitality which radiated from her whole person and was audible even in the quick, firm sound of her footsteps. It showed most of all in her conversation, which was alive with strong opinions and vigorous humour and an appreciative interest in the personality of whomever she was talking to. It was this capacity to respond that brought her and my grandfather together. She seems to have been the first girl to perceive the distinction of mind and character that lay beneath his nervous aloofness and to pierce through it so as to bring him out. In the warmth of her personality the shy bud opened: my grandfather fell in love. He proposed and was accepted. It only remained to announce the engagement to his father.

Here the trouble began. The Matador objected furiously to the marriage. His reason was primarily financial: Miss Alderson had no fortune. He took it for granted that his son must marry a girl with a fortune; otherwise he would not be able to live in the manner appropriate to his rank and to associate with his social equals. He also took the view that his son was proposing to marry beneath him. Georgina Alderson came from a world that the Marquess of Salisbury knew little of – and that little he did not like. Were not the Aldersons High Church people and as such likely to be on the way to Rome? Finally, he was against the match on the grounds that Miss Alderson was two years older than her prospective bridegroom. He communicated all these objections to his son in forcible terms, demanding at any rate that the couple should not meet for six months. Once again he met with a forcible answer.

'Your objections to my marriage', wrote his son, 'rested mainly on the "privations" it would entail. "Privation" means the loss of something I enjoy now. If the privation in question is the want of food, warmth, clothing, I am not prepared to face it. But I cannot lose anything else I now enjoy, for the simple reason that I do not enjoy anything. Amusements I have none. The persons who will cut me because I marry Miss Alderson are precisely the persons of whose society I am so anxious to be quit. My marriage therefore cannot entail upon me any privations. I have considered the matter for very many months, anxiously and constantly. I have come to the conclusion that I shall probably do well in Parliament if I do marry, and that I shall certainly make nothing of it if I do not. In the latter case, therefore, it will be useless to worry myself with so arduous a life. I have further come to the conclusion that Miss Alderson suits me perfectly . . . I have agreed to a six months separation for the purpose of testing my resolution: for the demand, I believe, is not an unusual one. But, as I never remember to have receded from a resolution once deliberately taken, I do not anticipate much result from the present trial . . . I am exceedingly sorry that my adherence to this marriage should cause you annoyance: but my conviction that I am right is too strong for me to give it up: and it is my happiness not yours, that is at stake.'

He was as good as his word. Six months later he wrote, 'I have thought on the arguments you have laid before me with care and patience: and, if the results of that consideration should displease you, I can only say that I am very sorry, and that they have been conscientiously arrived at. The question of age seems to me entirely a matter of individual taste, in respect to which argument would be inapplicable. The idea of a Romanizing tendency – of which I should have as great a horror as any man – is a pure misconception, which I am sure you would not entertain for a moment if you had a closer acquaintance with Miss Alderson. The objection on which you laid the greatest stress was poverty; and that is a solid objection as far as it goes. It is a truism to say that want of means must to some extent involve a want of comfort. But this is only to a limited extent . . . The privation to me will be more a privation of social position than of actual sustenance. Now social position is a thing which depends for its value almost wholly on each man's individual taste: and, after careful examination, I cannot find anything in my individual tastes which would suffer by the neglect of the whole Court Guide. Of all the enjoyments – such as they have been – that I have been conscious of during the last few years, I do not know any that would be impaired by an ostracism from the fashionable world.'

In July 1857 my grandfather and my grandmother were married. His father did not attend the wedding, and he refused to increase his son's modest allowance. For some years the two hardly met.

I think my grandfather comes well out of this interchange with his father: the controlled and stylish force of his letters is admirable. His father, on the other hand, demonstrates once more his inability to understand his son. For in fact my grandfather's marriage was the luckiest thing that ever happened to him and the turning-point in his life. His early experience, though unhappy, had not been altogether a misfortune for him. It had developed his intellect, strengthened his character and made him admirably independent-minded. But he had to pay a price for these advantages, in a prevailing mood of melancholy, a sense of alienation from others, and a lack of self-confidence which might have turned out a fatal obstacle to his political aspirations.

My grandmother happened to be exactly equipped to overcome these disabilities. She herself was not a perfect character. Along with a full share of her family's highly strung, uncontrolled nerves – fearless on horseback, she would yet refuse to cross the Channel if the sea was rough – she possessed the defects of her forceful vitality. She could be high-handed and rough-tongued, biased and insensitive. But never to my grandfather. Dominating to others, she looked up to him. He became the centre and guiding star of her life, to whom she submitted absolutely; and her whole pattern of existence was designed to serve him and his work.

In other respects, too, she was his ideal counterpart. On the one hand she was religious and political and humorous; she was also ill-dressed and unaesthetic. Was she not once heard to speak regretfully of a cousin's 'unfortunate love of music'? On the other hand, unlike my grandfather, she was sociable and high-spirited. She believed in life and believed in him and so could help him to believe in himself. Finally she was able to put him into touch with humanity. Not humanity in general – that was always to be impossible for him – but humanity as embodied in her and, later, in his children. Naturally affectionate, at last he found objects on whom to direct his affection, and who returned it. The effect of this was that, though his view of human existence remained to the end on the sad side, he himself knew happiness in its most secure and lasting form – that of a happy family life. This immeasurably improved his morale.

III

After their wedding my grandparents settled down to a modest life in London. On nights when the House of Commons sat late she used to go down and listen to the debate from the Strangers' Gallery; when it was over the two would walk home together across the Park, shadowy in the grey light of the coming dawn, and talk over the debate. In general my grandfather was never to discuss his work, even with close colleagues; but from his earliest years he consulted his wife about it. Wisely; for, though she had no expert knowledge of political questions, she had, unlike him, a sharp eye for human character, including the character of individual politicians, and could help him to understand them. Stimulated by her mind and her sympathy, his speeches grew easier and livelier.

It was a happy time for both of them, apart from a certain amount of financial worry. Between 1857 and 1864 they had five children; and in consequence their expenses became so heavy that my grandfather even considered giving up politics. Instead, however, he settled down to try to increase his income by journalism. He wrote regularly for the *Saturday Review* and the *Quarterly Review*: short pieces about novels and travel and fashionable life, and longer, more considered discourses on historical figures like the younger Pitt, and much of course on current politics.

These longer pieces are still worth reading. They are vigorously written in an incisive, polished eighteenth-century manner and contain ideas that can still set one thinking. These ideas are eminently 'un-liberal'. In a tough, lively way my young grandfather was against equality, against democracy and against the doctrine of progress. As in his parliamentary speeches, he tended to state his views in a provocative form. He said he did this to make them livelier reading; but in fact he leapt at a chance to give rein to the combative strain in his make-up: he enjoyed the role of gadfly. He was ready to sting on all sides, too. Muddle-

William Pitt the Younger making one of the speeches studied by the Third Marquess

Benjamin Disraeli

William Ewart Gladstone, and the Earl of Derby who, as Prime Minister, invited the 3rd Marquess of Salisbury to become Under Secretary for India

headed believers in progress were the main object of his attacks, but he also went hard for the idlers of Clubland and the follies of the fashionable world; and for time-serving, unprincipled politicians, including some of the leaders of his own party. He was never to be a party man. Years later he was once asked if he sympathized with the sadness felt by some lifelong Liberals obliged by their conscience to leave the Liberal Party. 'Certainly not,' he replied; 'if the Conservatives abandoned the principles for which I joined them, I should walk for the last time down the steps of the Carlton Club without casting a glance of regret behind me.'

This emphasis on strict principle might lead one to think my grandfather was priggish. Mistakenly: gadflys are seldom prigs. Besides, married happiness, by raising his spirits, had brought out his impish sense of fun, with the result that his gloomiest prophecies sparkled with an exhilarating intellectual gaiety. So did his parliamentary performances. On one occasion he accused Gladstone, then Chancellor of the Exchequer, of behaving like an attorney rather than a statesman. Gladstone, solemnly offended, rose to request an apology. Next day my grandfather demurely gave it. He said that he realized his words had been too strong: 'I am only doing justice to my own feelings,' he said, 'when I avow that I did a great injustice to the attorneys!' No wonder Disraeli was to describe him as a 'great master of flouts and jeers'.

Disraeli had reason to know it: some of the sharpest had been directed at himself, for my grandfather disapproved of him as an outstanding example of the unscrupulous career politician. However, Disraeli did not hold this against him; after all, he had done a good deal of flouting and jeering himself in the past. One weekend, soon after launching a peculiarly vehement attack on him, my grandfather arrived at Hatfield to find that Disraeli was one of the party. He escaped into the garden and turned on to a path only to find himself face to face with him. 'Robert, Robert, how glad I am to see you!' said Disraeli, and advancing upon my grandfather he enfolded him in his arms. Disraeli was not touchy: this is one of the many agreeable facts about him.

He was also clever enough to perceive my grandfather's more solid qualities; and in 1866 it was with Disraeli's support that the Prime Minister, Lord Derby, invited my grandfather to join his government as Secretary for India. He accepted, but only after some hesitation. He could not bring himself wholly to trust a government of which Disraeli was a member. All too soon his hesitation proved justified. The late Liberal Government had been defeated over a Bill to extend the franchise. Now, only nine months later, Derby and Disraeli decided that the best way to keep the Liberals out in the future was to bring in a Bill of their own which would extend the franchise even further than the Liberals had proposed. Such an act was all that my grandfather disapproved of most. As he saw it, it meant betraying a basic principle for the sake of advancing party interests; and he immediately resigned.

Unquestionably he was right to do so. Had he not for years girded against politicians for not sticking to their principles? All the same his resignation was to his credit; for it might have meant losing his first and last chance of political power. Conservative leaders in the future were likely to fight shy of giving office to a man who, after years as a back-bencher, threw up his job within a few months of getting it, and gave publicly as his reason that he thought his leaders had acted dishonestly. In the event the resignation turned out to do him nothing but good. It gained him a reputation as a man of honour which he was never to lose, while its only effect on Disraeli was to make him think that a man at once so intelligent and so audacious was likely to be a great asset to the Conservative Party.

Within two years the Conservative Government fell and was out of office for some time. During his period in opposition, my grandfather increased his reputation as a powerful debater, first in the House of Commons and later in the House of Lords. For in 1868 his father died and he became Third Marquess of Salisbury. In 1874 the Conservatives came back to power and Disraeli, now Prime Minister, offered my grandfather the post of Secretary of State for India. Warned by hard experience, he hesitated once again; but in the end it seemed folly to him, and also to my grandmother, to refuse this second chance. He accepted.

It was the start of a steady crescendo of success. There were, it seems, two reasons for this. The first was that he was wiser and more effective in office than in opposition; for in office the aggressive strain in him, which tended to get out of hand in opposition, was checked by his realistic respect for the hard facts that now conditioned his political actions. The other reason for his success was that within a short time Disraeli began to make use of him in foreign affairs. This was to be the field in which he shone most. Foreign affairs suited his temperament. Independent, outspoken, and not at all afraid of responsibility, my grandfather preferred working on his own and without having to bother whether other people approved of the course he was taking. This was impossible in home affairs, where the House of Commons and the public were always watching and advising, and taking offence if their opinions were disregarded. Foreign affairs, on the other hand, were conducted in secret by means of negotiations with foreign diplomats, with whom it was best to speak one's mind courteously, but also plainly.

My grandfather got his first diplomatic chance in 1876. The Turkish Empire, disintegrating for centuries, was at last breaking up under the stress of a series of rebellions. This time it was the Bulgarians who rebelled. Russia, anxious to help her fellow Slavs and also to extend Russian influence, hurried to their assistance. It looked as if a Turko-Russian war might break out which could involve the rest of Europe. To avoid this, the other European powers organized a conference in Constantinople. Disraeli sent my grandfather to it. He did not feel cheerful about his mission. 'Not at all in my line,' he wrote, 'involving sea-sickness, much French and failure.' So far as events were concerned, this gloomy prophecy proved correct. The mission failed to effect its purpose; it was conducted almost entirely in French, and my grandfather was very seasick on the voyage home. But he arrived back after having acquired a reputation. The foreigners had been struck by his skill in negotiation, and the English Government was impressed by his able dispatches. In 1878 Disraeli appointed him Foreign Secretary.

He found himself with plenty to do. War did break out between Turkey and Russia, in which Russia was victorious, and a treaty was signed at San Stefano. This treaty, in my grandfather's opinion, left Russia so powerful as to endanger the balance of power in Europe. England at this period was the strongest nation in the world; my grandfather set to work to make use of her strength to get the treaty modified. It was essential that the negotiations for this purpose should be kept secret, and he denied categorically in Parliament that they were taking place. I note this fact to illustrate that, for all his strict principles, he was not morally pedantic if he thought that the issue of war or peace was at stake. Once, when informed that a fellow politician would never tell a lie, 'I am glad I have been warned,' said my grandfather; 'I shall never tell *him* a secret.'

The negotiations ended in a satisfactory compromise; the Turks and the

Russians agreed to modify the treaty, and my grandfather took the opportunity to gain control of Cyprus for England so that she could use its ports as a base from which her fleet could safeguard peace in the Mediterranean. The result of the secret negotiations was confirmed by a public conference of European Powers in Berlin. At this the English delegates were Disraeli and my grandfather, who was accompanied by his schoolboy eldest son, to be shortly afterwards followed by my grandmother and two more children. He needed the company of his family, he said, as a compensation for that of the German royal family, to whom he had to pay a visit at Potsdam, and also of the foreign diplomats with whom he spent his days at Berlin. 'The place is detestable,' he had written to his wife. 'At Potsdam there are mosquitoes, here are Minor Powers – I do not know which is worse!' The conference ended in an agreement which was recognized as a triumph for British diplomacy. The delegates came back to London to be greeted by streets full of cheering crowds.

My grandfather disliked this; Disraeli revelled in it. However, they had at last grown to be friends. Indeed, they had various things in common. Both were patriots, both realists and both ironists who thought it possible to take human affairs too seriously. My grandfather retained some reservations about Disraeli; Disraeli's liking was less qualified. His romantic imagination was exhilarated by the spectacle of this intellectual patrician of historic lineage who said what he thought right, regardless of any trouble he might get into. 'Courage', he said to my Aunt Gwendolen Cecil, 'is the rarest of all qualities to be found in public men. Your father is the only man of real courage that it has been my lot to work with.'

In these years Disraeli came often to Hatfield, where he grew very friendly with my grandfather's children. Incurably youthful in spirit, he sought their company and charmed them. My father described him to me sitting immobile by the great fire in the Long Gallery of a winter evening, looking like an Egyptian mummy in a black suit, yellow, withered, with a pronounced squint and hair dyed dark purple. For much of the time he was silent; but when he spoke he was entertaining. One evening the young people were discussing a rumour that the French Ambassador, a notably commonplace person with the unexpected name of Monsieur Waddington, had been assassinated. Disraeli spoke – his first words for a long time; 'I hope it is not true,' he remarked with an impassive countenance; 'it would make assassination ridiculous.' No wonder my grandfather's children enjoyed Disraeli's visits.

Alas! these were soon to be numbered. In 1880 the government fell and there

The 3rd Marquess of Salisbury's eldest son, James, Viscount Cranborne, later the 4th Marquess

was a general election. It was the custom of the day for the Prime Minister, if he was a peer and therefore not standing for Parliament himself, to keep away from the contest. Disraeli stayed at Hatfield in the company of the two eldest Cecil sons. Every day he went for a drive accompanied by my father. Disraeli exerted all his powers to make the drives agreeable; my father was captivated. Then came the news of the Conservative defeat. 'Young man,' said Disraeli solemnly turning to my father, 'this is an incident in your life; it is the end of mine.' Within a year he was dead.

During the years of opposition that followed my grandfather was leader of the Conservative Party in the House of Lords. In 1885 the Liberals fell from power, and Queen Victoria asked him to form a new government. He cannot have contemplated the prospect with much satisfaction; for only three years before he had published an article entitled 'Disintegration' in which he had prophesied the speedy and inevitable decline of English greatness. However, there was no question but that he must accept. At fifty-five years of age my grandfather became Prime Minister of England. He was to remain so, apart from two short intervals of Liberal Government, for the next seventeen years.

IV

Since it was in this role that he has cut a figure in history, it seems an appropriate moment to stop and take a look at his mature personality. Mature is the word; profoundly changed from what he had been as a young man, he was already the venerable father-figure of my mother's reminiscences, bald, bearded and filled out to a majestic size. 'Put his Lordship in the carriage with the fresh horses,' my grandmother was once heard to say to her coachman. 'They cannot run away very far, with his weight to pull.'

His demeanour harmonized with his appearance. The nervous shyness of youth had softened to a benign aloofness, as of one who wished to be polite but was a little vague about whom he was talking to. He found it hard to recognize his fellow men, even his relations, if he met them in unexpected circumstances. Once, standing behind the throne at a Court ceremony, he noticed a young man smiling at him. 'Who is my young friend?' he whispered to a neighbour. 'Your eldest son,' the neighbour replied. He was also vague about people he did not know. Driving up from Hatfield station one evening, he found himself in the company of a man who seemed to know him and whom he therefore took to be some unrecognized old acquaintance. Suddenly the man spoke. 'Lord Salisbury,' said he in solemn tones, 'I am come to bring you a message from Almighty God.' My grandfather said nothing, but on arrival went to his study and, sitting down to work, summoned a manservant. 'I have left a madman in the front hall,' he said calmly; 'could you see that he is got rid of?', and then returned to his papers.

Calm was another characteristic of his mature personality. Basically he was still highly strung; this showed in his movements, twitching his foot, restlessly fidgeting with a paper-knife; and he was still capable of fits of black depression. He visited his sons at school only once – he found the memories it revived were too painful – and he still shrank from humanity in the mass, even if it professed to be friendly and admiring. This was an inconvenient reaction for a Prime Minister. It was said that going for a walk with him in a public place was like accompanying somebody wanted by the police and trying to avoid arrest. Dislike of admiration went with embarrassment at being paid a compliment, even at second hand. If one was repeated to him, 'Very good of them!' he would mutter, and would relapse into a gloomy silence which could last several minutes.

But in general – and this is where he had changed most from his youth – he communicated a sense of unruffled serenity. Nor, in spite of his apparent remoteness, was he insensitive to other people's feelings. Memories of his youthful sufferings made him quick to notice if someone was ill at ease, even if the cause was trivial. Blanche Balfour, a young cousin of his, once arrived at a big party at Hatfield having lost her luggage, a cause of great distress to a girl in those formal days. My grandfather noticed this and condoled with her so comfortingly that she was inspired to go through the evening incorrectly dressed but smiling. When, a few years later, she married, my grandfather sent her a diamond brooch accompanied by a card: 'For the young woman', he had written on it, 'who could enjoy herself without luggage.'

This spirit of sympathy blended with wit, unexpectedness and a sense of style gave its character to his talk. He was not a dominating talker; on the contrary, and especially when at home and relaxed, he would sit for long periods silent and with half-closed eyes, as if hardly listening. But when he did bestir himself to converse more continuously, the result was memorable and delightful. Not much of it has been recorded, but sentences in his letters give something of its flavour; as when he suggests that a troublesome Member of Parliament might be given a post abroad as 'he is a man who is likely to render much more distinguished service, if he is at a distance from his native land . . . I will not enlarge on this topic; it will explain itself before your own mind in all its seductive amplitude'; or, commenting on great thinkers, 'One of the difficulties about great thinkers is that they so often think wrong'; or, on experts, 'No lesson seems to be so deeply inculcated by the experience of life as that you should never trust experts. If you believe the doctors, nothing is wholesome: if you believe the theologians, nothing is innocent: if you believe the soldiers, nothing is safe.' Or again, 'I would not be too much impressed by what the soldiers tell you about the strategic

At Walmer in 1896: the 3rd Marquess of Salisbury

importance of places. If they were allowed full scope, they would insist on the importance of garrisoning the moon in order to protect us from Mars.'

These remarks showed that the gadfly in him never became wholly extinct. He knew he ought to keep it under. 'I am too tired to make a speech,' he once exclaimed. 'You are afraid of being dull?' said someone. 'On the contrary,' said my grandfather, 'I am afraid of not being dull enough . . . I find if I speak when I am tired, I always shock people.' He sometimes shocked them when he was not tired. Once joined in the political battle, he could argue as recklessly as in his youth. When for once lured by his children into a dispute, he was the same. 'He is not a good arguer,' said one of them; 'he is too unscrupulous, too much out for victory.'

However, these gadfly phases were short-lived. When the political battle was over, my grandfather relapsed into enigmatic detachment: the end of a family argument saw him sit back benign and aloof and with half-shut eyes, so that my grandmother could describe him as 'sitting as usual, humble and silent among his sons'. Indeed, except in relation to her, he was ultimately a recluse happy only with his family and even then apt to escape to the room which he had contrived for his solitude. It was an odd, characteristic apartment, cut off from the world by thick double doors and furnished in a fashion at once functional and amateurish, with large, ugly, useful pieces of furniture he had gathered from other parts of the house, and with various devices invented by him to suit his convenience: a writing table with two slits cut in its flat top to take his incoming and outgoing letters, a step-ladder up to a locked cupboard hidden in the panelling where he kept his secret files. On one side a door led to a dressing-room with a specially made sunk bath in the floor so that he should be able to walk down into it and without needing to heave his great weight over its edge; on the other side another door leading to a private laboratory. He still went in for chemistry, as a hobby.

All his life my grandfather retained his interest in science, and he liked to introduce recent scientific innovations into his home. Hatfield was one of the first places to have an inter-communicating telephone. My grandfather enjoyed testing its efficiency, by reciting nursery rhymes down it. Unsuspecting visitors, sitting as they thought alone, would be alarmed to hear, emerging from a mysterious instrument on a neighbouring table, the spectral voice of the Prime Minister intoning:

> Hey diddle diddle,
> The cat and the fiddle . . .

My grandfather was also a pioneer in installing electric light. This was even more alarming to the guests than the telephone. The naked uninsulated wires stretched on the ceiling of the Long Gallery would suddenly burst into flames.

My grandfather, conversing below, would look up; he or his sons would non-chalantly toss up a cushion to put the flames out and then resume their conversation. The fact that he was risking the destruction of a masterpiece of Jacobean interior decoration did not bother my grandfather.

His disregard of aesthetic considerations was impish and heroic. He thought nothing of cutting through a piece of ancient tapestry to make a door, or of nailing a tray for his letters on to the veneer of a beautiful table. 'Welcome to Hatfield,' he said genially to a prospective daughter-in-law with artistic tastes; 'its other name is Gaza, the capital of Philistia.' Here my grandfather was mischievously exaggerating. Philistines set as little value on intellectual things as on artistic ones. This was not at all true of him. Oxford was the recognized headquarters of the anti-Philistines; and he said that to have been chosen Chancellor of Oxford was the honour of which he was proudest. In any case, no out-and-out Philistine would, like him, have relaxed after a hard day's work over a volume of Goethe or Sophocles.

Indeed, my grandfather did not fall into any of the recognized categories of human character. In consequence people, then and since, have been mystified by him: the father-figure was also a sphinx. This was because, in age as in youth, he was a paradoxical mixture of scientific realist and religious mystic, of sceptical contemplative and combative man of action. But, whereas in his youth these diverse strains had warred distractedly and confusedly within him, he had managed by middle life, if not to reconcile them, yet to impose an armistice upon their strife. This was primarily the result of his happy family life, which helped him to rise above intellectual uncertainties. It was more profoundly the result of his mature religious convictions. He used to say that a man could not discover these by purely intellectual means, but only in the process of active living.

Certainly it had been so with him. My grandfather's religious views had become modified to reflect his nature more fully and exactly. This meant reflecting its complexities and uncertainties. Orthodoxy was still for him the best expression of his essential, most valued, religious convictions. But he refused to evade facing the difficulties involved in orthodox Christian belief; and he was impatient of Christians who tried to minimize them. 'God is all-powerful and God is all-loving; and the world is as it is! How are you going to explain that?' he once exclaimed. Nor did he find Christian ethics much easier to accept than Christian doctrine. 'They are so hard to put into practice that I can only accept them because they have Divine authority behind them,' he commented. All the same, he was certain that they did have Divine authority behind them. For, surveying his past life from the vantage point of late middle age, he knew that his religious experiences were and had been his highest, most significant experiences. Reading the Gospels and partaking of the Sacrament, he was aware of a living Divine presence – God incarnate in Christ – whom he could not but adore and worship. Thus my grand-father's spiritual vision did not square with his earthly experience. The relation between the two remained a dark riddle. Yet, in spite of everything, he found his faith unshaken.

This was the ultimate source of his serenity; and all the more because it freed him from any too painful sense of responsibility for the consequences of his actions. As he saw it, the consequences were not in his hands but in God's. 'I do not under-stand what people mean when they talk of the burden of responsibility,' he once said, standing at the door of Hatfield, and about to start for a walk on an overcast autumn afternoon; 'I could understand what they mean by the burden of decision – I feel it now, trying to make up my mind whether or not to take a greatcoat with me. I feel it in exactly the same way and no more when I am writing a dispatch upon which peace or war may depend. Its degree depends on the materials for decision that are available and not in the least on the magnitude of results which may follow.' He paused, and then in lower tones, as if to himself, he added, 'With the results I have nothing to do.'

In fact he seldom had much hope that the results would be satisfactory. He once disconcerted his children by telling them that he thought a young man of their acquaintance was mistaken in choosing a job on the ground that it would give him a chance to do good: this was bound to lead to disappointment. 'But good is sometimes done in the world,' one of the children objected. 'Yes, but not by you,' replied my grandfather with unusual vehemence, 'never by you – never allow yourself to believe that for an instant!' One should always try to do right, thought my grandfather, but one should never count on doing good. It is an ironical view; my grandfather's sense of the paradoxical nature of the human condition made him ironical through and through. But, so far as his religion was concerned, it was an irony not of doubt but of faith.

This kind of irony bewildered his Victorian contemporaries. Indeed, my grand-father was not a Victorian as the term is generally understood. His tone, his point of view, were those of an earlier age. Like his literary style, they recalled the eigh-teenth century: that characteristic English eighteenth century whose most famous representative is Dr Johnson, and which extended to include my grandfather's favourite Jane Austen. Like theirs, it was at once moral and realistic, judged good sense to be a better guide to conduct than fine feeling, and combined a firm Christian faith and morality with a down-to-earth unillusioned view of human nature and human prospects.

It is from such a point of view that he was to approach the political problems of his time. These were formidable. Like the first Cecils, he lived in an age of revolutionary transition. The sixteenth and seventeenth centuries had seen Eng-land change from a medieval and feudal branch of Christendom to an independent

national state ruled over first by the Crown and then by the aristocracy. Now –
under pressure from the liberal ideals of the French, and the practical facts of the
Industrial, Revolution – the nineteenth century was to see this settlement give
way in its turn to a society whose ideals, summed up under the slogan 'Liberty,
Equality and Fraternity', were to find expression at home in the liberal and democratic movements, and abroad in popular movements towards national independence. People had begun to divide themselves on the one hand into Liberals who,
in varying degrees, approved of the new movements, and Conservatives on the
other, who in varying degrees opposed them. As Victorian Gilbert put it, every
Englishman

> Born into this world alive
> Is either a little Liberal
> Or else a little Conservative.

There was no question of my grandfather's being anything but a little Conservative. His Johnsonian view of the human situation made it inevitable. Belief
in original sin, together with his own experience, had convinced him man was
incurably imperfect. Civilization was not a sign that man had 'progressed', but
rather a thin crust precariously formed during a phase of tranquillity, beneath
which seethed the forces of barbarism, ready to burst out at any serious disturbance.

Nor did the slogans of Liberalism stir my grandfather to enthusiasm. Liberty,
the right of a man to do and think what he liked without fear of tyrannical interference, he did indeed passionately believe in. But he did not equate it with democracy. Democracy meant the right of the majority to impose its will on others;
and this he thought a peculiarly dangerous threat to individual liberty, for the
majority represented tyranny rendered confident by superior numbers. As for
equality, he thought it a meaningless term, as applied to politics. Government
must always in practice be run by the few who make it their job; and the doctrine
that all have an equal right to choose these few merely means that they are
chosen by a majority of inevitably ignorant persons. Here again he was a pre-
nineteenth-century man. He saw as little objection to the idea of a hierarchical
society as Dr Johnson had done or, for that matter, his own ancestor Burghley.
Nor, any more than they, did he believe in the holy right of nationality, the right
to rebel against an established government only because it was a foreign one. For
good or ill my grandfather was not a Liberal.

Yet he was not 'reactionary' either. Detached and objective, he recognized
change as the law of life, and a wise statesman, he thought, should always be
alert to note what changes were on foot in order to adjust existing institutions
to fit them. 'Constant revolution is not a food on which English people desire to
be fed,' he said, 'but changes there must be.' Moreover, once change has taken

place it must be accepted; to force a change backward was as likely to disturb peace and order as to force a change forward. Altogether my grandfather's conservatism had come to be qualified at every turn by his realism and his detachment. His basic political aim was to preserve civilization by maintaining peace and order; and he judged that this was best done by a process of continual, cautious day-to-day adjustment. For, he explained, whereas he had originally thought of a statesman as the man who, as it were, directed the political traffic, he had come to realize that he was at best a man who managed to drive the coach of state through the traffic without getting involved in an accident. It was with this modest objective that in 1885 he set about governing what was then the most powerful nation in the world.

V

Here it is that his personal history merges, as Burghley's had merged earlier, into general history, a subject too vast and complex to be tackled in this book. I can do no more than take a glance at the part he played in it and note how this illustrates his character and outlook. Home politics did not illustrate them much. In them, according to his general principles, he went in for cautious adjustment to changed circumstances, though his Christian conscience did lead him to be actively in favour of measures to improve working-class housing and education. The domestic scene was too quiet to demand much of his attention. Two things, however, did disturb his tranquillity enough to throw light on him: the Irish question and Lord Randolph Churchill.

Randolph Churchill was a source of trouble only during my grandfather's early period of power. Brilliant and very ambitious, he had swept to fame in the previous ten years, partly by his splendidly impudent attacks on the revered Mr Gladstone and partly as a leader of the Tory democrats, a young ginger group, who sought to win working-class supporters by presenting themselves as likely to do more for them than the Liberals would. By now, the thirty-six-year-old Churchill, with his protuberant eyes and ferocious moustache, was easily the most sensational figure in the Conservative Party: there was no question in the minds of most of its more influential members that he should have high office.

When forming his 1885 administration my grandfather therefore made him Secretary of State for India, and in his 1886 administration Leader of the House of Commons and Chancellor of the Exchequer; but with foreboding. He foresaw that Churchill was bound to be a nuisance. Indeed, he was the last person to get on with my grandfather: an arrogant temperamental egotist, not without generous impulses but liable, if thwarted, to explode in fits of emotional temper generally followed by fits of emotional reconciliation. My reserved and rational grand-

Lord Randolph Spencer Churchill in 1889, and Lord Salisbury drawn by Sir John Tenniel as Sisyphus struggling with the problem of Ireland

father found tempers and reconciliations equally embarrassing – and both un-intelligible. Already in 1884 he had compared Randolph Churchill to the Mahdi, the fanatical leader of a Muslim sect at that time ravaging the Sudan, and not to Churchill's advantage. 'Randolph and the Mahdi', he had written to a friend, 'have occupied my thoughts almost equally: the Mahdi pretends to be half mad and is very sane in reality: Randolph occupies exactly the converse position.'

For a short time the two managed to be friendly. Then Churchill, in my grand-father's view at least, began to grow intolerable, quarrelling, intriguing, inter-fering in his colleagues' departments and, at cabinet meetings, generally in an angry minority of one. 'My task', commented my grandfather satirically, 'is leading an orchestra in which the first fiddle plays one tune and everybody else, including myself, wishes to play another.' The result was that the same Conserva-tive magnates who had pressed Churchill's claims to be Chancellor of the Ex-chequer, now pressed the Prime Minister to get rid of him. 'The time is not yet,' said my grandfather. They must wait till Churchill had put himself in the wrong with the Party as a whole. He soon succeeded in doing this; he asked that less money should be spent on defence so that the rest could pay for his social schemes. My grandfather judged the foreign situation too dangerous to risk cutting down on defence; and he knew that starving the Army and Navy would never be popular with Conservative voters. He rejected the proposal. Churchill, who thought himself indispensable, decided to force my grandfather's hand.

In the December of 1886 a large house party was assembled at Hatfield, which included Churchill's mother, the Duchess of Marlborough. On Sunday evening a manservant was observed to deliver a note to my grandfather, who was talking to one of the lady guests. He glanced at it impassively, put it in his pocket and continued his conversation. Next morning my grandmother, lying in bed beside him, said she must get up to say goodbye to the Duchess of Marlborough, who was leaving by an early train. 'Send for *The Times* first,' said my grandfather sleepily. 'Randolph resigned in the middle of the night; and, if I know my man, it will be in *The Times* this morning.' He was right; he realized that Churchill would do his best to embarrass the government by announcing his resignation publicly before its leader had time to consider it. The poor Duchess left the house in tears. 'Why, oh, why are my sons so unlike other people's sons?' she was heard lamenting as she was assisted down the Grand Staircase.

Events proved my grandfather's calculations more accurate than Churchill's: the country backed the Prime Minister. It was reported to him that Churchill had said he had been driven to his action by Lord Salisbury's manner, which, after the first friendly weeks, had grown cool. My grandfather was not softened. 'Coldness of manner may be an excuse for an erring wife,' he said, 'but not for an overbearing colleague'; and when, later, he was pressed to give Churchill another chance, 'Did you ever know a man who, having had a boil on his neck, wanted another?' asked my grandfather with some amusement. Randolph Churchill never got office again.

My grandfather's handling of this issue shows his political skill at its most effective. His record over Ireland, on the other hand, reveals his limitations. This was the period of the first campaigns to give Ireland Home Rule; my grandfather was violently opposed to the idea. He judged, truly enough, that Home Rule must in the end lead to independence, and he thought that this, besides being a potential military danger to England of the most serious kind, also involved a shocking betrayal of those Irishmen who had been loyal to England. On his side he proposed to heal Irish discontent by introducing measures to make the people more prosperous, at the same time suppressing lawlessness by what he called 'resolute' government.

While he was Prime Minister, this policy was tried out, not unsuccessfully. But it was bound to fail in the long run. For it did not take account of the one permanent and overriding factor in the situation, the feeling of the Irish that they were fundamentally different from the English and could never be content to be united with them. It is odd that a man as clear-sighted as my grandfather should not have recognized this. Here it was that his eighteenth-century outlook was a disadvantage to him. He simply had not understood in Ireland or elsewhere the irrational, irresistible power of the new popular nationalism; and he was peculiarly sensitive to the threat to civilized order presented by seeming to yield to the lawless violence so enthusiastically practised by the Irish. Nothing is to be had for nothing in this hard world. For once it was a misfortune for my grandfather not to be a typical man of his time.

But in foreign affairs his attitude was on the whole a gain; it enabled him to take a more far-sighted view. Luckily, for they occupied most of his attention. During the larger part of his period of power he was Foreign Secretary as well as Prime Minister, and it was on the international highway that he was chiefly occupied in guiding the coach of state. The two aims of his foreign policy were simple and orthodox: first the legitimate interests of his country, and secondly peace. Both aims were to be achieved by maintaining the balance of power between the leading nations. This was a traditional type of policy going back at least as far as Burghley's time; and my grandfather's individual gifts showed less in his aims than in the methods by which he sought to achieve them. As he saw things, circumstances were always changing, with some nations increasing in strength and others losing, so that the balance of power was continuously shifting. To preserve it, my grandfather therefore believed in a plan of continuous consultation between the great nations by means of which necessary adjustments were made in good time to meet new shifts in power. He took the lead in this because, since England was then the most powerful nation, her influence was likely to be decisive.

At the same time he opposed her committing herself to any permanent alliance. For one thing, he thought that the situation might always alter in such a way as to make such an alliance undesirable, and for another he thought that, in the new democratic England, popular opinion might at any time change in such a way as to force the government to repudiate a previous alliance. For the rest, he believed profoundly in maintaining the sanctity of international agreements, was against interfering in the internal affairs of other countries, especially on ideological grounds, disapproved of any kind of bluff – 'Never threaten unless you have the power to carry out your threat,' he said – and preferred diplomatic activities to be pursued behind the scenes.

'War is the worst evil,' he once said; 'the second worst evil is an obvious diplomatic triumph: because it makes harder any later reconciliation between the two powers involved.' These were the principles that guided him during the period of power. He had an anxious task, for it was an anxious, unsettled period in which the world was, unknown to itself, preparing for the catastrophic struggles of the twentieth century. My grandfather realized this. 'Nations', he once said, 'may be roughly divided between the living and the dying . . . for one reason or another – from the necessities of politics or under the pretence of philanthropy – the living nations will gradually encroach on the territory of the dying and the cause of conflict among civilized nations will speedily appear. These things may introduce causes of vital difference between great nations whose mighty armies stand opposite threatening each other. These are the dangers I think which threaten us in the period which is coming.'

They were threatening indeed. Turkey was declining, Russia's power was growing; so, more alarmingly, was Germany's. The Far East was witnessing the defeat of old China and the lightning rise of Japan. In the West the United States grew ever mightier. All these movements were, during my grandfather's reign, to involve England in crises of varying intensity. By the exercise of his diplomatic skill – mingling firmness and reasonable concession – my grandfather helped to settle them. Each time war was averted.

Within eleven years of his death, England found herself engaged in the First World War. In the intervening period the government, abandoning his principles, had contracted permanent alliances and pledged themselves to go to war, without knowing for certain that the country would be behind them. It looks as if my grandfather was wiser than his successors. However, it is doubtful whether by 1914 his policy could have prevented catastrophe. It had depended for its success on England's being the most powerful nation; and she was so no longer. My grandfather himself, by the time he died, had come to the conclusion that peace could no longer be maintained by hand-to-mouth diplomatic means but only by an establishment of an agreed established international system. 'The federated action of Europe', he said sombrely in 1897, 'is our sole hope of escaping from the constant terror and calamity of war, the constant pressure of the burdens of an armed peace, which weigh down the spirits and darken the prospect of every nation in this part of the world. The federation of Europe is the only hope we have.'

He spoke of European federation because in his time Europe still dominated world politics. But the issues which the European Powers quarrelled about were for the first time largely non-European. By far the most important happening of late nineteenth-century history was the entry on to the international scene of the Third World; its most momentous event was the partition of Africa. This was a hurried affair, rightly called the scramble for Africa. The scramble involved conflict. Not between Europeans and Africans – the Africans were not in a position to put up much of a fight, even had they wanted to do so – but between competing Europeans. My grandfather was concerned to see that this conflict did not lead to war; also that, since it seemed inevitable that Africa should be divided up, England should get her fair share of it. He proved so successful, and the other nations so maladroit, that in the end England gained far more than anyone else. Under my grandfather a hundred million inhabitants and six hundred million square miles were added to the British Empire.

It is a crowning irony of his career that he himself was not an imperialist. He believed in conserving rather than acquiring; he was reluctant to add to his country's responsibilities; and he was possessed by no idealistic vision of England's mission to rule other people for their own good. For him, England's acquisition of an African Empire was a by-product of his usual policy of preserving peace and safeguarding British interests. An English trader's adventure in Africa would lead to an agreement with a native ruler which gave England a right to protect her trade in his territory. An invasion was likely to follow, by a mixed mob of adventurers and missionaries and competing foreigners. This, in its turn, would produce a state of chaos, to be ended only by England's moving in and taking over.

Taking over, my grandfather thought, did entail a moral obligation to impose order and justice and to promote the well-being of the natives. As a Christian, he was particularly determined to stamp out slavery; as a Christian, too, he sympathized with the work of the missionaries, though he often thought them foolishly anxious to impose English habits on Africans, who in his view should be encouraged to develop on their own traditional lines. He also strongly disapproved of racial prejudice, what he called the 'damn-nigger' attitude. He said with prophetic insight, 'I look upon it as not only offensive and unworthy, but as representing what is now and will be, in a highly magnified proportion, a serious political danger.' On the other hand, no more in Africa than in Ireland did he respect national sentiment as such. Rational and old-fashioned, my grandfather saw nothing wrong in one people, whether black or white, ruling another, so long as they ruled them well. He hoped that the English people might prove able to do this. But the prospect did not exhilarate him; it was likely to raise too many problems. Thus detachedly, unhopefully, but effectively, he presided over the establishment of what was to be, during the short time it lasted, the largest empire in the history of the world.

His fears were not shared by his fellow countrymen. It was the age of the Diamond Jubilee and *Land of Hope and Glory*. The hearts of the people of England swelled to bursting with enthusiastic imperial pride. Their enthusiasm extended to include the Prime Minister among its objects. Unexpectedly, my undemocratic grandfather had in his later years a considerable success with the new democracy. His speeches to popular audiences were received more warmly than his speeches in Parliament; and, while his political colleagues still found him disconcertingly inscrutable, the public revered him as a pillar of bearded and benevolent wisdom. Undemonstratively, he returned their friendly feeling. His experience as a landlord and agriculturalist had led him to discover in the common people of England a strain – shrewd, cautious and undoctrinaire – with which he felt an affinity.

If the English people approved of him, so did their Queen; and more passionately. Queen Victoria took to my grandfather the moment he became Prime

Minister. All her life she combined a regal will with a feminine desire for a man to whom she could look for advice and support; more than ever now that she was growing old. My grandfather was exactly the man to fill the role. For, as well as thinking him wise and virtuous, she found him entertaining. Queen Victoria – it was one of the unexpected features of her unique character – had not the Victorian taste for seriousness, at least not in her male advisers. She had much preferred Melbourne and Disraeli to Peel and Gladstone, and largely because their talk was more amusing. So, in its own way, was my grandfather's. He soon became a central and necessary figure to her existence. On him, by means of frequent talks and a continuous flow of telegrams and of emphatic, opinionated, heavily underlined letters, she poured out the full force of her naïve and formidable personality. Her affection and admiration grew with the years; till at last, 'Who has been my greatest Prime Minister?' she asked one of her courtiers. 'Lord Beaconsfield,' he suggested. 'No! Lord Salisbury,' replied Queen Victoria.

On his side, he became much attached to her. Secretly he was amused by her underlinings, her outbursts of unbridled sentimentality about anniversaries and mementoes; at times, too, he found himself tried by her demands on his time and by her violent partisanship. He writes in 1886, 'I have four departments – the Prime Minister's, the Foreign Office, the Queen, and Randolph Churchill; the burden of them increases in that order.' But he grew enormously to respect her loyalty, her honesty and her power to forecast English public opinion. Further, like Melbourne before him and for the same reason, he responded to her charm: the charm that simple, high-hearted positive natures have for complex, melancholy and sceptical ones. She commanded his homage and raised his spirits and touched his heart. He grew fonder of the Queen than of anyone outside his immediate family.

VI

Not that his affection for her could be compared with what he felt for them. If his serenity of spirit was the product of his faith, his pleasure in existence came from his family life. He never enjoyed society; he had no close friends. Their place was supplied by his wife and children. Luckily they were more than equal to it. My grandmother's personality had grown with the demands made on her by her husband's eminence. These were formidable; for, though my grandfather supervised the management of his estates – he had begun to take a scientific interest in farming – he left everything else to his wife. She ran family life, social life – this involved official entertaining on a big scale – and took charge of a great patriarchal and feudal establishment, with its houses in town and country, its gardens and its stables. These last were usually looked on as the province of the master of

the house; 'but', said my grandfather, 'it has taken me years to know the difference between a horse and a cow, please do not expect me to do anything more.' My grandmother also took an active part – necessary in the days before the Welfare State – in looking after the needs of the poor people of Hatfield, getting cottages built and seeing that the sick were looked after.

All these things she did decisively and confidently, and with plenty of time left over to talk and to read. Her way of doing things was unconventional. My grandmother never became a correct Victorian great lady; she did not even dress like one. On a certain occasion she arrived at a ball, given for meeting the royal family, arrayed in rich satin and the family diamonds. But, when she raised her skirt to curtsey, she disclosed grey woollen stockings and walking shoes. She had forgotten – or, more likely, had not bothered – to change them. She never bothered about things she thought unimportant, with the result that her activities were a curious mixture of effectiveness and inefficiency. She got what she wanted but paid too much for it: the food at her table was lavish but not good; her servants were numerous but idle; and her horses had a habit of running away. This my grandmother did not mind. Once, when she was driving a pair of them, the lady who accompanied her interrupted the talk, nervously calling attention to the fact that one horse had bolted. 'What does it matter, my dear?' said my grandmother. 'I can make the other one go just as fast.' And, whipping it up, she continued her conversation.

I think she must have felt a temperamental sympathy for the runaway horse. The square, short figure with the piercing blue eyes moved through life and through Hatfield with a reckless energy and impatience. 'She was like a rushing mighty wind in the house,' my mother relates, 'from the time that she was heard approaching Chapel in the morning, her firm footsteps moving to the accompaniment of a large bunch of keys of the House and garden attached by a chain round her waist, to the time, which might be any hour if she was interested, when she went to bed, having probably finished the evening after leaving the Drawing-room by standing talking to the family at the bottom of the staircase and waving her bedroom candle to punctuate her points, with a fervour that was the death of many good evening gowns. There was never a cessation to her activities, and she was the quickest worker I have ever seen. All her letters for the day would be written between Chapel and breakfast, which if there were many, might mean breakfast about eleven, when she would appear, with a triumphant sense of duty done, to rally her family on their idleness, they, poor things, having been conscientiously keeping the guests going in her absence. Breakfast was always a

Queen Victoria in 1900

tremendous feature. Papers were read, letters discussed, and any exciting political development torn to pieces. After breakfast, she would move into the Gallery in the winter, into the Summer Drawing-room in summer, where she would sit, surrounded by the newspapers, which she would glance through, and keeping up an endless conversation with all and any she could lay hands on.'

Her part in politics was not confined to discussing the news. As well as acting as her husband's chief confidante in political matters, she sometimes took a discreet hand in them herself. When Gladstone proposed abolishing the University seats in Parliament, it was my grandmother who went round to see him, as her husband's emissary, and persuaded him not to do so. She was not afraid of confronting Gladstone; she was not afraid of confronting anyone. The Prince of Wales, afterwards Edward VII, alarmed most people. 'Lady Salisbury,' he once said, eyeing her costume with distaste, 'I have seen that dress before.' My grandmother rightly thought this remark impertinent. 'Yes, Sir,' she replied briskly, 'and you will see it very often again.'

All this is attractive; and my grandmother's personality was attractive. But it was not easy. Unlike her husband, she did not mellow with the years. On the contrary, in age as in youth she remained dominating, wilful and stormy, sometimes with comic results. One day she entered the Dining-room at Hatfield to find that a caller, whom she disliked, had been invited to stay for lunch. She vented her displeasure by making discouraging signs to any servant whom she saw approaching the unwanted guest with a dish, with the result that the poor man left the table after the meal virtually unfed. Power also made her behave as if the same rules did not apply to her as to other people. If she wanted to take a short cut through a neighbour's park, she thought nothing of commanding her coachman to take a locked gate off its hinges to let her through. On the other hand, if she found an unauthorized person trespassing in Hatfield Park she denounced him with unmeasured roughness of language. Never ill herself, she gave short shrift to the ailments of others. 'Her attitude to illness', said my mother, 'was great sympathy for two days, expectations of recovery on the third, and vigorous indignation on the fourth if the sufferer had not recovered.'

She was an affectionate but outspoken mother and a difficult mother-in-law. Not that she was a jealous one: once her son was married, she accepted his wife as a member of the family, whose part she would take, if necessary, against her own son. But her conception of family life was a matriarchal one, according to which she felt she had a right always to have her family around her. Her unmarried son and daughter lived at home till she died, by which time they were well into middle age; her second son, William, the Rector of Hatfield, lunched and dined together with his family at Hatfield House every day; my mother and father, the eldest son and daughter-in-law, lived there the whole winter. If they ever went away for

Hatfield House: the South-West Wing today

a weekend, my grandmother complained so loudly, both before and after, that they hardly ever thought it worth while to go. In London they did have a house of their own; but, unless invited elsewhere, they dined every night with my grandparents. My mother sometimes found this trying. But she said that it had its compensations; dining with my grandparents was much more entertaining than dining in most places. She also said that my grandmother's infirmities of temper were ultimately kept in check by my grandfather. She was too much under his influence for her to act in such a way as to offend against his basic standards.

He depended on her absolutely and delighted in her company; also in that of his children. There were seven of them: two girls, Maud and Gwendolen, followed by five boys, James, William, Robert, Edward and Hugh. The family was given to nicknames, most of them odd; only Maud was called by her name. Of

the rest Gwendolen was known as T.T., James as Jem, William as Fish, Robert as Bob, Edward as Nigs and Hugh as Linky. Though highly individual physically and mentally, they also possessed common characteristics. All were pale and bony, with strongly marked features and long restless hands; all were vital, high-spirited, intelligent and uncompromising.

Their relations with their parents were close and continuous. I have heard it said that the English aristocracy of this period seldom saw their children, who were left to be brought up by nurses and governesses. The opposite was true of my grandfather's children, and equally of his grandchildren. They did have nurses who dressed them and washed them; but their mental and moral life was shaped and coloured wholly by their parents. The girls were educated at home, and the boys also up to the age of thirteen. Then my grandfather sent them to Eton; surprisingly, seeing how he himself had suffered there. I suppose he thought it was time they saw a little of the outside world, and no doubt he had learned that Eton was a less barbarous place than in his day. In fact his sons were not tormented there. But neither did they like it; life was much more interesting at home. 'The level of conversation at Eton is deplorably low,' commented the thirteen-year-old Hugh.

This was the consequence of seeing so much of his clever father and mother. While they were very young, their mother had most to do with them; my grandfather did not feel at ease with his children till he could conduct some sort of conversation with them. But, since they were, boys and girls alike, clever, talkative and not at all shy of him, these conversations began early and after that he saw as much of them as he could. He took his eldest son and daughter, while still in their early teens, to the conferences at Constantinople and Berlin, in order to have some congenial company with him. At home, when he was not shut away working, he liked to be in his children's company, sitting silent and amused, listening to their flow of uninhibited talk and now and again interrupting to supply a piece of information or make an apt or mischievous comment.

There was no question of my grandmother sitting and listening. She equally enjoyed her children's company, but joined animatedly in arguments and discussions. Now and again her Alderson nerves got the better of her; something would be said to rouse her temper, and she would flare up. But soon the moment of temper would pass, and the talk would enthrallingly continue. Even when the house was full of guests, she could be observed in the morning walking up and down the terrace with one of her sons, absorbed in discussion; at night, after the guests had gone to bed, she and the children gathered together at the foot of the

The Van Dyck Room at Hatfield House

stairs to indulge in one last delicious bout of talk. This happened from an early age; for, from an early age, the children had all their meals with their parents and went to bed as late as they did.

It was a new epoch in the history of Hatfield House. The painted countenances of Burghley and Queen Elizabeth looked down to observe a fresh and different phase of Cecil family life. My grandmother was responsible for its form, which was Aldersonian: a united family existence, alive with common interests and pleasures, with its own idiosyncrasies and nicknames and family jokes; heated discussions on politics and religion and ethics, alternating with hard-fought games of tennis and reckless gallops round the Park. For, though none of the family were sporting or athletic in any serious sense, they had plenty of physical energy and required an outlet for it. The family spirit fused in equal proportions their father's and their mother's: it blended aristocratic self-confidence and authority with professional-class standards of expertise and hard work. It was an independent-minded, liberty-loving spirit like my grandfather's; but, like my grandmother's, it was also hopeful and fiery.

By the standards of any period, the upbringing was free and unconventional. The children were not required to be tidy or punctual or even very clean, and my grandfather benevolently allowed them to take every kind of risk with horses and firearms. 'Nigs has been very hard put to it to find something to do,' he writes of his fourth son when still a schoolboy, 'having tried all the weapons in the gun-cupboard in succession – some in the riding school and some, he tells me, in his own room – and having failed to blow his fingers off, he has been driven to reading Sydney Smith's essays and studying Hogarth's pictures.'

Nor were his children made to be silent or acquiescent in the presence of their elders. Middle-aged visitors were disconcerted to find their views disputed politely – my grandfather's belief in liberty did not include the liberty to be rude – but firmly by a boy or girl of twelve. As a matter of fact, the children were more polite to visitors than to their father; a foreign girl staying at Hatfield thought that 'goose' must be a word of endearment, since she had heard it so often used by the Cecil children when addressing their father. He does not seem to have addressed them as geese – on the contrary, 'My father talks to me as if I was an ambassador,' said one of his sons, 'and I must say I do like it.' This did not imply, however, that his father deferred to his opinions. He was not in the habit of deferring to any ambassador's opinions. Treating his son on equal terms meant that he made no concession to youthful ignorance or stupidity. 'Would you mind defining?' he would ask courteously and formidably; or, in answer to some excited state-ment, 'do let us look at the question chemically', by which he meant with scientific detachment. Humorously and relentlessly, he kept his children's minds at work, questioning vague statements and deflating cloudy sentimentalities, especially

Lady Maud left *and Lady Gwendolen Cecil in 1870, and the Salisbury family in 1896:* left to right, back *Lord Selborne, Lord Hugh and Lord William Cecil, Lord Salisbury, Lord Edward and Lady Robert Cecil;* centre *Lady Selborne, Lord Cranborne, Lady Salisbury, and Lord Robert Cecil;* front *Lady Cranborne, Lady Gwendolen Cecil, Lady Florence the wife of Lord William Cecil, and Lady Edward Cecil*

if they involved praise for some quixotic but foolish action. 'A display of moral vanity masquerading as virtue': so he would describe it.

He also refused to make up his children's minds for them. If one of them asked him for his advice on a course of action, he would give what he considered to be the facts necessary to know in order to form a decision; and then, 'Now it is for you to decide,' he would remark, and decline to say any more. This method presented a teen-aged boy or girl with an ordeal. The children were inexperienced; they admired their father and wanted very much to do what he thought right. Often, in frustration, one of them would ask another to try diplomatically to find out their father's true opinion. Once his children had grown up, my grandfather was even more determined to let them judge for themselves. He thought it morally wrong to exert pressure to influence a grown son or daughter's choice in the matter of marriage or profession. He remembered how he had suffered from his own father's interference, and he resolved to be as different from him as possible.

All the same my grandfather and grandmother did influence their children, and more than most parents. The Hatfield system of education operated inevitably within the framework of religious convictions which conditioned and guided the lives of the two powerful and magnetic personalities responsible for it. Unconsciously and undesignedly my grandparents had created a mental atmosphere in which these convictions could not be regarded with detachment. 'Read what rubbish these people write,' said my grandfather to his fifteen-year-old daughter Gwendolen, tossing over to her an anti-Christian article by Frederic Harrison. Introduced in such a tone, the arguments of the solemn and secular Mr Harrison were not likely to make much impression. To set up as an atheist in my grandfather's family would have been like setting up as a Christian Scientist in a medical school.

Luckily none of the children felt any temptation to do so. Their faith was more militant than their father's. Their minds, unqualified by his strain of scepticism, were positive and fiery like their mother's. It was she who was responsible for their religious education. Coolly – for my grandparents distrusted emotional religion – she taught them some elementary theology, encouraged them to read the Bible for themselves and laid great emphasis on the value of religious practice. They learned from her that, since God is a living spirit continuously aware of each individual man, it is clearly of the first importance that each individual man should be in direct touch with him. There were prayers in the Chapel every day, although the children only attended them if they wanted to do so. At twelve years old they were confirmed, and after that the weekly service of Communion became for them, as it was for their parents, the centre and mainspring of their religious lives.

This was rare in those days, and led to trouble when the oldest boys went first to Eton. They wrote back saying that their housemaster objected to the weekly Communion on the grounds that it interfered with the school routine. Within a few hours of getting their letter, my grandmother was at Eton giving orders that her sons' boxes were to be packed and themselves removed from the school for ever, unless they were allowed to take part every week in the central rite of their faith. Faced by my grandmother at her most alarming, the housemaster capitulated. The incident left its mark on the boys' attitude not only to sacramental religion but also to schoolmasters. They learned that their parents did not think them infallible nor expect their sons to do so. The sons profited by the lesson. Forty years later my father visited me at Eton and interviewed my housemaster. 'It must be trying for you to spend much of your time with such an inferior man,' he said to me afterwards. I had already come to this conclusion myself; but it was reassuring to have it confirmed by someone whose standards I knew to be as impartial as my father's.

For my grandfather's influence on the moral conduct of his children was as strong as it was on their ideas, and this in spite of the fact that he was so reluctant to give them moral advice. My aunt Gwendolen was once asked how he exerted his influence. 'He never said anything,' she replied, 'but it was so evident that he was miserable if he thought any of us was not doing his best, that it was too uncomfortable to go on.' His code was an expression of his beliefs. Life should be lived with a Christian purpose. Since neither of my grandparents was contemplative, this meant a life of action. My father and his brothers and sisters grew up with formidably developed social and political consciences. From their early years they flung themselves into the task of righting wrongs and furthering good causes, religious, social, political. While still in their teens my father and his sister Gwendolen were so indignant at what they felt to be the Liberal Government's shabby treatment of Gordon that, without stopping to think whether they could afford it, they hired a lecturer to go round England pleading Gordon's cause.

They were encouraged to do such things by the sense of their duties as members of a governing class. These were strongly impressed on them. My grandfather had no doubt that a governing class was a good thing, but only if it carried out its obligations. If it failed to do so, he told his children, the sooner it was done away with the better. They were as ready to follow him in this as they were in matters of religious belief. It came naturally to them to take a lead, and their interests were all public interests. Their attitude towards them, however, was a very individual one, the consequences of their unusual upbringing. This had made them, within a common framework of Christian belief, strongly idiosyncratic and independent. They were indifferent to the opinion of the outside world and often disagreed with each other.

Among my earliest memories is that of the voices of my aunts and uncles enthusiastically arguing. These arguments had begun in childhood; so hot were they liable to get that my grandmother had to forbid her children to discuss certain subjects. One of these was the morality of duelling. The boys were against it, the girls were in favour – because, said the boys, they would not be expected to fight duels themselves. I doubt if this was the reason. My aunts were too powerful intellectually to claim any privileges on the grounds of their sex. The elder daughter, my Aunt Maud, was later in life to become an active though moderate supporter of equal rights for women. She was less moderate in youth. As a debutante, she once got into an argument with a young man who stood out for male superiority. 'What can you do that I can't?' asked my Aunt Maud. 'You can't knock me down,' said he. 'Can't I?' said my aunt; and she did.

My grandparents' children were influenced in other ways by their upbringing. In particular, their minds and souls had been developed at the expense of their senses. Not only were they unluxurious – their parents had actively discouraged any taste for luxury – but they took little pleasure in eating or drinking or dress: and they played down the whole subject of sex. If they mentioned it at all, which was rare, it was in distant generalized terms, and they disliked any book or play that made much of it. Like Jane Austen, the family's favourite novelist, they took for granted that passion should be ruled by virtue and good sense. According to many accepted authorities on the subject, this attitude of theirs should have led to dangerous psychological inhibitions; and I think my father, who was unusually sensitive, did as a result suffer in youth from unnecessary feelings of guilt in these matters. But the rest of the family do not seem to have been bothered. Five of the seven married, and four of them with a conspicuous and lasting success, surely impossible without a fulfilment that was physical as well as mental. There was something normal and vigorous about them that rendered them immune to puritanical inhibition. Indeed the word 'puritan' cannot be applied to them. They enjoyed themselves too much, were too amused and too amusing.

For, luckily, along with his strain of austerity, my grandfather had bequeathed to his children his sharp sense of comedy. It pervaded their family life, and no subject, except religion, was protected from it. Robust and incisive, its cool, strong light sparkled over their most dogmatic assertions, their most impassioned arguments, disinfecting them from any taint of heaviness or solemn folly. To the end of their long lives they were capable of falling into fits of uncontrollable laughter, often at inappropriate moments. My Uncle William, when Bishop of Exeter, was openly overcome with laughter when something went wrong while he was taking part in a solemn procession round the cathedral in full vestments; my seventy-year-old Uncle Hugh could barely contain his mirth when listening to a lady detailing a long and circumstantial tale of trivial misfortunes. 'There is no greater strain on one's gravity,' he said to me afterwards, 'than listening to such an accumulation of calamities.'

Laughter is a sign of happiness. Family life in Victorian Hatfield was happy. My grandmother had laid the ghosts of her husband's sad and lonely boyhood. Joyously the children talked and read and climbed about the roof and skated on the pond and galloped on horseback over the turf of the Park. Their mode of life, with its mixture of privilege and freedom, animal energy and moral purpose, gave them an extraordinary self-confidence; and also a feeling of solidarity. For good or ill they were self-sufficient, each other's closest friends, perhaps each other's only close friends, and needing no company but each other. Even when the house was full of guests, the children generally managed to sit next to one another at meals and gathered together to talk after everyone else had gone to bed. If ever they found themselves outside the family circle – as the boys did when they went to Eton – they did not like it and returned with relief to the home, where alone their personalities could freely blossom.

This self-sufficiency did not mean that the family was generally alone. Hatfield was a patriarchal establishment with aunts, uncles and cousins frequently on long visits there. It was also one of my grandparents' duties to entertain. The parties were sometimes grand and formal; the huge house was filled to welcome the Emperor and Empress of Germany or the Italian Crown Prince or the Shah of Persia, with their respective retinues. More commonly there were large mixed gatherings for the weekend – 'packs' the children called them – made up of people that my grandmother thought she ought to ask but who, as likely as not, had little in common with each other. They ranged from cabinet ministers to archbishops, from Lewis Carroll to Gladstone. Gladstone, though the Liberal Leader, shared my grandmother's religious views, and she liked him. During one visit he met in the passage my Uncle Hugh, only five years old, but already an ardent Conservative. 'You are a very wicked man,' he said. Gladstone was disconcerted. 'My dear boy, what would your father think if he heard you say that?' he said. 'He thinks you are, too,' replied my Uncle Hugh implacably, 'and he is coming to kill you in a quarter of an hour.'

Gladstone was only one of the crowd of statesmen and proconsuls and generals and ambassadors and bishops and archbishops who came to spend their weekends at Hatfield during this period of its history. Most of the time my grandfather kept aloof from the company, appearing, benign and distant, mainly at meals. It was his family who threw themselves into the task of entertaining these heterogeneous assemblies. In their early years his children's idea of doing this was sometimes surprising, as when, in a desperate effort to break the ice, they organized an elderly group of guests in a game of follow-my-leader round the stairs and passages, or sat them down on the floor of the Long Gallery to compete at blowing a feather across a stretched-out sheet. This was in the intervals of taking them on a lively and informative tour round the antiquities of the house, or drawing them in to assist at discussions about House of Lords reform or the Christian attitude to capital punishment, or the character of Lord Randolph Churchill.

The guests must have often been bewildered at Hatfield; but they seemed to enjoy themselves. 'The family are really delightful,' wrote Lewis Carroll to a friend, 'perfectly at ease and kindness itself and make a guest feel at their ease too.' Such guests as had a taste for the curious varieties of the human scene must also have savoured the piquant contrast between the stately and venerable house and the pack of young people who were its inhabitants; untidy, ungainly and with grotesque nicknames like Fish and Nigs, but bursting with intelligence and individuality and life.

VII

My grandfather lived till 1903. Various causes combined to cast a shadow over his last years. The years 1895 to 1899 were made anxious by a series of international crises, culminating in the Boer War; and these crises were symptoms of the coming of a new age, an age of change, dangerous and restless, in which he did not feel at home. Not even in his own party; the last quarter of the nineteenth century saw the birth of a new kind of Conservatism. The old Conservatism had been landed, aristocratic and paternal; the new Conservatism, a late by-product of the Industrial Revolution, was middle-class, industrial and managerial. Led by Joseph Chamberlain, the able, forceful son of a Midland manufacturing family who had started his career in politics as a Radical, it set out to present Conservatism as a creed of the future rather than the past, go-ahead, up to date and hopeful, combining plenty of social reform with a belief in the infinite opportunities for increasing Britain's wealth and glory offered by her newly acquired Empire.

All this represented a point of view very unlike my grandfather's, which was sceptical and cautious, and that of a landlord. His own kind of Conservatism remained more concerned with preserving than expanding, less with imperialist adventures than with driving the coach of state through the traffic of a chaotic world in such a way as to avoid an accident.

Yet his feelings towards the new Conservatism were more mixed than hostile. He seldom disagreed with its specific proposals; and his later speeches show that he could even at moments be fired by the blaze of patriotic and imperial sentiment that was sweeping through the country. Moreover he had long ago accepted the fact that, in a changing world, one had to accept change; and all the more because he saw himself now as a man of the past surviving into a period he did not fully understand. Under his calm exterior there had always been more uncertainty than people perceived; now more than ever he doubted what was the right course for a statesman to take. Uncertainty led to inactivity; so much so that some of his enterprising followers grew impatient. The ambitious young George Curzon described him as 'that strange powerful inscrutable and brilliant obstructive dead-weight at the top'. This was not an accurate description. My grandfather did not obstruct; he stood back. He was still too formidable, intellectually and morally, not to get his way if he chose to do so; but more and more he let others, and especially Joseph Chamberlain, take over. Though he himself backed the Boer War as both just and inevitable, yet he used to speak of it as 'Joe's War'. My grandfather's political influence during his last years was declining.

Lord Salisbury in old age, drawn by E. Fuchs

This decline was not due only to uncertainty of purpose. Even more were its causes physical. His health was beginning to fail. Judged by his photographs he looked, in his middle sixties, more like eighty: bowed, dim-sighted, enormously heavy. He felt permanently tired, so that he was liable to go to sleep in inopportune moments, dictating a dispatch, or presiding over a Cabinet meeting. To get rest, he went abroad as often as he could. In earlier years he had owned a villa at Puys in Normandy, to relax in while his children bathed and boated. Now he bought one on the French Riviera where he might recoup his spent forces in a warm climate. In England he sought to reduce his weight by taking exercise. This led to a last and comical manifestation of his Philistinism. The pastoral glades and immemorial avenues of Hatfield Park were, under his orders, disfigured by paths of black municipal-looking asphalt, down which, attired in a shabby cloak and wide-brimmed felt hat, he took a daily ride on a tricycle. Since he was too infirm to start the machine rolling, he was usually accompanied by a groom or a grandchild whom, when he found himself forced to slow up, he would politely request to push him from behind till he had achieved the required impetus. In spite of his and their efforts, my grandfather's weight did not noticeably diminish.

In the autumn of 1899 came a terrible blow. My grandmother died. For months she had been ill and growing gradually worse. It is a sign of what she meant to my grandfather that for once he seems to have found it impossible to face a painful fact. Insisting that surely she could be cured, he desperately sought out new doctors, anxiously persuaded her to try new kinds of treatment, hailed the slightest sign of improvement as evidence of solid hope. Not till the last few weeks of her life did he accept what others saw to be inevitable. Then his habitual self-command took over. But the shock of her death, when it did come, was such that he never recovered from it.

He wanted to resign; but the Queen, now close on eighty, said she could not do without him and begged him to stay. Loyalty, and affection as well, made him unable to refuse. He lingered on in office for two years more. But he felt growingly unequal to it. Though his intellect was still keen, his health and sight were both weakening daily.

All the same, and in spite of sorrow and declining faculties, my grandfather continued to give an impression of serenity. Indeed, his last years, though sad, were not tragic. He was surrounded by a devoted family, and he was supported by a detachment of spirit born of his realism and also of his faith. There is a saying

Georgina Alderson, 3rd Marchioness of Salisbury, with her son Viscount Cranborne, afterwards 4th Marquess of Salisbury, painted by George Richmond

of Bishop Butler's often quoted in the Cecil family: 'Things are what they are, their consequences will be what they will be; why, then, should we desire to be deceived?' These words might have been written by my grandfather. He had never desired to be deceived: self-deception, he once told his son Robert, was the most dangerous of all human weaknesses. But the things whose existence he recognized and whose consequences he accepted included, among much that was dark and disillusioning, the saving truths of the Christian religion. One of these was that the Kingdom of Heaven was not of this world, and that man therefore should not despair because he had not found it here.

At last, worn out at seventy-two, my grandfather retired from public life in the summer of 1902. The following year, on the 22nd of August, his family gathered round his bed at Hatfield to assist at his last hours. His son, William, now Rector of Hatfield, read aloud the prayers for the dying. 'Depart, O Christian soul,' ran the solemn words. My grandfather died that evening, as the sun was setting.

This sunset, as subsequently historians have not failed to point out, was symbolic; and not just of my grandfather's death. To the contemporary observer his career had remained to its close a success story. He died still a revered national figure, with his party in power and his policies apparently successful: he had been Prime Minister of England at the Diamond Jubilee of 1897, which celebrated the highest point of dominion and glory ever attained by the English. In fact Fate, in a spirit of irony which my grandfather would have appreciated, if grimly, had designed these triumphs as though to provide a contrasting prelude to a period of spectacular catastrophe, which entailed, incidentally, the decline of most of what my grandfather had stood for: British greatness, aristocratic government, individual liberty and international peace. Within fifty years of his death, British greatness had dwindled, aristocratic government had disappeared, individual liberty had lost its prestige and England had been involved in the two greatest wars in the history of mankind.

Robert Cecil, 3rd Marquess of Salisbury, in his robes as Chancellor of the University of Oxford, by George Richmond, 1870–2

2

THE CHILDREN
of the Third Marquess

AS THEY HAD BEEN in youth, so were my grandfather's children in maturity: strong personalities, able and argumentative, unconventional and uncompromising, unpunctual, unaesthetic and notable for the way they contrived to combine high-spirited humour with passionate moral convictions. Brought up to be Christians and members of a governing class, they lived disinterested lives dedicated to public service in a Christian context. One or other of them was always to be found in the forefront of some movement he or she believed in; on behalf of Church schools or women's suffrage, for improving working-class housing or the promotion of world peace, or fair treatment for lunatics. Like their father, they were at the same time old-style Conservatives and extreme individualists, each taking his own line and drawing his own conclusions and inclined equally to question the opinions of experts and the verdicts of majorities. In some of them this individualism flourished rampantly and eccentrically; none of them can be described as like other people.

My father, who in 1903 became the Fourth Marquess, might seem an exception to the family type. Unlike his brothers and sisters, he was punctual, unargumentative, with some taste for the arts and not instinctively hostile to orthodoxy. But his likeness to his relations was far greater than his unlikeness. For he too was intensely religious, dedicated to public activities, moved by passionate moral convictions and liable to surprise one with an odd unexpected opinion. For the rest, he was a very attractive personality – I never met anyone, even among his opponents, who did not like him – with his light-limbed soldierly figure, his well-cut, clear-eyed countenance, his beautifully courteous manners and a boyish, candid sweetness of nature which, now and again, shone out in a sunburst of boyish enjoyment.

Not often enough, though: my father's prevailing mood was melancholy,

James Cecil, 4th Marquess of Salisbury, centre *with his three surviving brothers* left to right *Hugh, Robert, and William, painted in 1928 by Frederick Shepherd*

darkening to occasional fits of black depression, which sometimes lasted for weeks on end and which, one gathered from various hints, were associated with a sense of his own sinfulness. This was, to say the least of it, unnecessary. He had extraordinary qualities of courage and compassion and very little to reproach himself with except too autocratic a temper, which, however, he strove to keep under control, and a tendency to worry too much about his health. 'I do not feel ill,' he once said to me, 'but I do feel rather as if I was going to feel ill!' His melancholy had some obscure nervous origin, exacerbated by a hypersensitive conscience which had been developed to a point of obsessive scrupulosity.

My father's ideal of Christian conduct was too high for mortal man to live up to. His attempt to reconcile the precepts of the Gospel with the facts of ordinary life in twentieth-century England produced in him a Tolstoyan tension. His efforts to do so could have comic manifestations. He once visited the studio of the painter James Shannon to see a picture he had painted of my mother, and found himself torn between a sense that it was his moral duty to speak the exact truth and his unwillingness to hurt Shannon's feelings. After a struggle, 'I think', said my father, 'it is a picture one might get to like very much in time.'

The same scrupulosity, on the other hand, was responsible for good and un-common actions. It led him, on finding himself the owner of some slum property, to refuse, against all professional advice, to sell it; he feared it might get into bad hands. Instead, he had it reconditioned at his own expense to be let to the sitting tenants at the same low rents. This was extremely characteristic of him. He looked on his privileged position as a trust only to be justified by a life given up to work for the good of others. I never knew anyone who worked harder or allowed himself less time for pleasure. On myself as a boy the spectacle produced a mildly muti-nous reaction. What was the good, I asked myself, of having all these advantages and getting so little fun out of them? Thinking it over now, I see I was wrong. My father's course of life was justified by the good he did; it also came naturally to him to dedicate himself and take responsibility. In appeasing his conscience, he also fulfilled his nature.

He tended to credit others, among them his children, with a moral sensibility as acute as his own. This was flattering but embarrassing. I remember once in 1919, when I was seventeen, pouring out to him my enthusiasm for the idea of a League of Nations as a means for stopping war. My father approved my feelings but thought such a league might possibly fail, and he gave me his reasons. What they were I forget; but I do remember his obvious concern at the distress of mind he thought I was likely to feel if my youthful idealism was to turn out unjustified. I did not like to say – what I already realized – that I was not suffi-ciently public-spirited for this kind of disillusionment to worry me much. Four years later, just after I finished my final examinations at Oxford, he took me aside to tell me that during the previous year he had received several letters from shopkeepers asking him to settle some unpaid bills of mine. He had done so, he said, but had not told me about it till now for fear that the pangs of conscience I might suffer for the trouble I had caused the shopkeepers – who, he explained, often found it hard to make ends meet – might distract my attention from my studies. Once again I did not like to say that my conscience was made of too coarse a stuff for the inconvenience I had caused the shopkeepers to have come between me and my books.

Lord David Cecil about 1933, by Henry Lamb

He was plunged into politics at the age of twenty-four when he was elected Conservative Member of Parliament for the Darwen division of Lancashire. His political vision was more limited than his father's; he was not so detached or so acute. This made his Conservatism less realistic and more a matter of loyalty and sentiment. He responded, as his father had not, to the new Imperial Dream, which he envisaged from a strictly idealistic point of view; he valued the British Empire only as a means by which the British might help less fortunate peoples. Otherwise his Conservatism was against the new kind and very much in favour of the old: feudal, paternal, traditional. My father revered what was ancient: the Monarchy, the High Court of Parliament, the University of Oxford. This feeling for the ancient extended beyond politics to make him instinctively regret change.

He even hated seeing the walls of Hatfield stripped of ivy, though he knew it was necessary for their preservation. He was also made uneasy by the 'capitalist' strain in the new Conservatism. Though he accepted the fact that money-making was a legitimate occupation, if done for the good of the community, he thought better of professions – clerical, academic, military – of which making money was not the object. He felt more sympathetic to Socialism, he once told me, than to the *laissez-faire* Liberalism of his youth, because the motives behind it appeared more disinterested.

His gifts and his position helped him to rise early in politics. Before he was forty-five he had held office as Under Secretary for Foreign Affairs and Lord Privy Seal. Later, though he always remained important, the political tide flowed against him. He differed from the new Conservatives about Protection – all my family were Free Traders – and, much more, from the Liberal Party who were in power after 1906. He was a leader of the 'Die-hard' resistance to the Parliament Act of 1911, which broke the power of the House of Lords. To accept it, thought my father, would be to abdicate his inherited responsibilities.

During the First World War, he made a success as a very conscientious chairman of the tribunal that tried the cases of conscientious objectors. This was an appropriate role for my father, whose principles, though they taught him that a man should fight for his country, also required him to treat with respect and sympathy the scruples of an individual conscience, however much it might differ from his own. After the war he returned to party politics, where in 1922 he played the most important part of his life as leader of the Conservative group which brought down Lloyd George's government on account of what they considered its corruption. He continued to serve in Conservative governments till 1931, and was for a long time Leader of the House of Lords. Then and afterwards he was largely occupied in fighting for lost or losing causes, such as resistance to Home Rule in India and elsewhere; he felt that England was once more abdicating her responsibilities, this time for the well-being of peoples committed by Providence to her charge.

More successfully he concerned himself, during his later years, with the management of his property. Here for once pleasure coincided with duty. For one thing, this work involved him in a subject that had always interested him, working-class housing: he designed many of his cottages himself. For another it meant personal contact with his tenants. Unlike his father, he enjoyed such contacts. He visited every cottage on his estate as often as he could, listening with sympathy and interest to complaints and queries and reminiscences. Especially at Cranborne did he enjoy this; relationships of such a kind were less self-conscious in the rural remoteness of Dorset. Besides, people there often suffered from a Thomas Hardy type of melancholy which my father could well understand.

He was once asked, as a magistrate, to sign an order committing a young woman to a lunatic asylum. He asked what grounds there were for thinking she was mad, and was told that she said that she thought herself a great sinner. My father easily entered into this feeling. 'She may have good reasons for saying so,' he said with sympathy. 'What right have we to deprive her of her liberty for that?' And he refused to sign the order.

In this work – indeed in all his work – he was helped by my mother. He was as lucky in his marriage as his father had been; and his wife was as considerable a personality, in her very different way, as was my grandmother. She was Lady Alice Gore, second daughter of the Fifth Earl of Arran, and descended through her maternal great-grandmother, Lady Palmerston, from the Melbourne family. The story of her childhood reads like the gloomier passages of a Victorian novel; for her mother had died of consumption very young, leaving four children to be brought up by their grandmother, Lady Jocelyn, a sad widow, made sadder by a stern,

Cranborne Manor, by Rex Whistler

puritanical evangelical religion, which she imposed on her grandchildren. Their life was not made more cheerful by the fact that Lady Jocelyn's other children all died of consumption, too, so that till the age of thirteen my mother was never dressed in anything but black. However, she had the vitality and natural good spirits to survive this sombre start. In 1886, at the age of seventeen, she was launched on London society: a tall, dark-haired, charming girl confronting her destiny, full of zest and curiosity and endowed with the intelligence and breadth of view and practical capacity to take a leading role on the stage of the great world, should she get the chance. Her luck was in, and she got it. Before she was twenty my father had met and married her. From that moment, and for ever after, she was absorbed into the life of Hatfield and the Cecils.

I find it hard to write about my mother. Unqualified praise is insipid and, what is worse, unconvincing. Yet, if I am to speak sincerely, I can find even less to criticize in her than in my father. Her outlook was inevitably limited by her circumstances and her period, but less so than that of many persons; and for me she remained, throughout her long life, stimulating and understanding, illuminating and heartening and delightful. She was too sensitive and had seen too much sorrow during her childhood not to realize life's power to hurt; and secretly she was often apprehensive and anxious. But this never weakened her sense that life was worth living, and it intensified her outstanding quality, that of imaginative sympathy. My mother had a clever heart and a great deal of it. Even when she came across a character or phase of feeling unlike her own, she generally knew by instinct how best to deal with it. My father's mysterious fits of depression, for example, corresponded to nothing in her own experience. But, when he was suffering from one of them, she was the only person he wanted near him. For she knew by intuition the best way to comfort him.

She was also to play an important part in the history of the Cecils by introducing an element into it which was noticeably to modify the family pattern established by my grandparents. Her descent from the Melbournes meant that she was bred to the social and cultural tradition of Whig society of the eighteenth and early nineteenth centuries. This was the most attractive society ever produced by the English aristocracy, combining as it did a warm, easy naturalness, with the grace and culture and sense of style of a finished social accomplishment. The eighteenth century lingered on in the English upper classes well into my mother's time, and when I read the letters of the great Whig ladies of the eighteenth century – Lady

Hatfield House: the Armoury

Overleaf *the Long Gallery*

Bessborough, Lady Granville, Lady Sarah Lennox – I am struck how much their tone of voice and turn of phrase recall hers. It is a very different tone and turn from that of my father's forceful female relations, and I take it that the difference attracted him. There was something tender and fastidious in him that responded to the appeal of a charming and civilized femininity.

On his side he had much to give her: not only a spacious and interesting life in the centre of things, but also an opportunity to satisfy her philanthropic impulses. These were very strong. If on one side she looked back to the eighteenth-century Whigs, on another she was filled with a Victorian concern for the lot of those less fortunate than herself. Natural sympathy here had been increased by her evangelical upbringing, which, together with its sternness and gloom, did emphasize the Christian's duty to help his neighbour; and also, I think, by the influence of another relation, for Lord Shaftesbury, the man who did so much to relieve the sufferings of the boy chimney-sweeps and the children working in the mines, was her great-uncle. She saw something of him as a child; and, though she could not help being amused by the way he talked of everything in religious terms – he would describe an incident as just lasting 'the time of a short prayer' – he made a deep moral impression on her. Marriage to my father gave her scope and money and power to fulfil this philanthropic strain in her; and all the more because she was able to do so in a personal way. It was not natural to her to help people at second hand. She liked to do so directly, spontaneously, personally, as the member of a community in which she knew the individuals and could enter into their individual joys and sorrows. She shared these inclinations with my father. It helped to cement their union.

Under their sway the form of life at Hatfield continued in broad outline the same as under my grandparents, but modified by the different character of its new master and mistress. Up to 1914 the annual traditional rituals went on pretty much unaltered. I remember the Christmas rituals especially well: Christmas Eve in the Armoury, dark but for the candles on the great tree at the top of the steps at the end, twinkling among the shadows on the pieces of armour that lined the walls, and the gust of chill air that blew in as the front door opened, so that we could hear the thin clear voices of the choir-boys from Hatfield church singing carols outside in the starry darkness of the winter night; and afterwards going down to the cellar, where, along with my brother and sisters, I helped my parents to distribute beer and bread to the people on the estate; and, earlier in the winter, the Tenants' Dinner in the Marble Hall, an all-male celebration with my father sitting at the centre of the High Table dressed in white tie and tail-coat and, on one

The Library at Hatfield House

occasion, my six-year-old self also dressed in my best – a blue satin tunic with a lace collar and a long fringed sash – being stood up on the table to say 'Thank you' to the company on behalf of my mother for drinking her health.

In other respects the change in ownership showed itself. It showed in the look of the place. My father had a taste for architecture, especially for the Elizabethan and Jacobean styles, and his grandfather had offended against his sense of period by putting plate glass into the mullioned windows of the great state rooms. My father had them reglazed with the correct leaded panes. He also restored what was left of Queen Elizabeth's old Palace of Hatfield; and he further satisfied his personal aesthetic impulse by designing some bronze table-lamps for the Library. My mother's part in the embellishment of the house was a matter of rearrangement rather than creation. She had been brought up in a well-informed tradition of eighteenth-century Whig taste. Accordingly she weeded out bad pieces of furniture and disposed good pieces in such a way as to show them to advantage. She also made the great rooms more intimate by breaking them up into lesser units, divided from each other by vases filled with tall spreading boughs of evergreen.

Her modifying influence showed also in the way her children were brought up. For it was modification, not revolution; our upbringing was a milder version of my father's. We were required to be reasonably tidy and clean and were urged, mostly in vain, to be punctual. Further, by example and precept, my mother sought to instruct us in the art of making ourselves agreeable socially. Broadly, however, my grandparents' tradition of education persisted. In particular, the boys were educated at home till they were thirteen. Like my uncles and aunts, too, we were brought up to converse on equal terms whether with relations or visitors, and were allowed to express our views but expected to be able to defend them. Especially was this so when we found ourselves in the company of my Cecil aunts and uncles. They listened attentively to what we had to say, but came down on us, with all the force of their vigorous minds, if we said anything they considered mistaken or silly. At the age of thirteen, I described someone to my Uncle Hugh as 'good'. 'What do you mean by good?' inquired my uncle. 'Someone who makes other people happy,' I suggested; it was the best I could do at thirteen. It was not enough for my uncle. 'Any capable licensed victualler can do that,' he commented. I burst out laughing; I found my Uncle Hugh immensely amusing. But I also made a mental note to the effect that I should take the trouble to think more precisely.

Viscount and Viscountess Cranborne with their eldest daughter Lady Beatrice,
now Dowager Lady Harlech

The Cecils of Hatfield House

Our association with our parents was, as in the previous generation, close and continuous. My father, hard-worked and delicate, saw less of us than did my mother, at least till we were in our teens: she managed to spend a great deal of time in our company. I was especially lucky in this, for, since I was the youngest by seven years, she was worried that I would be bored or lonely if left alone. As well as driving out with her in the afternoons to visit cottages on the estate, I used to spend the mornings at Hatfield playing in her sitting-room while she interviewed people or wrote her letters. As I was talkative, my company must have been distracting. I do not think that she minded being distracted. She always sat with the door open for fear, so she once told me, that she might miss something interesting that might be happening outside. Meanwhile she encouraged me to talk about anything that especially interested myself.

This attitude arose primarily from spontaneous sympathy; but also from principle. Later she told me that she looked on it as one of a mother's chief functions to discover a child's bent and then to encourage it. Certainly she

The 5th Marchioness of Salisbury, drawn by John Singer Sargent in 1923, and her son Lord David Cecil as a boy at Eton

followed this principle with me. From an early age I was interested in the arts. Though educated in a cultivated tradition, the arts meant nothing important to her. But she managed to enter into my interest; she would have done the same if it had been in botany or medicine. She took me to museums, concerts and theatres; she read to me by the hour, beginning with *Alice in Wonderland* and going on to Scott and the Brontës and Jane Austen. She also listened while I read aloud my first attempts at authorship. Later, when I was an Eton boy, she contrived to come down to the school nearly every week for an hour or so, and I would talk to her about what I had been reading and, if I had written anything, show it to her. On her side she told me about any drama that was being enacted in the life of her family or friends. I found these confidences enthralling – the human drama always interested me almost as much as the arts – and I was gratified that, while still a schoolboy, I should be thought mature enough to be the recipient of them.

It was on the social life of Hatfield, however, that my mother made her deepest impression. She much enjoyed social life and had a great gift for it both as a guest and as a hostess. She was a delightful conversationalist, spontaneous, responsive, amusing, and her quick sympathy made her peculiarly skilful in bringing out the best in other people's talk.

When, in 1903, she became Lady Salisbury these gifts, inevitably subdued during the reign of her mother-in-law, flowered. In London she gave luncheon parties and dinner parties and was at home on most days for tea; at Hatfield there were weekend parties. Here also she modified a tradition rather than broke with it. Since the life of the house still centred in public affairs, many of the guests were still statesmen and proconsuls: the meditative countenance of Lord Balfour, the headmasterly glance of Lord Curzon, Kitchener's crimson face, and the face of the youthful Winston Churchill pale 'with the pallor of one who had lived in the limelight', rise from the mists of childhood memory to confront my mental eye. But the guests were selected, as they had not been in my grandmother's day, to compose a pleasant harmony, and the public figures were interspersed with people chosen for personal and social reasons; because they were my mother's friends – she had many close friends, both male and female – or because they were agreeable and charming people. The result of my mother's efforts were that her parties got a name for being unusually enjoyable.

Now and again, however, there was a failure, notably the only visit of King Edward VII and Queen Alexandra. Unlike his mother, King Edward VII did not care for my family, whom, I imagine, he thought both highbrow and strait-laced. On this particular occasion matters were made worse by the fact that he wanted my parents to invite a lady to whom he was at that time attached and whom they disliked and disapproved of. Though loyal, they were not servile, and they refused. In consequence the King was grumpy throughout the weekend.

The young Winston Churchill, and Earl Kitchener, painted in 1890 by Hubert von Herkomer

There were other weekends less disastrous than this but only moderately enjoyable. The nature of the formal social life of those days made it inevitable. For parties sometimes had to include people asked out of politeness and not because they were agreeable. The consequence was that some guests were likely, some of the time, to be bored. As a little boy I remember hearing my mother say to my elder sister, 'We must give your Aunt Nelly an amusing place at dinner this evening; she sat between two such dull men last night.' It did not strike me then – as it strikes me now – that there was something unsatisfactory about the kind of party which entailed inviting two dull men. I suppose they had been asked from a sense of duty, because they were colleagues of my father or foreign diplomats to whom my parents had been asked to be civil. My mother accepted such obligations without complaining. In a sense I think she was glad of them. For her evangelically trained conscience was often at odds with her Whig sense of social enjoyment: if she had not thought that her social life was in part the fulfilment of a duty, she would have doubted whether she was justified in giving up so much time and energy to it. However, while accepting the duty, she recognized the hardships it could involve; and not for herself alone. I remember her saying with a rueful smile after an unusually arduous weekend, 'Learn to laugh at nothing; because very often there is nothing to laugh at.'

This old-fashioned type of social life lingered on at Hatfield till the Second World War. Then abruptly it stopped. My father offered the house as a military hospital, and the offer was accepted. The effect was strange. In the great state rooms planned for 'feasts and triumphs', the narrow iron hospital beds lay side by side against the carven panelling and beneath the sculptured ceilings. Stranger still, the place was purged of its characteristic smell; the odour of disinfectant replaced that of beeswax and wood smoke. The effect on me, when I went there, was, by a sort of reversal of the Proustian process, to deprive Hatfield of its power to evoke memories.

Meanwhile my parents, now old people, lived on the ground floor in a corner of the house. But they did not seem displaced or dispirited. They took it as natural and right that, in a time of national danger, they and their home should be of use and in the thick of things; and they preferred it so. My mother visited the patients and made friends with them; my father talked to the doctors and, when he could, went up to London for the day to attend the debates in the House of Lords. His spirits, sadly accustomed to accept human life as an ordeal, was in time of calamity undismayed and reassuring.

Edward VII with Queen Alexandra, and the 4th Marquess of Salisbury in the Armoury, Hatfield House, during the 1930s

He survived the war to die in 1947. My mother lived for eight years longer. Within a very short time of his death she had packed up and left and settled in a modest house in London. I once asked her if she minded leaving Hatfield, where she had lived for half a century. 'No,' she said, 'why should I? I loved Hatfield because Jem was there. It means nothing to me without him.'

II

My grandfather's other children were all of them unusual and interesting enough to deserve a detailed description. Alas! I have no space here to give more than a glimpsed impression of their figures as they passed across the Hatfield scene.

First, the two eldest, the daughters; the fact that they were of a different sex from their brothers was less important than in most families. '*Il n'y a que les hommes dans cette famille là,*' remarked a French diplomat after a visit to Hatfield. My aunts had masculine interests and a masculine type of intelligence. They were not beautiful: when they first appeared in London society they were nicknamed the 'Salisbury Plains'. But, if they were ugly, it was with a heroic majestic ugliness that in later life, when I got to know them, made them better worth looking at than many women who had been beauties.

The elder, my Aunt Maud, had a head like that of a formidable but good-humoured senator of ancient Rome and a strong, pleasant voice in which, uncompromisingly, she uttered controversial opinions. She carried to an extreme point her family's imperviousness to sensuous impressions. Her youngest son, when a schoolboy, played a practical joke on her at a lunch-party by handing her a plate of pudding which he had mixed with ink and blotting paper. The joke fell very flat, for my aunt just ate the pudding apparently unaware that there was anything unusual in its taste.

She was married happily to the Second Earl of Selborne, an Oxford friend of my father's and, like him, a strong churchman and Conservative politician. He had a successful career, was at one time First Lord of the Admiralty and later High Commissioner in South Africa. My aunt was of great assistance to him in his work, especially in South Africa, where she became the centre of a group of progressive and able young Empire-builders who found her conversation stimulating and exhilarating. So did her children. She brought them up on her parents' system, allowing them to be as untidy and dirty and unpunctual as they liked, but deeply interesting herself in their religious and intellectual education. When her sons

James Cecil, Viscount Cranborne, afterwards 4th Marquess of Salisbury, in the uniform of the Hertfordshire Yeomanry Cavalry, painted in 1882 by Sir William Blake Richmond

were at Oxford, where they did very well, she studied the same philosophical and historical books as they did, to be able to discuss them when they came home. She had time left over from these family activities to occupy herself with various public causes, notably that of women's suffrage. Here she followed her father, who, as was natural in a man with daughters like his, thought women fully capable of making valuable political judgments.

My Aunt Maud did not often come to Hatfield. When she did, I was amused to notice that she treated my father not as head of the Cecil family, but as a younger brother who needed at times to be put right. She would start some topic that they were likely to disagree about; and, if my father began tentatively to dissent, 'Nonsense, Jem,' she would say, 'it is notorious that . . .', and go on to enforce her view by stating as unquestioned some fact which was, to say the least of it, disputable.

Her sister, my Aunt Gwendolen, was an equally memorable personality. If Aunt Maud looked like a Roman senator, my Aunt Gwendolen's rugged, sensitive countenance and ardent short-sighted gaze recalled a scholar depicted by Rembrandt. Ardour was one of her outstanding characteristics: she listened with ardour and replied in a flood of ardent, animated words. She lived at Hatfield all her life; for she never married, but identified her life wholly with her father's, for whom she acted as a sort of unofficial and confidential private secretary. When he died, she retired to a little Jacobean house hidden in a sequestered glade of Hatfield Park to devote herself to writing his official life.

Although she spent forty years at this task, she never finished it, partly because she had a lust for perfection which led her to revise and scrap and rewrite again and again, and partly because she allowed herself frequently to be distracted – it might be by a book she picked up casually which instantly absorbed her whole attention, but more often by some appeal to her compassionate heart, easily inflamed to forget all else in a desire to relieve suffering. A beggar-woman met on a walk who told her a tale of woe, a letter from an unknown lunatic complaining that he was unjustly confined in an asylum: these were enough to make my aunt throw all her work aside in order to get wrong righted. How often do I remember her arriving at Hatfield House at any hour of the day or night, on fire with pity and indignation, to pour out vividly and at length some story of this kind into the sympathetic but sceptical ears of my father and mother! She had a specially soft spot for lunatics; and her efforts on their behalf were so strenuous that she sometimes got them released. More often than not, it was soon found necessary to send them back to the asylum. So also did the beggar-woman often turn out an unworthy object

Lord David Cecil about 1943, by Augustus John

of my aunt's charity. This did not stop her from believing the next hard-luck story she heard and taking up the cause of the next discontented madman who might come her way.

She was an extraordinary mixture of simplicity and wisdom. For, along with an incurable innocence that led her to believe improbable tales of misfortune, she possessed an unusually powerful intellect – my grandfather thought her the cleverest of his children – always working at full pitch, reflecting, analysing, drawing interesting conclusions on religion, on social reform, on politics. Her political judgment was penetrating; so much so that when she was over seventy and living away from current affairs, my brother, then an Under Secretary of State, found it helpful to consult her. This judgment appears in the unfinished biography of her father which, though ponderously written – my aunt was not a stylist – is a remarkable exhibition of psychological and political insight.

Her habit of life was eccentric; though, indeed, to call it a 'habit' is misleading, for the course of her day was irregular and unpredictable. She followed no routine but got up and ate and went to bed only when it occurred to her to do so. The times that it did so occur varied astonishingly. This came partly from her propensity to get distracted by chance trains of thought. She was aware of this and made efforts to check it. She once told me that, lost in reflection, she stayed far too long in her bath, and that she had tried to avoid this by starting, as she stepped into it, to recite Byron's poem *The Destruction of Sennacherib*, continuing her recitation while she washed, and getting out as she reached the last word of the last line. However, she admitted this ingenious device had proved a failure. If a stimulating thought struck her, time and Byron were alike forgotten.

This taste for do-it-yourself devices of her own was another of the things that made her mode of life surprising. For instance, she found it tiresome to get out of her car to open the gate into her drive every time she came home. She therefore devised a mechanism which operated to open the gate automatically if the car was driven towards it at a moderate pace. If, however, the pace was too fast or not fast enough the mechanism failed to work and the car ran into the gate. This often happened, with damaging consequences to the car, to the gate and some-times to my aunt. Before she had a car, she drove a pony and trap, in which she used to travel round the country on her various charitable activities, with her dog running behind. The only trouble was that the dog barked all the time. To stop this my aunt evolved a plan based on the concept of what is now called the conditioned reflex. She knew the dog was frightened by gunfire; so, she argued, if every time the dog barked it heard a gunshot, it would associate the two events and stop barking. She put her theory into practice. The pony cart set forth, the dog barked, my aunt fired a revolver. Alas! the only effect was that the pony ran away and the dog barked more than ever. Such episodes filled her day-to-day

Lady Maud and right *Lady Gwendolen Cecil*

life with unexpected adventures and misadventures which, when related, added a touch of extra dramatic interest to her torrential and enthralling discourse.

III

After the daughters came the sons: first my father, then his clergyman brother William. My grandfather appointed him Rector of Hatfield at the age of twenty-five in 1888. He stayed there till 1916, when he was made Bishop of Exeter, so that he was a well-known figure in the place for twenty-eight years. Also an ornamental one; for, unlike his sisters, he was picturesquely handsome.

Tall and broad-shouldered, with golden curly hair and beard and deep-set blue eyes, which sometimes twinkled with mirth but in repose gazed out at the world with a profound and pitying sadness, he looked like one's idea of some ancient prophet. Like an ancient prophet, too, he was unkempt. I remember him most characteristically as dressed in a stained and faded cassock and with his shapely hands ingrained with soil; for he was fond of his garden and liked working there. He was a very active priest, who spent much of every day bicycling round Hatfield in company with his wife – they were a devoted couple – to visit his parishioners, into whose troubles he entered with a peculiarly intense sympathy. This did not prevent him from taking an interest in far-away China, where he wanted to establish a Christian University; he travelled over the world in a vain effort to get it started. At home he took a special interest in outcast persons – gypsies and tramps – partly out of pity for their hard lives but also because he felt a temperamental kinship with anyone who could not fit in with the conventional world. His nickname Fish was an abbreviation for 'queer fish'; not surprisingly, for he arrived at his opinions by queer, devious mental processes and had a queer, unpredictable temperament which sometimes showed itself in difficult moods and fits of nervous gloom.

In his habits he was as eccentric as his sister Gwendolen. He took the same pleasure in inventing odd devices of his own to serve practical purposes. It was typical of him to warm his bed not with a commonplace hot-water bottle, but with a naked electric bulb, encased in two old fencing masks fastened together with bits of wire, and then, after being plugged into a point in the wall, thrust between the sheets for just enough time to warm them without setting the bed on fire. He was not unaware that his taste for inventing gadgets had its comic side. He told me once of a plan he had thought of for heating a room by putting radiators under the armchairs. 'But,' I objected, 'one could not move the chairs; it does not sound a comfortable plan.' My uncle's eyes began to twinkle. 'My dear boy,' he said, 'when one is putting in a heating system, comfort must go to the wall.' His power of invention could also be stimulated by a spirit of mischief. One winter during the First World War there was billeted on his house an army chaplain, talkative and pushing, who insisted on spending every evening uninvited in the rectory drawing-room, tediously holding forth. It gradually became more than my uncle could stand; so one evening when the chaplain arrived he made an excuse to leave the room, and then, climbing up on to the roof, filled the drawing-room chimney with straw. He then descended and, hidden behind some bushes in the garden, watched with schoolboyish enjoyment clouds of billowing smoke issue from the drawing-room fireplace till they filled the room and drove the chaplain out. It

Lord William Cecil, Bishop of Exeter

was unusual conduct for a middle-aged clergyman; but my uncle was very unusual. He was also very absent-minded. Once he lost his railway ticket on the way to taking a confirmation. 'It is all right,' said the guard, 'we know Your Lordship.' 'But I cannot remember where I am going!' exclaimed my uncle bemusedly.

In spite of eccentric habits and schoolboyish impulses, my Uncle William was a deeply impressive personality. To hear him preaching in Holy Week was a strange and poignant experience. It was as if he had been an actual witness of the Passion of Christ, so moved was he by His sufferings and by the despair and bewilderment of His disciples. My uncle's noble sadness of countenance was a true expression of the man within. His spirit was soaked in a sense of Christianity as a tragic and realistic religion that recognized suffering and evil as an inevitable part of the human condition but held that this suffering, if rightly accepted, was a means by which the soul of man could be illuminated and redeemed. This faith was put to the test. My uncle was passionately devoted to his family of seven children: of these, three sons were killed in the First World War and his youngest daughter died of typhoid at the age of eighteen. My Uncle William suffered these losses with agonizing acuteness, but his faith and charity of heart were unshaken.

IV

The next brother, my Uncle Robert, did not live at Hatfield; but he visited it often, so that I was early aware of his tall, big-boned figure and hunched back, the result of an accident in boyhood, bald domed forehead and countenance at once hawk-like and genial. He was the most eminent and widely known of his generation of Cecils; at one time there was even talk of his becoming leader of the Conservative Party like his father. He took after him in many ways, spoke in identical deliberate tones, dressed with the same arresting shabbiness; it was rumoured that the shapeless, crumpled trousers he wore in the House of Commons had been cobbled together for him by his wife's parlourmaid. He had the same feeling for individual liberty as his father, the same intense religious faith, and in politics shared both his father's indifference to party ties and party sentiment and his interest in foreign affairs.

But there were important differences between the two men. My Uncle Robert lacked his father's melancholy and scepticism. He was sanguine and positive and impetuous like his mother. Moreover, unlike the rest of his family, he was not a congenital Conservative; for, while he had no more sympathy than they for specifically 'liberal' ideals, there was in him a strong streak of the born reformer who, when he sees anything he thinks wrong or incompetent, feels an immediate impulse to take action about it.

This streak involved him in disagreeing with a great many people and taking part in movements which brought him into conflict with them. From Eton days when, as Captain of the House, he sought to stop the big boys from overworking their fags, he spent much of his time in campaigns for reform: to rationalize the procedure of the Oxford Union Society, to procure juster treatment for young barristers – he went to the Bar after leaving Oxford – for getting women the vote. Most of these campaigns were unsuccessful, as he himself in later life readily admitted. For, though what he thought wrong generally was wrong, he was not always perceptive about the wisest way to get it put right.

In 1904 he entered Parliament. Here he soon found himself involved in a more momentous conflict, and one which, for once, was not the result of his reforming impulse. The clash between the old and the new type of Conservatism, implicit for the last ten years, now broke openly out over the question of Tariff Reform, by which the soul of man could be illuminated and redeemed. This faith was put to the British Empire. Both my uncle's traditional and his idealist side made him an opponent of the new Conservatism. The victory of the 'moneyed interest', as he called it, meant in his view the rule of the businessman whose aim was personal gain, instead of that of the landowner, who saw himself as a trustee.

'The old conception', he once wrote, 'coming down from feudal days that a man had no unqualified right to his property but held it only as a trust, the condition of which was his readiness to discharge his public duties, was demoded. Instead, the new doctrine was that a man had a right to what he could get, so long as it was honestly come by and, with a similar qualification, could do what he pleased with it. Unpaid service was neither asked for nor much approved.' My uncle was against Tariff Reform because he thought it was a policy whose deliberate purpose was to enrich the British at the expense of foreigners. As a result of his opposition to it, he had to fight a Tariff Reform faction on his own side in his own constituency, and this in the end drove him out of the House of Commons for two years. He got back in 1911, and by the time the First World War broke out had made enough name for himself soon to enter the government, first as Under Secretary for Foreign Affairs and later as a Minister of Blockade.

Once again like his father, my Uncle Robert proved more effective in office than in opposition; he was a great success. This was the more remarkable because to administer the blockade was a peculiarly distressing job for a Christian; it meant starving the German people out. My uncle, however, had no doubt that a blockade was necessary to prevent the more dreadful suffering caused by a prolonged war, and he enforced it with unwavering efficiency. The fact, however, that he had felt forced to do something so repugnant to his nature made an indelible mark on him and one that was to affect his whole subsequent history. The rest of his life was given up to campaigning to prevent war. Inspired by his father's ideas, he thought this could be best done by the establishment of some international system for the purpose. My uncle played more part than any other Englishman in promoting the League of Nations and drawing up its constitution.

Meanwhile, in 1919, he resigned from the Coalition Government because it had decided to disestablish the Welsh Church. Even the cause of international peace could not eclipse for my uncle the cause of the Church. Indeed, both were expressions of that Christian faith without which he saw no hope for the future of the world. 'I am confident', he once declared, 'that no healthy political or international system can be built except on a religious foundation.'

His war record meant that he emerged from it a leading statesman. It was now that some important Conservatives began to look on him as a possible future leader. However, a large number of others were against him. They were suspicious of the League of Nations as a rival to the British Empire; and they doubted if my uncle was a good party man. Was he not too idealistic, too independent, too indifferent to public and party opinion? It must be said that my uncle did nothing to reassure them. He was by nature an autocrat and, though friendly enough to his fellow-men, was not quick to notice their reactions or, if he did, to pay much attention to them. It was characteristic of him that, when Asquith, a Liberal, stood for Parliament against a Conservative, my uncle sent an open telegram supporting him because he thought him more likely than his opponent to be of use in the House of Commons. He may well have been right in this; but the average Conservative could hardly be expected to agree with him. The consequence of his attitude was that, though he continued for a time to be a member of a Conservative Administration – he was made Lord Privy Seal and called to the Lords in 1923 as Lord Cecil of Chelwood – any hope of his ever becoming a leader faded.

In time he drifted out of office and out of the Conservative Party. He joined no other but, as an Independent, devoted himself to supporting the cause of the League of Nations at home and abroad. He was always a respected figure, was awarded the Nobel Peace Prize in 1938 and honoured throughout the western world as a man of ideals. This did not alter the fact that he ceased to have much political influence and that he lived to see the collapse of the League of Nations, to which he had devoted so large a part of his life.

All this should have made his later years sad. If it did, he never showed it. My Uncle Robert in his later years appeared vigorous, forward-looking and far too much interested in what was taking place in the international scene to bother about what had happened to himself. He could get very indignant about Appeasement or any other policy he disapproved of; but it was with the sanguine, hopeful indignation of youth, not the sour disillusioned indignation of age. Nor had disappointment extinguished the impish, cheerful sense of fun which gave salt to his conversation. A quotation from some reminiscences he wrote at the age of eighty-five may give my readers something of its flavour. He is talking about his experiences as a young barrister:

> There was one criminal case at Leeds of a remarkable character. A nervous householder was in the habit of having a loaded gun within reach when he went to bed. It happened that he engaged a new cook, and a night or two after she arrived he was woken up about four in the morning by the noise of someone moving in the house. He accordingly got up and, taking his gun with him, went cautiously downstairs. As he came round the corner he saw a figure approaching him, and instantly fired, and found he had killed his cook. He was accordingly tried for manslaughter, when it became evident that he was a highly nervous individual and the jury acquitted him. But it only shows how rash it is for cooks to get up very early. Few of them would do so now.

He also found compensation for public disappointment in private happiness. In 1889 he married my Aunt Nelly, a daughter of the Second Earl of Durham. He writes in the same reminiscences, 'It was certainly the cleverest thing I have ever done and has been of supreme advantage to me.' He was right. Like those of his two elder brothers, his marriage was exceptionally successful. Exquisitely pretty, with small fine features and large dark eyes, my aunt combined a sharp,

Robert, Viscount Cecil of Chelwood, 1919, by Augustus John, and right *Hugh Cecil, Baron Quixwood, 1920, by John Singer Sargent*

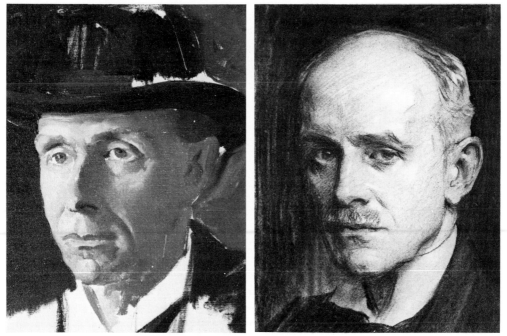

strong, witty intelligence with a delicate artistic and literary sensibility – she was a friend of Walter De la Mare and Virginia Woolf – and in ardent sympathy with my uncle's ideals. Their life, however, was not without its troubles. They were childless; and my aunt early became afflicted with deafness, so that soon only my uncle could easily make her hear. But these troubles, though inevitably they cast a shadow, only served to increase their devoted dependence on each other. They seemed to live in an enclave which set them apart from other people, and within which, for nearly seventy years, their delight in each other unfadingly bloomed.

Lady Robert Cecil, wife of Robert, Viscount Cecil of Chelwood

V

The fourth son of the family, my Uncle Edward, nicknamed 'Nigs', figures least in my memories of Hatfield, for he was rarely there. I recall him on four or five visits: fair, tall, exuberant and surrounded by a group of his relations whom he kept in fits of laughter by his talk. He had a special power of exhilarating his brothers and sisters. This was partly because in some important respects he differed from them. He was ready to plunge, as they were not, into the strange unknown world that existed outside the bounds of Hatfield, Oxford University and the Houses of Parliament. For though as intelligent and religious and talkative as the rest of his family, my Uncle Edward also possessed a venturesome bohemian strain that led him to frequent bars and restaurants and the green-rooms of theatres and to fall in love and make friends in such places. Moreover he went into the Guards, a choice of profession surprising to his relations and not least to his father, who, however, according to his usual practice, set himself to study military matters in order to be able to talk to his son about them, and soon was the more expert in them of the two.

My uncle was an effective though unorthodox soldier, and was twice decorated in the Boer War. A hero of besieged Mafeking, he returned home to be greeted at Hatfield by cheering crowds and a torchlight procession, with my grandfather standing on the steps of the North Front. After the war he left the army to become financial adviser to the Khedive of Egypt. Since his own finances were always in confusion, he might have seemed an unlikely man to make a success of this job. In fact he proved very efficient. He also got on well with the Egyptians. Casual, unconventional and interested in the varieties of human character, he enjoyed Cairo life and wrote some lively sketches of it. He settled there for his remaining years. These were not many. During the First World War he contracted consumption, was taken to a sanatorium in Switzerland, and died there in 1918 at the early age of fifty.

VI

There remains the youngest of the family, my Uncle Hugh. A confirmed bachelor, he made his home with my parents for most of his life, so that he figures continuously in my early memories of Hatfield: tall, thin and angular, with a bald round forehead, high-pitched voice and an old-fashioned, precise mode of speech – he used to pronounce claret as 'clarrit' and say 'ain't' for 'isn't' – and long pale knobbly hands, so shaky that I early learned to associate his presence at meals with a perpetual clink of fork on plate or clatter of cup against saucer. His education had been even more exceptional than that of his brothers; for he was so delicate that, except for a few months at Eton, where he soon became ill and had to be taken away, he never left home. Instead he stayed at Hatfield, a very clever, very precocious child, conversing argumentatively and excitedly with his elders – he had a high-strung, irritable nervous system – and, like his father before him, thinking about politics and theology.

At eighteen he went up to Oxford, where he made an outstanding success, revealed himself as possessed of an extraordinary talent for public speaking, got a first-class degree in history and subsequently became a Fellow of Hertford College. He left the University uncertain whether to become a clergyman or to go into Parliament. His mother, ambitious for the future glory of what seemed to be her most brilliant child, persuaded him to choose Parliament. It was a mistake. My uncle, unlike his brothers, was not a man of action. He had neither taste nor talent for practical affairs and was interested less in getting things done than in discovering what he thought. Furthermore his thoughts were usually eccentric and controversial, and were made more so because he liked to follow them uncompromisingly to their logical conclusions whatever practical difficulties those might raise, and also to express them in their most extreme and paradoxical form. As a Fellow of Hertford College, he once attended a meeting to decide whether an undergraduate should be punished for being found one morning drunk and incapable outside the College gate. My uncle thought he should not. 'I see no more reason', he said, 'for punishing a man for drinking so much that he cannot walk than for eating so much that he cannot sleep.' The other Fellows of Hertford College did not agree with him.

Nor often did his fellow politicians. His mode of thought unsuited him for the blend of intellectual compromise and practical ingenuity needed to make a success in political life. He made a great name for himself as an orator, and many good judges thought him the finest of his time; but that was all. No one, so far as I know, thought of him as a possible minister. His early career was further hampered by the fact that, like his brother Robert, he was a Free Trader with the Tariff Reformers in his own party against him, so that for several years he was out of Parliament.

During these first years he made a more successful name for himself in a different sphere. Unlike the rest of his family, he had a taste for social life, but he hardly discovered it during his parents' lifetime. Afterwards he did and, since he was agreeable and out of the ordinary and a son of a late Prime Minister, he found himself welcome. He was soon a well-known personality in Edwardian fashionable society. In it, but not of it: Hatfield remained his spiritual as well as his actual home and, though he made many friends in the fashionable world, his upbringing had left him always a little suspicious of its standards, as of things of which he must not let himself wholly approve. Now and again he salved his conscience by explaining this in formidable terms to his fashionable friends, who were flustered but unrepentant.

The First World War brought an end to all this. From the beginning my uncle hated the war and especially when it led to the introduction of military conscription, which he looked on as perhaps inevitable but a disastrous blow to the sacred cause of individual liberty. Himself, he believed the war to be justified and proceeded to join the Air Force: a gesture heroic but comical, for no one had less gift for operating any kind of machine. The Air Force recognized this and, after he had managed shakily to pass his first flying test, found work for him on the ground. Joining the forces did not change his principles. He got special leave from the Air Force to go and make an impassioned speech in the House of Commons in defence of the right of conscientious objectors to act as their individual consciences dictated.

After the war he continued to sit in Parliament, but he took less and less part in debates. The post-war political world, concerned as it was with economic and social problems, was not his world. Instead he turned his mind to Church affairs, where his intellect and his eloquence made him a leading layman in the Church Assembly. In 1936 he was made Provost of Eton; and thus, at the age of sixty-seven, left home for the first time. After seven years at Eton, where he impressed and amused the boys and impressed and disconcerted the masters, he retired to Bournemouth. He lived there till his death in 1956. He was now Lord Quixwood: in 1941 he had been raised to the peerage by his old friend Winston Churchill.

His life at Hatfield, which is what concerns this book, was regular and idio-syncratic. He had his own manservant, his own bedroom and sitting-room and his own routine. He was never seen till lunchtime, when he appeared about twenty minutes late. After lunch he went for a walk; from the age of thirteen I usually went with him, both of us talking animatedly. For, unexpectedly, there was in him a youthful, light-hearted, irresponsible strain which made him like the company of young people and caused them to be happy in his. Between tea and dinner he retired to his sitting-room, an apartment on the ground floor, which he insisted on keeping bleakly and tastelessly furnished in heavy mid-Victorian style, as in his parents' days. He could be found there reclining awkwardly on a hard sofa, upholstered in dingy-coloured rep and reading, it might be, a news-paper or a sermon of Cardinal Newman's or a detective story he had chanced to pick up in the Drawing-room. At dinner he appeared, again twenty minutes late, to pass the evening in talk.

He had the same appetite for conversation as the rest of his family. Like them he had strong views on every subject and enjoyed stating them. This could lead to trouble; for, if one of his views involved what he thought a serious moral issue – one could never be sure of what he would consider a serious moral issue – the statement of a contrary opinion would throw him into a state of violent agita-tion which found vent in an outburst of highly articulate indignation. 'Your opinion is both irrational and immoral!' he might exclaim, much in the manner of Dr Johnson in a similar situation. This did not matter if the object of the outburst was a friend; for his friends knew my uncle to be essentially a man of kindly and humble disposition who was distressed and remorseful if he discovered that he had inadvertently hurt someone's feelings. But he was perfectly capable of bursting out to a stranger, who, naturally enough, took offence. The result was that my uncle, again like Dr Johnson, was not liked by everyone. On the other hand, those who enjoyed his company did so as enthusiastically as Dr Johnson's friends enjoyed his.

Indeed, he was an admirable talker. It was partly what he said: the endless stream that flowed from him of odd, entertaining, thought-provoking ideas and fancies. It was even more the way he said it: the apt, unpredictable images that sprang to his mind, his gift for the happy, witty phrase. This gift of phrase it was that made his public speeches so famous; as when, in an attack on the Parliament Act of 1911, he spoke of 'the Liberal Party making hay of the Constitution while the setting sun of Liberalism still shone', or rebuked Lloyd George, with splendid bitterness, for the crimes committed by the Black and Tans in Ireland: 'With so much dishonour, you might have brought us a little peace!'

My uncle's private talk was equally well worded. He once told me that the best way to learn to write with ease was always to try to express oneself as well as possible in ordinary conversation. Certainly he did. Examples throng my mind, as when he said of the Chamberlain Government of the 1930s, 'They aspire to

Lord Robert Cecil and James, 4th Marquess of Salisbury, and Lord Hugh Cecil, as 'Cecils in Conclave' by Max Beerbohm, and David Lloyd George by Poy

common sense but only achieve commonplace'; or of a bereaved wife who, in his view, advertised her bereavement too much, 'I do wish B. had not set up as a *professional* widow'; or of another acquaintance who had adopted a child – my uncle had a characteristically eccentric disapproval of adoption – 'It bores me to see V. going through all the *antics of maternity* with a child I know not to be her own.' Someone asked him, when he was Provost of Eton, whether he had enjoyed the festivities connected with the Eton and Harrow match, a big social event at the school. 'Not at all,' replied my uncle, 'I feel like a prostitute, sitting there smiling at everyone and with nobody smiling back.' He also had the art of saying much in very few words. Once a tedious talker, launched on a flood of reminiscences, paused to ask him, 'Am I boring you, Lord Hugh?' 'Not yet,' replied my uncle courteously.

Unlike many wits, he never repeated his witticisms; nor did he go in for monologue. There was nothing egotistical about his conversation. He listened as keenly as he spoke; and he was at his best when talking to someone able to meet him on conversationally equal terms. I have heard described a fine exhibition bout of conversational in-fighting between him and Winston Churchill in the thirties. They had been great friends in earlier years – my uncle had been Churchill's best man at his wedding – but later they had drifted apart because they disagreed on politics. Now they chanced to meet at a friend's house at the height of the international crisis brought about by the Italian invasion of Abyssinia and when Italy had defied the League of Nations. My uncle provocatively opened the conversation. 'I understand, Winston,' he said in his high, precise tones, 'that you have become in favour of the League of Nations now that it seems likely to lead to a war.' Though unprepared, Churchill was equal to this attack. 'There is a mischievous plausibility in what you say,' he rumbled out. After this they fell to it, hammer and tongs, on the subject of Churchill's political record, each making use of the full resources of his rich vocabulary, his full power of rhetorical invective. The rest of the company listened with some anxiety; but in fact both combatants were enjoying themselves, and at the end, like boxers at the close of a fight, they shook hands.

I should make clear that my uncle's first remark indicated no disapproval of the League of Nations for taking a warlike line. He was always for standing up to the dictators: the appeasement policy met with his sharp disapproval; so did the men who promoted it. 'Neville Chamberlain', he said to me, 'is no better than a Mayor of Birmingham, and in a lean year at that. Furthermore he is too old. He thinks he understands the modern world. What should an old hunks like him know of the modern world?' The word 'hunks' was unknown to me, and afterwards I looked it up in a dictionary. I found it defined as 'an irritable, disagreeable old person'. As often before, I was impressed by my uncle's command of the

English language. A fellow Christian, who supported appeasement, also provoked his scorn. 'He even tried to speak kindly of Hitler,' he commented, 'which is a caricature of Christian charity.'

The war, when it came, found my Uncle Hugh unmoved. He was having dinner when the first bomb fell on Eton with a shattering din and only a stone's throw away from his house. 'Tucker,' he said calmly to his manservant, 'bring me a glass of claret'; and the next day he alarmed the school staff by going to inspect an unexploded bomb and poking at it with his umbrella. Earlier, and with less justification, he had opposed providing air-raid shelters for the boys, should a war happen; he thought it fussy.

His last years were spent at Bournemouth in a poky, shoddy-looking villa he had bought for himself: a distressing contrast, one would have thought, to the antique splendours of Hatfield and Eton. But my Uncle Hugh noticed such things as little as his father had done. Old age, with weakening health and fading sight, proved a trial for him, and he was far too realistic and outspoken not to admit it. But it did not blunt the cutting edge of his wit. 'Old age,' he said to me on one of my last visits to him, 'old age, David, is the out-patients department of Purgatory.'

VII

The life-story of his children shows the magnetic strength of my grandfather's personality. For, in spite of the fact that they were so vital and so diverse and that he made a conscious effort not to impose his point of view on them, they grew up wholly and lastingly committed to it; and especially in regard to what they thought the two most important subjects in life, religion and politics. Even my Uncle Robert, who broke away from the Conservative Party of which his father had been leader, still adhered to his father's basic political principles, and saw the League of Nations, to which he had dedicated his life, as a development of ideas that he had learned from his father.

My grandfather's influence, though pervading, was not enfeebling. Morally and mentally his children were a credit to him. All were strong and individual personalities; and his sons, guided by his knowledge and wisdom and growing up in the inner centre of political activity, rose early to become distinguished figures in public life. Yet, in the event, they did not turn out to be influential figures. My father spent most of his life campaigning on behalf of losing causes; my Uncle William was generally odd-man-out among his fellow bishops; my Uncle Robert was a reformer whose reforms were rarely carried through; and my Uncle Hugh was noted for putting forward passionately and eloquently views with which hardly anyone agreed. He who contemplates the lives of this generation of Cecils must be struck by the fact that, in spite of all their worldly and intellectual advantages, they did less to affect the course of English history than have some more mediocre persons.

Their upbringing was partly the reason for this. Politics, secular or ecclesiastical, are largely concerned with managing men. Life at Hatfield did not teach this. If central, it was also segregated. At once privileged and unconventional, free and sheltered, it separated the young Cecils from other people. They saw little of their contemporaries. When they did so at Eton, they did not feel at home with them; and all the less because their education, with its stress on individual freedom, had encouraged each to develop on his own lines, however unorthodox and eccentric the result.

The consequence was apparent when, as grown-up people, they came out into the world. None of them were very good judges of character – they had known too few people intimately; and they found it hard to adapt and harder still to compromise. If one of them found himself in a minority – this was very likely to happen – his impulse was not to come to terms with his opponents but to resign. The Cecils, it has been said, are addicted to resigning. Certainly it was true of this generation. It had been true of their father; here again they followed in his footsteps. Resigning, however, did not prevent him from coming back to power later. But that was in the nineteenth century, when the Conservative Party was led by Disraeli. It is unlikely that, in the twentieth century and under a less adventurous leader, my grandfather would so easily have got a second chance.

In following his example his children belonged to the past. But they belonged to it in a wider sense. Here we come to the fundamental cause of their inability to influence history and their age. Their view of life – which they had learned from their father – was pre-twentieth century, even pre-nineteenth. I realized this when I was old enough to note how surprisingly unaware they were of the intellectual world of their generation, of the thinkers who, when my uncles and aunts were young, were having a disturbing, sometimes a revolutionary influence on so many of their intelligent contemporaries. Marx and Ibsen and Nietzsche meant nothing to my clever aunts and uncles; and this was not just because they disagreed with them. Even more it was because the whole mode of thought of these writers and the angle from which they looked at life were so remote from theirs as to make their words unintelligible. On the other hand Burke and Johnson spoke to them as contemporaries; and, if they chanced to go to one of Shakespeare's historical plays, they were much better at entering into its ideas and sentiments – about kingship and degree and the sanctity of law – than are many present-day professional teachers of English literature.

Indeed, the Cecils' political and religious views and the terms in which they discussed them had still something in common with those of Shakespeare's time. It was not a question of their looking back wistfully to the past; there was nothing

wistful about this robust-minded generation of Cecils. Nor was it that they were out of touch with reality. Possibly they were more in touch with it than were some of the 'modern' thinkers. Basic realities have not changed much since the sixteenth century; and, to judge by results, the political and religious ideas that inspired the age of Queen Elizabeth I have more to be said for them than those that inspired the age of King George V. But, insofar as they held them, these twentieth-century Cecils were out of tune with their contemporaries. They were survivals: vigorous, confident, intelligent survivals from a hierarchic and religious period, living on into one growingly democratic and secular, in which people were accustomed more and more to question assumptions which the Cecils took for granted, and understood less and less of the assumptions on which the Cecils based their lives. In consequence – and this was almost as true of the conservative-minded as of the 'progressive' – though people respected the Cecils, they were not influenced by them. To influence one's age one must, for good or ill, be more in tune with it than they were.

The tradition of royal hospitality: a garden party at Hatfield House about 1899, by A. Faulkner, showing left Prince George, later George V: third from left the Princess of Wales; centre the Prince of Wales, afterwards Edward VII, with the 4th Marchioness of Salisbury; and immediately to the right the 3rd Marquess of Salisbury

EPILOGUE

MY CHRONICLE ends here. For the figure of the Fifth Marquess of Salisbury (1893–1972) is still too close for the historian to be able to see it in perspective. I would only note, for the benefit of any reader interested in the genetic aspect of my subject, that he united in equal proportions the two diverse and dominating strains in his heredity. On the one hand he continued the parental tradition in making a distinguished name for himself as a Conservative statesman, mainly concerned with foreign affairs and scrupulous to the point of resignation. On the other, he took after his mother's family in that he was sociable, and a man of taste who occupied his leisure hours in beautifying Hatfield and setting in order its manuscripts and Library.

For the rest, the story told in these pages has a curious and unintended symmetry. It spans, roughly speaking, the period of aristocratic ascendancy in England and shows the Cecils of Hatfield most prominent at its beginning and at its end. There is a likeness also in the part they played during these two phases of their history. In each a venerable Cecil, noted for his brains and his piety, assists a Queen of England to preside over an age of outstanding glory which is also an age of transition between one political dispensation and another: from medieval to modern in the first, from aristocratic to democratic in the second. Finally, the policy of the Cecils in both ages was prudent and realistic and pacific.

Yet there is contrast as well as likeness between the two. The sixteenth-century Cecils were men of the future, leaders of the conquering army of the age to come. The Cecils of the nineteenth and twentieth centuries were men of the past fighting a rearguard action, temporarily successful during my grandfather's time, defeated in that of his children. Moreover, though religiously akin, the two were morally very different. The sixteenth-century Cecils had some of the less amiable characteristics to be found in men out to better themselves in a tough world: though disturbed at times by a sense of sin, they were ambitious, not overscrupulous and relentlessly persistent at sticking to power. In contrast to them, the twentieth-century Cecils resigned from power whenever their exacting consciences told them they should do so. They were devoid of personal ambition and, if anything, more scrupulous than they needed to be. It seems that three hundred years saw an improvement in the moral character of the Cecils of Hatfield.

Robert Cecil, 5th Marquess of Salisbury

Sad to say, this did not delay the eclipse of their influence; nor did it help to avert the defeat of most of the causes for which they fought. For these were mainly lost causes, lost because they represented a social order growingly obsolete and expressed ideals which, for the time being at least and whether or not they were true, had ceased to speak with a living voice to the fickle hearts of men. This apparent failure, if indeed they ever thought about it, did not ultimately dishearten these latter-day Cecils. Like their father, they saw their lives, as they saw the lives of all men, in the light of their faith in a Divine Reality, whose creatures they were; and in relation to whose being – timeless, changeless, all-powerful, benignant – all that happened in this dimension of fleeting time was, when all was said and done, insignificant.

Genealogy

Members of the Cecil family who are
not mentioned in the text are not
named here.

b. born
d. died
= married

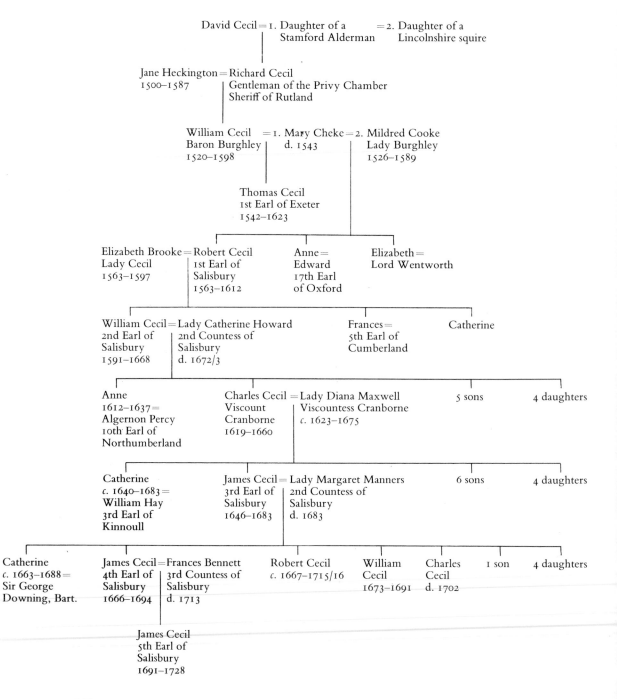

David Cecil = 1. Daughter of a   = 2. Daughter of a
            Stamford Alderman   Lincolnshire squire

Jane Heckington = Richard Cecil
1500–1587   Gentleman of the Privy Chamber
                  Sheriff of Rutland

William Cecil = 1. Mary Cheke = 2. Mildred Cooke
Baron Burghley   d. 1543   Lady Burghley
1520–1598   1526–1589

Thomas Cecil
1st Earl of Exeter
1542–1623

Elizabeth Brooke = Robert Cecil   Anne =   Elizabeth =
Lady Cecil   1st Earl of   Edward   Lord Wentworth
1563–1597   Salisbury   17th Earl
                   1563–1612   of Oxford

William Cecil = Lady Catherine Howard   Frances =   Catherine
2nd Earl of   2nd Countess of   5th Earl of
Salisbury   Salisbury   Cumberland
1591–1668   d. 1672/3

Anne   Charles Cecil = Lady Diana Maxwell   5 sons   4 daughters
1612–1637 =   Viscount   Viscountess Cranborne
Algernon Percy   Cranborne   c. 1623–1675
10th Earl of   1619–1660
Northumberland

Catherine   James Cecil = Lady Margaret Manners   6 sons   4 daughters
c. 1640–1683 =   3rd Earl of   2nd Countess of
William Hay   Salisbury   Salisbury
3rd Earl of   1646–1683   d. 1683
Kinnoull

Catherine   James Cecil = Frances Bennett   Robert Cecil   William   Charles   1 son   4 daughters
c. 1663–1688 =   4th Earl of   3rd Countess of   c. 1667–1715/16   Cecil   Cecil
Sir George   Salisbury   Salisbury   1673–1691 d. 1702
Downing, Bart.   1666–1694   d. 1713

James Cecil
5th Earl of
Salisbury
1691–1728

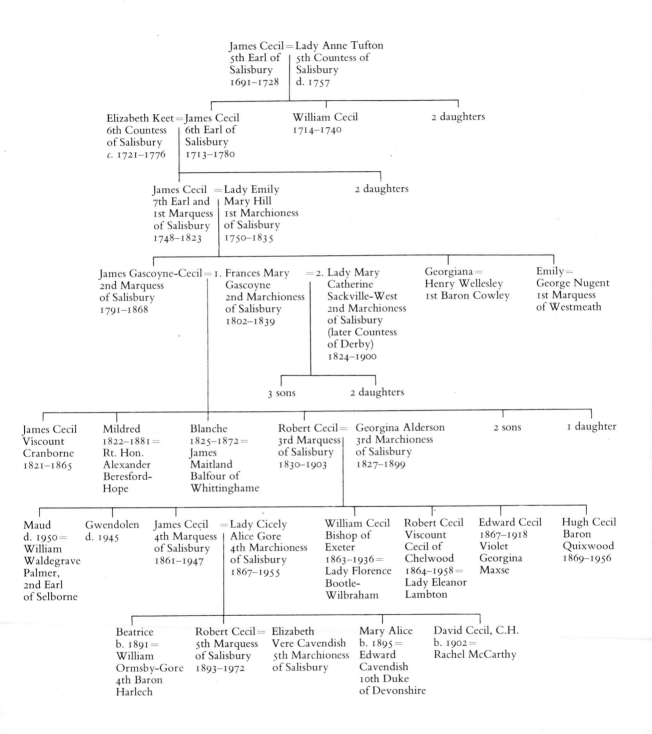

James Cecil = Lady Anne Tufton
5th Earl of | 5th Countess of
Salisbury | Salisbury
1691–1728 | d. 1757

Elizabeth Keet = James Cecil   William Cecil   2 daughters
6th Countess | 6th Earl of   1714–1740
of Salisbury | Salisbury
c. 1721–1776 | 1713–1780

James Cecil = Lady Emily   2 daughters
7th Earl and | Mary Hill
1st Marquess | 1st Marchioness
of Salisbury | of Salisbury
1748–1823 | 1750–1835

James Gascoyne-Cecil = 1. Frances Mary   = 2. Lady Mary   Georgiana =   Emily =
2nd Marquess | Gascoyne   Catherine   Henry Wellesley   George Nugent
of Salisbury | 2nd Marchioness   Sackville-West   1st Baron Cowley   1st Marquess
1791–1868 | of Salisbury   2nd Marchioness   of Westmeath
         | 1802–1839   of Salisbury
                                     (later Countess
                                     of Derby)
                                     1824–1900

3 sons   2 daughters

James Cecil   Mildred   Blanche   Robert Cecil = Georgina Alderson   2 sons   1 daughter
Viscount   1822–1881=   1825–1872=   3rd Marquess | 3rd Marchioness
Cranborne   Rt. Hon.   James   of Salisbury | of Salisbury
1821–1865   Alexander   Maitland   1830–1903 | 1827–1899
                Beresford-   Balfour of
                Hope   Whittinghame

Maud   Gwendolen   James Cecil = Lady Cicely   William Cecil   Robert Cecil   Edward Cecil   Hugh Cecil
d. 1950=   d. 1945   4th Marquess | Alice Gore   Bishop of   Viscount   1867–1918   Baron
William   of Salisbury | 4th Marchioness Exeter   Cecil of   Violet   Quixwood
Waldegrave   1861–1947 | of Salisbury   1863–1936=   Chelwood   Georgina   1869–1956
Palmer, | 1867–1955   Lady Florence   1864–1958=   Maxse
2nd Earl   Bootle-   Lady Eleanor
of Selborne   Wilbraham   Lambton

                Beatrice   Robert Cecil = Elizabeth   Mary Alice   David Cecil, C.H.
                b. 1891=   5th Marquess | Vere Cavendish b. 1895=   b. 1902=
                William   of Salisbury | 5th Marchioness Edward   Rachel McCarthy
                Ormsby-Gore   1893–1972 | of Salisbury Cavendish
                4th Baron   10th Duke
                Harlech   of Devonshire

311

Concise Bibliography

Among the many literary sources consulted in writing this book are the following:

Antrobus, Jocelyn, *Bishop's Hatfield, Some Memories of the Past*

Bacon, Francis, *Essays*

Beckingsale, B. W., *Burghley*

Blake, Robert, *The Conservative Party from Peel to Churchill*

Blake, Robert, *Disraeli*

Buxton, John, *Elizabethan Taste*

Cecil, Algernon, *Robert Cecil, First Earl of Salisbury*

Cecil, Lord Edward, *The Leisure of an Egyptian Official*

Cecil, Lady Gwendolen, *Life of Robert, Marquis of Salisbury*

Cecil of Chelwood, Viscount, *All the Way*

Clarendon, First Earl of, *History of the Grand Rebellion*

The Creevey Papers

Creighton, Mandell, *Queen Elizabeth*

Dennis, George Ravenscroft, *The House of Cecil*

Dugdale, Blanche, *Family Homespun*

Duschinsky, Michael Pinto, *The Political Thought of Lord Salisbury*

Feiling, K. G., *England under the Tudors and Stuarts*

Gardiner, Samuel Rawson, *History of England*

Garvin, J. L., *Life of Joseph Chamberlain*

Handover, Phyllis Margaret, *The Second Cecil*

Hansard, *Parliamentary Debates*

Hare, Augustus, *The Story of My Life*

The Harleian Miscellany

The Hatfield Papers

Hurstfield, Joel, *The Queen's Wards*

James, Robert Rhodes, *Lord Randolph Churchill*

Jenkins, Elizabeth, *Elizabeth the Great*

Kennedy, A. L., *Salisbury* `

Mathew, David, *The Jacobean Age*

Milner, Viscountess, *My Picture Gallery*

Montgomery and Buckle, *Life of Disraeli*

Neale, J. E., *Queen Elizabeth*

Oman, Carola, *The Gascoyne Heiress*

Peck, Francis, *Desiderata Curiosa*

Pepys, Samuel, *Diary*

Read, Conyers, *Lord Burghley and Queen Elizabeth*

Read, Conyers, *Mr. Secretary Cecil and Queen Elizabeth*

Rowse, A. L., *The Elizabethan Age: 1. The England of Elizabeth*

Rowse, A. L., *Ralegh and the Throckmortons*

Rowse, A. L., *Shakespeare's Southampton*

Smith, Paul, editor, *Lord Salisbury on Politics*

Spedding, James, *Life of Bacon*

State Trials from Richard II to George III

Stone, Lawrence, *The Crisis of the Aristocracy*

Walpole, Horace, *Letters*

Notes on the Illustrations and Acknowledgments

Unless a separate attribution is made here, the paintings, sculptures and works of art illustrated in this book belong to the Marquess of Salisbury and are to be found at Hatfield House. Special thanks are due to the Courtauld Institute of Art and to the National Portrait Gallery for providing reference photographs of items in this collection. The museums, art galleries and photographers who provided illustrations are acknowledged below.

The following abbreviations are used:

BM   The Trustees, British Museum, London
Courtauld   Courtauld Institute of Art, London
Mansell   Mansell Collection, London
NPG   National Portrait Gallery, London
V&A   The Trustees, Victoria and Albert Museum, London

In giving the titles of members of the Cecil family 'Salisbury' is omitted.

Jacket front 1st Earl, later than 1606, after John de Critz the Elder. Photo: Derrick Witty.
Jacket back and frontispiece Lady Cicely Alice Gore, 4th Marchioness, with her son Lord David Cecil, 1908, by Sir James Shannon. Photo: Derrick Witty.
Reverse of frontispiece Cecil coat of arms, in the Great Hall. Photo: Derrick Witty.
Page 12 South Front, completed 1611. Photo: Edwin Smith.
Page 14 South view from House. Photo: Edwin Smith.
Page 15 East view from House. Photo: Edwin Smith.
Page 17 Grand Staircase. Photo: Edwin Smith.
Page 19 View of House from south-east. Photo: Edwin Smith.
Page 20 Great Hall. Photo: Edwin Smith.
Page 22 *Left* Hat and stockings of Queen Elizabeth I. Photo: A. F. Kersting. *Right* Crystal posset set attributed to Benvenuto Cellini.
Page 24 Chapel Gallery. Photo: Edwin Smith.
Page 27 Yew Room. Photo: Edwin Smith.
Page 29 Old Palace. Photo Edwin Smith.
Page 30 Elizabeth I, Ermine Portrait, 1585, attributed to Nicholas Hilliard. Photo: Derrick Witty.
Page 31 Elizabeth I, Rainbow Portrait, c. 1600, attributed to Isaac Oliver. Photo: Derrick Witty.
Page 32 Cranborne Manor. Photo: Angelo Hornak.

Page 36 *Left* Henry VIII, c. 1542, early 17th-century copy by an unknown artist. NPG. *Right* Elizabeth I as a Princess, c. 1542–7, by an unknown artist. Windsor Castle. Reproduced by gracious permission of Her Majesty the Queen.
Page 41 Mildred, Lady Burghley, c. 1563, attributed to Hans Eworth. Photo: Derrick Witty.
Page 42 1st Baron Burghley, c. 1565, attributed to Hans Eworth. Photo: Derrick Witty.
Page 44 *Left* Edward Seymour, Duke of Somerset, by an unknown artist. Photo: Mansell. *Right* Edward VI, c. 1546, studio of William Scrots. NPG.
Page 47 Possibly Lady Jane Grey, c. 1555–60, by an unknown artist. NPG. Photo: Mansell.
Page 49 Engraving from Foxe's *Book of Martyrs*, 1st edn 1563. Photo: Mansell.
Page 50 Medal of Philip II, 1555, by Jacopo da Trezzo. NPG.
Page 51 Mary I, 1554, by Antonio Moro. Prado, Madrid.
Page 54 Woodcut of bull- and bear-baiting in the Fechthaus, Nuremburg. In *Curiöser Spiegel*, 1689 (as reproduced in the 1793 edn). V&A. Photo: John Freeman.
Page 56 1st Baron Burghley, c. 1590, probably by Marcus Gheeraerts the Younger or John de Critz the Elder. Photo: NPG.
Page 59 1st Earl, later than 1606, after John de Critz the Elder. Photo: Derrick Witty.
Page 60 1st Earl, c. 1608, mosaic portrait after John de Critz the Elder. Photo: Derrick Witty.
Page 65 Burghley House, Stamford. Photo: A. F. Kersting.
Page 66 Mary Queen of Scots, 1559, by Hieronymus Cock. BM. Photo: John Freeman.
Pages 68–9 Map of London, 1572, attributed to Joris Höfnagel. Guildhall Library, London. Photo: John Freeman.
Page 73 Robert Dudley, Earl of Leicester, c. 1585, attributed to William Segar. Photo: Courtauld.
Page 78 *Left* Lord Burghley riding a mule, by an unknown artist. *Right* Map, 16th century. Photo: Derrick Witty.
Page 81 Double portrait of 1st Baron Burghley and 1st Earl, after 1606, by an unknown artist. Photo: NPG.
Page 86 Spanish ship plans, 1587, from *Coleccion de*

Incunables Americanos siglo XVI, Vol. VIII. Museo Naval, Madrid.

Page 90 1st Earl, *c.* 1608, after John de Critz the Elder. Photo: Courtauld.

Page 94 Spanish citadel in Antwerp, 1597. Koninklijk. Museum voor Schone Kunsten, Antwerp. Photo: ACL, Brussels.

Page 95 Alexander Farnese, Duke of Parma, 16th century, by an unknown artist. Musée Royal des Beaux-Arts, Brussels. Photo: ACL, Brussels. *Right* Maurice of Nassau, 16th century, by an unknown artist. Musée Royal des Beaux-Arts, Brussels. Photo: ACL, Brussels.

Page 96 Woodcut in *The Booke of Falconrie*, 1575, by George Turbervile. BM. Photo: John Freeman.

Page 100 Robert Devereux, 2nd Earl of Essex, 1590, by William Segar. National Gallery of Ireland.

Page 105 *Left* Sir Francis Bacon, 16th-century engraving by Simon Passaeus. BM. Photo: John Freeman. *Right* Engraving of Cadiz, *c.* 1596. BM. Photo: John Freeman.

Page 106 Henry IV of France, early 17th century, by an unknown artist. Musée de Versailles. Photo: Giraudon.

Page 109 King James Drawing-room. Photo: Edwin Smith.

Page 110 James I, 1623, possibly by John de Critz the Elder after Paul van Somer. Photo: Derrick Witty.

Page 113 *Top* Nonesuch Palace, 1568, by Joris Hoefnagel. BM. Photo: John Freeman. *Bottom* View of London, *c.* 1616, by J.C. Visscher. BM. Photo: John Freeman.

Page 117 Effigies of Elizabeth I and courtiers, *c.* 1823, by James George Bubb. Photo: Edwin Smith.

Page 121 Raleigh and his son, 1602, by an unknown artist. NPG.

Page 124 Sir John Harington, 1583, by an unknown artist. NPG.

Page 125 Funeral procession of Elizabeth I, early 17th century, probably by William Camden. BM. Photo: John Freeman.

Page 127 North Front. Photo: Edwin Smith.

Page 128 Chapel. Photo: Derrick Witty.

Page 130 Title page, *The Workes of James I*, 1616. The Trustees, National Library of Scotland.

Page 131 James I as a child, *c.* 1575, attributed to Arnold Bronkhorst. Scottish National Portrait Gallery.

Page 134 Anne of Denmark, 1610, by Isaac Oliver. Windsor Castle. Reproduced by gracious permission of Her Majesty the Queen.

Pages 138–9 Guy Fawkes and the Gunpowder Plot conspirators, from a 17th-century engraving. BM. Photo: John Freeman.

Page 141 Raleigh's study at Sherborne. Photo: John Crampton.

Page 143 Title page, *The Noble Art of Venerie or Hunting*, 1611. BM. Photo: John Freeman.

Page 145 Ben Jonson, possibly *c.* 1620–30, after Abraham Blyenberch. NPG.

Pages 148–9 Salisbury House, London, *c.* 1630, from a drawing by Wenceslaus Hollar in the Pepysian Library, Cambridge. Photo: Mansell.

Page 150 *Left* John Tradescant the Elder, *c.* 1630, by an unknown artist. Photo: A. C. Cooper. *Right* Staircase decoration. Photo: Edwin Smith.

Page 152 Robert Carr, Earl of Somerset, *c.* 1620–5, after John Hoskins. NPG.

Page 159 Tomb of 1st Earl, *c.* 1615, by Maximilian Colt. Photo: Edwin Smith.

Page 162 6th Earl, 1733, by Rosalba Carriera. Photo: Courtauld.

Page 166 *Left* Detail, Charles I, *c.* 1628, by Daniel Mytens. Photo: NPG. *Right* Algernon Percy, 10th Earl of Northumberland, with his wife and a daughter, *c.* 1634–5, studio of Sir Anthony Van Dyck. Photo: Courtauld.

Page 167 *Left* Sir Thomas Fairfax and the New Model Army, by Joshua Sprigge. From *Anglica Rediviva*, 1647. BM. Photo: John Freeman. *Right* Oliver Cromwell, 1652, a Dutch engraving. BM. Photo: John Freeman.

Page 169 4th Earl and his sister as children, *c.* 1668–9, by Michael Wright. Photo: Derrick Witty.

Page 170 2nd Earl, 1626, by George Geldorp. Photo: Derrick Witty.

Page 171 Catherine Howard, 1626, by George Geldorp. Photo: Derrick Witty.

Page 172 5th Earl, *c.* 1703, attributed to Charles Jervas. Photo: Derrick Witty.

Page 174 *Left* 4th Earl, *c.* 1687, painted over a portrait of James, Duke of Monmouth, both by William Wissing. Photo: NPG. *Right top to bottom* (1) Charles, Viscount Cranborne, *c.* 1645–55, by Sir Peter Lely. Photo: NPG. (2) Diana Maxwell, Viscountess Cranborne by Sir Peter Lely. Photo: NPG. (3) 3rd Earl, 1680–1, by Sir Godfrey Kneller. Photo: Courtauld. (4) Frances Bennett, *c.* 1686, attributed to William Wissing. Photo: Courtauld.

Page 179 *Left* The Hon. William Cecil, by William Wissing. Photo: NPG. *Right* The Hon. Robert Cecil, 1689, by Charles Beale the Younger. Photo: Courtauld.

Page 182 Lady Anne Tufton, possibly *c.* 1715, by Charles Jervas. Photo: Courtauld.

Page 183 Detail of a landscape view of House, *c.* 1740, by an unknown artist. Photo: Courtauld.

Page 185 Elizabeth Keet, 1774, by Benjamin van der Gucht. Photo: Courtauld.

Page 186 1st Marquess, 1781–3, detail from a painting by George Romney. Photo: NPG.

Page 189 *Left* Georgiana, Duchess of Devonshire, and her daughter, 1786, by Sir Joshua Reynolds. Chatsworth, Derbyshire. By permission of the Trustees of the Chatsworth Settlement. *Right* Charles James Fox, 1793. BM. Photo: John Freeman.

Page 190 View of the house, *c.* 1785, attributed to William or Charles Tomkins. Photo: Courtauld.

Page 192 Lady Emily Mary Hill, 1790, by George Engleheart. Photo: B. King.

Page 193 Handel Festival, 1784. Photo: Mansell.

Page 195 View of the West Wing, after 1835, by an unknown artist. Photo: B. King.

Page 199 *Left* Frances Mary Gascoyne, 1828–9, by Sir Thomas Lawrence. Photo: NPG. *Right* 2nd Marquess, 1844, by John Lucas. Photo: Courtauld.

Index